best
hikes
with
dogs

SAN FRANCISCO
BAY AREA & BEYOND

best hikes with dogs
SAN FRANCISCO BAY AREA & BEYOND

Second Edition

JASON FATOR &
THOM GABRUKIEWICZ

THE MOUNTAINEERS BOOKS

THE MOUNTAINEERS BOOKS
*is the nonprofit publishing arm of The Mountaineers,
an organization founded in 1906 and dedicated to the exploration,
preservation, and enjoyment of outdoor and wilderness areas.*

1001 SW Klickitat Way, Suite 201, Seattle, WA 98134

© 2013 by Jason Fator and Thom Gabrukiewicz

First edition, 2004. Second edition, 2013

Manufactured in the United States of America
Copy Editor: Jane Crosen
Cover and Book Design: The Mountaineers Books
Layout: Jennifer Shontz, redshoedesign.com
Cartographer: Benjamin Pease/Pease Press Maps
All photographs by the author unless otherwise noted

Cover photograph: *Paul plods along the trail with the summer slopes of Mount Shasta in the background.*
Frontispiece: *Paul stands tall among the giant redwoods along the Pipeline Road Trail.*

Library of Congress Cataloging-in-Publication data on file.

Maps shown in this book were produced using National Geographic's *TOPO!* software. For more information, go to www.nationalgeographic.com/topo.

ISBN (paperback): 978-1-59485-703-4
ISBN (ebook): 978-1-59485-704-1

Certified Chain of Custody
SUSTAINABLE FORESTRY INITIATIVE   Promoting Sustainable Forestry
www.sfiprogram.org
SFI-01268

SFI label applies to the text stock

CONTENTS

Part 1: Hiking with Your Dog

Part 2: The Trails

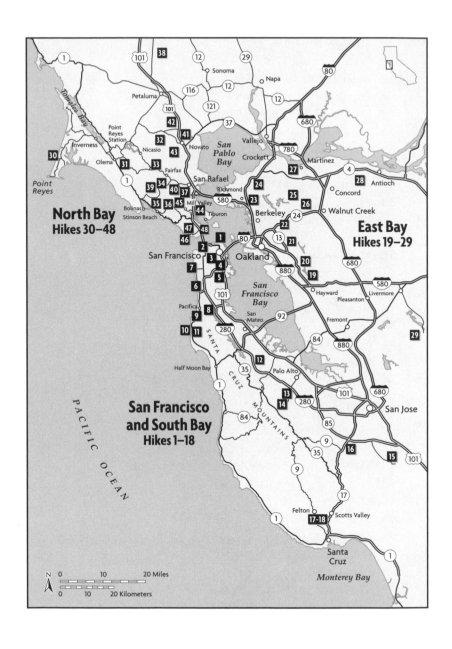

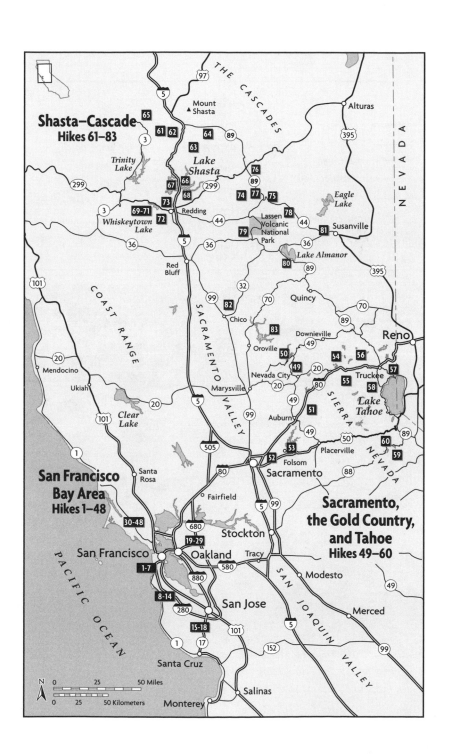

Map Legend

━━━━━ Freeway	(80) (280) Interstate		℗ Trailhead parking		
──── Highway	(50) (395) US highway		⚑ Campground		
═════ Dirt road	(1) (299) State highway		⛩ Picnic area		
▪▪▪▪▪ Featured trail	[47] [3522] Forest road		⌣ Bridge		
▪▪▪▪▪ Other trail			▪ Point of interest		
～～ River/creek	N↑ True north		▲ Peak		
▭ Body of water			⌶ Gate		
⊢⊣ Waterfall	**1** Hike location on locator maps				

The girls, Scully, left, and Trinity take a break during a dayhike to Boulder Creek Falls in Whiskeytown National Recreation Area

HIKE SUMMARY TABLE

Trail	Easy on paws	Easy hike, about 4 miles	Possible overnight	Water for swimming	Unleashed OK	Solitude	Alpine scenery	Forested	Good for senior dogs	For fit dogs
SAN FRANCISCO BAY AREA										
San Francisco and South Bay										
1. Golden Gate Promenade	•								•	
2. Inspiration Point	•	•							•	•
3. Mount Davidson Park	•	•							•	•
4. Glen Canyon Park	•	•							•	
5. McLaren Park	•	•		•	•				•	
6. Fort Funston Sunset Trail	•	•		•	•				•	
7. Ocean Beach Esplanade	•			•					•	
8. Sweeney Ridge	•	•				•			•	
9. Rockaway Point	•	•		•					•	
10. Gray Whale Cove	•	•							•	
11. Montara Beach to North Peak	•					•			•	
12. Pulgas Ridge	•	•							•	
13. Arastradero Preserve	•	•							•	
14. Coal Mine Ridge	•	•							•	•
15. Stile Ranch Trail	•	•							•	
16. Saint Josephs Hill Open Space Preserve	•	•							•	
17. Pipeline Road Trail	•							•	•	
18. Graham Hill Trail	•	•						•	•	
East Bay										
19. Anthony Chabot Loop	•				•			•	•	
20. Bort Meadow	•				•	•		•	•	
21. West Ridge Loop	•	•						•	•	
22. Sibley Volcanic Regional Preserve	•	•				•		•	•	
23. San Pablo Ridge Trail	•					•			•	
24. Sobrante Ridge Trail	•	•			•	•			•	
25. Briones Crest	•					•				•
26. Lafayette Ridge	•					•	•			•

Trail	Easy on paws	Easy hike, about 4 miles	Possible overnight	Water for swimming	Unleashed OK	Solitude	Alpine scenery	Forested	Good for senior dogs	For fit dogs
27. Franklin Ridge	•				•	•				•
28. Black Diamond Mines Regional Preserve	•	•	•		•				•	
29. Murietta Falls					•	•				•
North Bay										
30. South Beach Trail			•			•			•	
31. Bolinas Ridge	•					•		•		•
32. Indian Tree Open Space Preserve	•	•				•		•		
33. Roys Redwoods Trail	•	•						•	•	
34. Cascade Falls Trail	•	•		•			•	•	•	
35. Cataract Falls and Laurel Dell						•		•		•
36. Mount Tamalpais East Peak Trail						•		•		•
37. Dawn Falls Trail	•	•		•				•	•	
38. Crane Creek Regional Park	•	•						•		
39. Pine Mountain Summit							•			•
40. Phoenix Lake	•	•						•		
41. Deer Island	•	•				•		•	•	
42. Mount Burdell	•					•		•		•
43. Waterfall Trail and Indian Valley	•	•						•		
44. Ring Mountain	•	•						•	•	
45. Blithedale Ridge	•	•				•				•
46. Rodeo Lagoon	•	•						•		
47. Miwok and Bobcat Trails	•					•				•
48. Fort Baker	•	•				•		•		
SACRAMENTO, THE GOLD COUNTRY, AND TAHOE										
49. South Yuba Independence Trail	•			•					•	
50. Bullards Bar Trail	•		•	•			•	•	•	
51. Codfish Creek Trail	•	•		•	•				•	
52. American River Parkway	•			•					•	
53. Folsom Lake and Mormon Island Dam	•		•	•					•	
54. Crooked Lakes Trail to Penner Lake	•		•	•	•		•	•		•

Trail	Easy on paws	Easy hike, about 4 miles	Possible overnight	Water for swimming	Unleashed OK	Solitude	Alpine scenery	Forested	Good for senior dogs	For fit dogs
55. Loch Leven Lakes	•		•	•	•	•	•	•		•
56. Summit Lake Trail	•	•	•	•			•	•	•	
57. Martis Creek Lake and Wildlife Area	•		•				•		•	
58. Alpine Meadows to Five Lakes	•		•	•			•	•		•
59. Caples Lake to Emigrant Lake	•		•	•			•	•		•
60. Lake Margaret	•		•	•		•	•	•	•	
SHASTA–CASCADE										
61. PCT to Seven Lakes Basin			•	•			•	•	•	•
62. Castle and Heart Lakes		•	•	•			•	•		•
63. Squaw Valley Creek Trail	•		•	•		•		•	•	
64. McCloud Waterfalls	•	•	•	•				•	•	
65. Mount Eddy and Deadfall Lakes			•	•		•	•	•		•
66. Bailey Cove Loop	•	•		•				•	•	
67. Waters Gulch Creek to Packers Bay	•			•	•			•	•	
68. Clikapudi Trail	•			•					•	
69. Boulder Creek Falls	•		•	•				•	•	
70. Mill Creek Trail	•			•		•		•	•	
71. Whiskeytown Falls	•		•	•				•	•	
72. Meiners Loop to Mule Mountain Pass	•				•			•	•	
73. Sacramento River Trail	•			•					•	
74. Magee Peak			•	•	•		•	•		•
75. Baker Lake to Hat Creek Rim				•	•					•
76. Crystal and Baum Lakes	•			•	•				•	
77. Hat Creek Trail	•			•	•	•	•	•	•	
78. Caribou Wilderness Area	•		•	•	•	•	•	•	•	
79. McGowan Lake Trail				•	•		•	•	•	
80. Lake Almanor Recreation Trail	•		•				•	•	•	
81. Bizz Johnson Trail	•		•	•	•				•	
82. North Rim to Middle Trail Loop						•				•
83. Feather Falls	•		•	•			•	•	•	

AUTHOR'S NOTE

When my good friend Thom Gabrukiewicz asked if I'd be interested in writing a new edition of this book for The Mountaineers Books and becoming a co-author with him in the process, I was completely excited and, as a first-time author, also more than a little overwhelmed.

For this new edition of *Best Hikes with Dogs San Francisco Bay Area & Beyond*, I have added nineteen new hikes, most of which are in the San Francisco Bay Area. I've also updated all the hikes from the previous edition to make sure the information contained in this book is as accurate as possible. Also new are the difficulty ratings and regulations added to the information blocks. Each hike has been rated as easy, moderate, strenuous, or somewhere in between. The regulations notes contain the official rules about leashes and any other special dog rules for each hike.

When I think back on my experiences writing this book, what stands out are the times when Paul, my six-year-old Great Dane, and I stopped to take a break on the trail and sat quietly for a while, taking in the views. The companionship of a good dog is pretty hard to beat. An early November trip to Tahoe was especially memorable—due to the later-than-normal onslaught of winter, we saw the most stunning fall colors display I've ever had the pleasure to witness. This experience and many others ensure that we will be back out there on the trail for many more trips in the years to come.

My hope is that with this book Thom and I—along with his dogs Scully and Trinty and my dog Paul—have given you the extra nudge you need to get outside with your dog. This is all about your connection to your canine and the natural world around you. Let this book be the encouragement you need to venture into the parks, wilderness areas, and open spaces of Northern California. What could be better than a great hike with your dog?

—*Jason Fator, author of the second edition*

Tiny Heart Lake makes an excellent place for Paul to rest after the steady climb from Castle Lake.

PREFACE

Over half of all households in the United States can't be wrong. That's the number of Americans who have at least one dog or cat living with them in their home, according to the Pet Food Institute (www.petfoodinstitute.com). In fact, there are an estimated 67 million dogs in the United States, and a huge percentage of Californian households contribute to that number. We are a state that has gone to the dogs, and we want to share our open lands with our four-legged friends. Indeed, several high-population counties have dog political action committees to help plan open spaces for multiple use.

In Northern California, we are blessed with space—from national forests and regional parks to U.S. Bureau of Land Management lands and state parks. Still, the presence of canine companions on the trail continues to be a contentious situation. There are those who advocate having no dogs on trails. Some groups contend that dogs don't belong in the wilderness, since they might chase wildlife, harass other hikers, and foul trails and campsites. It's up to dog owners to soothe the fears of this small segment of the hiking population, with education—and with good trail manners.

There is a huge segment of the population who fear dogs. And any sort of trail encounter—even just your dog running up to a hiker to say hello—can be trouble. It's up to dog owners to be good stewards for all 5 million dog-owning households in California. Training goes a long way, as does a stout leash.

The question remains, however, "Are dogs harmful to the backcountry?" To that, I say, "No more than human wanderers."

Just as there are irresponsible hikers who cut switchbacks, camp too close to water sources, and don't bury their waste, there are problem dogs who have no business being on-trail. Sadly, this is a symptom of poor training. Even if you have voice and hand control of your dog, you should always hike with a leash or harness.

Basically, dogs should adhere to the same backcountry ethics as their human masters. Dogs should defecate at least 200 feet from a water source, and the waste should be buried in a cat hole from 6 to 8 inches deep. Dogs shouldn't be allowed to cut a switchback. Dogs should never be encouraged to chase wildlife. Done right, dogs on trails can actually help hikers see more wildlife, since their senses of smell, sight, and hearing are superior to ours. That's been my experience with dogs on the trail—in fact, that's why there are so many dog breeds, each one created to increase the likelihood of seeing wildlife during a hunt.

But not all dog owners should just rush out and hit the trail. First, you need to know where dogs are allowed and where they are not. Most national parks and monuments allow dogs to enter, but trails are off-limits, even for the best-trained dog. Know the laws and land management rules governing each area you intend to visit with your canine companion, whether your destination is a state park or a national forest.

Each hike in this book allows dogs to share the trail. However, trail regulations can change from year to year because of conditions and new regulations. Hikers should always call the land manager to find out the current trail regulations and the current trail conditions of any new route.

Hikers also need to be aware of changing weather conditions and be prepared for anything. You can easily twist an ankle or jam a wrist crossing loose talus, and you may need to stay the night while waiting for an able-bodied hiker to walk out and summon help. Dogs also need care and tending: they can tear up their pads, fall off a slope, or get too close to some wildlife and get injured.

It all comes down to being prepared. An enjoyable time on your public lands depends on both you and your dog being ready not only for the elements but for dispelling the myth that dogs cause havoc on the trail.

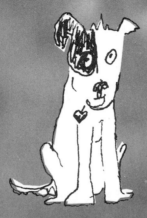

PART 1

Hiking with Your Dog

Packing up your dog and hitting the trail seems like a carefree, easy outing. But there are some things to consider, and preparations to make, before setting out. The following will help you and your dog stay safe and will go a long way toward making sure that you both have a good time—and that you don't affect the good time of other trail users.

Good Dogs Require Good Owners and Training

Think about how many hours of enjoyment and amusement your dog brings. Now think about the amount of training it takes to transform a mischievous puppy into a well-behaved older dog. Well-behaved pets are a direct reflection of their owners. Too often, pets are made to suffer for the sins of the master—and they often bear the brunt of any negative feelings generated by an irresponsible pet owner.

Paul cools off in the clear, chilly waters of the McCloud River.

It seems strange that certain pet owners can't even meet the basic responsibilities of pet ownership—caring for a dog, feeding him, and keeping him healthy. You must also be responsible for your dog's exercise and recreation. Despite the 100,000 years since man first domesticated wolves, your dog still has a basic, wild need to run, jump, and swim.

It all begins with training.

I tend to believe that there are many more bad owners than there are "bad" breeds of dogs. However, there are those breeds that have been bred to bring out aggressive behavior. Consider this when selecting a new puppy or if you're about to adopt an older dog from a rescue organization or shelter. Internet research can lead you to basic breed traits that you can expect from your dog—even if that dog is a mixed breed.

Next step: work with your dog, daily if he or she is a puppy and weekly for an older dog. The first commands of sit, shake, stay, and lie down form the foundation of a "well-heeled" pet.

Most communities have dog-training classes, either through the parks and recreation department, community college, or some of the larger chain pet stores. Take a class. And back that training up with even more training. One of the better Internet sites for dog training comes from the University of Wisconsin–Stevens Point. Dr. P's Dog Training (www .uwsp.edu/psych/dog/dog.htm) is packed with information.

Another important component is "socializing" your dog with other dogs—and people. Take your pet to places where there are other dogs playing. Get your puppy used to crowds of people. All such efforts allow your pet to be a popular fixture along the trail, since a well-trained dog is a delight to encounter.

Happy, Healthy Trails

Even responsible pet owners can have trouble realizing their dogs aren't invincible bundles of muscle and energy. While I was recuperating from knee surgery, my own dogs were left with nothing more than running around the yard for the ten weeks that I couldn't bear weight on my mangled knee. First hike out, both dogs cut their pads, and I had to carry Scully out on top of my pack—8 miles with an extra 50 pounds on my back. (Don't tell my doctor.)

Dogs that do nothing but lie in the living room or the backyard all day cannot be expected to challenge steep grades, gravel paths, and mountain trails without some ill effects. Like a human couch potato, dogs can get stiff, sore muscles, bruised and blistered toes, and all sorts of scrapes and bug bites.

To avoid this, you and your dog must stay active. Nothing extreme is required: just 30 minutes of walking a day does your body good, and that of your dog. As with any new exercise program, start gradually and build slowly. After a few weeks of walking, try running for 10 to 15 minutes, or quicken your walking pace.

This will help build muscle tone in both you and your pet, but more importantly, exercise will help toughen the pads on your dog's feet, making them ready to go off-road when you are. Those first hikes are where you should go slow. Make your first several outings day hikes, on paved trails where you can get your dog used to hiking and to what's expected on the trail. Just as a good pair of hiking boots is essential for a positive backcountry experience, your dog's pads need to be in their best condition. There are pad-toughening agents for sale, but nothing beats good, clean exercise.

If you are partial to more extreme hikes farther in the backcountry, I recommend you buy your dog a set of booties. There are several brands and styles on the market; with a little training, your dog will get used to—and even excited by—your pulling out the booties for a hike.

Also, remember that your dog can get stiff and sore after a day of hiking. Trying to get a sore dog to move out of camp after a day of rigorous hiking can be a chore. You either have to poke, prod, or resort to carrying your dog to get her moving. Some simple medications, like ordinary aspirin, can help. These are covered in detail under "Canine First Aid" later in the introduction.

Snow Hikes

Many of the trails in this book can be hiked or cross-country skied in the winter. If you've never tried a snow hike, I urge you to try it. Winter can be an absolutely fantastic time to revisit a trail you know by heart in the summer. While there is a slight learning curve to cross-country skiing, the basics of snowshoeing have never changed. If you can walk, you can snowshoe.

Snowshoeing is gaining in popularity, and it's considered the fastest-growing of all winter sports. Compared to other winter activities, snowshoeing ranks as one of the easiest to enjoy—and one of the best winter fitness regimes. Hiking uphill in unpacked snow can easily burn 1000 calories an hour, according to fitness experts. Those willing to spend a little extra time learning how to cross-country ski will reap the additional benefits of speed and efficiency enabled by the sport's gliding stride. On skis you can cover even more distance, at higher speed and with less effort.

While snow hikes with your dog can be a lot of fun and great way to get a different take on a trail you may have hiked before, there are some additional risks and things to watch out for when venturing into the snowy backcountry. Any time you travel in potential avalanche terrain, you should have the proper avalanche gear (avalanche beacon, probe, and shovel) and training to know how to use them correctly. You should also know the terrain and the areas where hazards may exist. Go with a partner who is also trained and has the proper gear, talk to a ranger, and consult a report on the surrounding snowpack to make sure you aren't venturing into an overly risky situation. Use caution around streams or lakes frozen over with ice or covered with snow that may not be thick enough to support your or your dog's weight.

Other things to be aware of are the fact that dogs (and humans) may need extra, protective clothing and gear for winter travel, such as a jacket if your dog is prone to getting cold and/or booties to protect his or her feet from ice buildup and abrasions. You'll both tire more quickly in deep, soft snow, so allow extra time for your journey, pick a shorter route, and be sure to bring extra food and water.

What to Expect from Your Breed

On-trail, I've seen perky Pomeranians and lackadaisical Labradors, bulletlike border collies and plodding poodles. A good trail companion, it seems, depends more on training than breeding.

With that said, you're probably going to get more miles out of a golden retriever than a Chihuahua. Some short-legged breeds, like dachshunds and bassets, can't carry packs and will probably be able to go only short distances.

The best advice is to pick a breed that fits your lifestyle. If you plan on taking your dog with you often into the backcountry, a working breed, sporting breed, or something from the herding group will make a better companion than a dog from the toy group.

I fully believe in a dog carrying his or her own supplies. In talking to several veterinarians, I've found that dogs can carry a third of their body weight. Generally, my own dogs carry about 20 percent, including their food and treats, collapsible bowls for food and water, their first-aid kit, and the leashes. Puppies can't carry any weight until their bones finish growing. In some breeds, this can take up to two years. But do get your puppy used to a pack. Let her carry it empty around the yard. That way, when the time comes to get into the backcountry, your dog isn't going to try to buck the pack like a miniature bull.

Other considerations include a vest or sweater for short-haired breeds that can get cold in the backcountry.

Permits and Regulations

Simply put, know the rules and regulations of the areas where you plan to hike. Dogs are not allowed past the parking lots of national parks and monuments. Some regional parks allow dogs, but with certain restrictions (like leashes). Some require only that you have voice or hand control over your dog. Generally, national forests, wilderness areas (unless they are in national parks), and Bureau of Land Management (BLM) lands have no restrictions on bringing your dog with you to hike.

There are other, not necessarily dog-specific, considerations though.

If you plan on camping and on building a fire, you'll need to carry a free campfire permit—and know whether or not certain fire restrictions are in place, especially when it's dry. Fire permits can be picked up at national forest headquarters, ranger districts, and BLM offices. They are good for six months.

Some wilderness areas require that you carry a backcountry camping permit. Again, these free permits can be picked up at ranger district offices.

Some of the hikes described in this book are in areas that require

It's important to pay attention to leash restrictions on the trails.

a recreation pass, parking fee, or use fee, so you should always come prepared to pay fees where required.

So far, most Northern California national forests don't require the so-called Adventure Pass to recreate. The $5 day pass ($30 a year) is required at Los Padres, Angeles, San Bernardino, and Cleveland national forests in Southern California and selected locations in Washington and Oregon. California has nineteen national forests that encompass 20 million acres.

Leave No Trace

The Leave No Trace principles of outdoor ethics are paramount (see www.leavenotrace.org):

Plan Ahead and Prepare

- Know the regulations and special concerns for the area you'll visit.
- Prepare for extreme weather, hazards, and emergencies.
- Schedule your trip to avoid times of high use.
- Visit in small groups. Split larger parties into groups of four to six.
- Repackage food to minimize waste.
- Use a map and compass to eliminate the use of marking paint, rock cairns, or flagging.

Travel and Camp on Durable Surfaces

- Durable surfaces include established trails and campsites, rock, gravel, dry grasses, and snow.
- Protect riparian areas by camping at least 200 feet from lakes and streams.
- Good campsites are found, not made. Altering a site is not necessary.
- In popular areas: concentrate use on existing trails and campsites; walk single file in the middle of the trail, even when wet or muddy; keep campsites small; focus activity in areas where vegetation is absent.
- In pristine areas: disperse use to prevent the creation of campsites and trails; avoid places where impacts are just beginning.

Dispose of Waste Properly

- Pack it in, pack it out. Inspect your campsite and rest areas for trash or spilled foods. Pack out all trash, leftover food, and litter.
- Deposit solid human waste in cat holes dug 6 to 8 inches deep at least 200 feet from water, camp, and trails. Cover the cat hole when finished.
- Pack out toilet paper and hygiene products.
- Carry wash water 200 feet away from streams or lakes and use small amounts of biodegradable soap. Scatter strained dishwater.

Leave What You Find

- Preserve the past: examine, but don't touch, cultural or historic structures and artifacts.
- Leave rocks, plants, and other natural objects as you find them.
- Avoid introducing or transporting nonnative species.
- Don't build structures or furniture, or dig trenches.

Minimize Campfire Impacts

- Campfires can cause lasting impacts to the backcountry. Use a lightweight stove for cooking and enjoy a candle lantern for light.
- Where fires are permitted, use established fire rings, fire pans, or mound fires.
- Keep fires small. Only use sticks from the ground that can be broken by hand. Burn all wood and coals to ash, put out campfires completely, then scatter cool ashes.

Respect Wildlife

- Observe wildlife from a distance. Don't follow or approach animals.
- Never feed animals. Feeding wildlife damages their health, alters natural behaviors, and exposes them to predators and other dangers.
- Protect wildlife and your food by storing rations and trash securely.
- Control pets at all times, or leave them at home.
- Avoid wildlife during sensitive times: mating, nesting, raising young, or winter.

Rest and hydration breaks are essential to a successful hike.

Be Considerate of Other Visitors

- Respect other visitors and protect the quality of their experience.
- Be courteous. Yield to other users on the trail.
- Step to the downhill side of the trail when encountering pack stock.
- Take breaks and camp away from trails and other visitors.
- Let nature's sounds prevail. Avoid loud voices and noises.

Trail Etiquette for Dogs

Just as it's important for humans to follow Leave No Trace ethics, it's important that your dog—and you—follow a standard of trail etiquette. As a hiker, you are responsible for your actions; as a dog owner, you are also responsible for your dog's actions.

The hard-and-fast rule is to observe common sense and common courtesy. Here are some other rules to live by on the trail:

- Have your pet on a leash or under strict voice command at all times. Strict voice command means that your dog heels immediately when told, stays at heel, and refrains from barking.
- When you and your dog meet other trail users, you should yield the right-of-way, stepping well clear of the trail to allow the other users to pass without problem.
- When you and your dog meet a mountain biker or horse, you should yield, and make sure your dog stays calm and under strict control. Stay off the trail—with a firm grasp on your dog—until the horse or biker is well clear of the area.
- When you meet other hikers, the group heading uphill has the right-of-way. It's much easier for descending hikers to break stride and find a safe place to step off the trail.
- Always stay on-trail, and never make, or take, shortcuts; this leads to erosion. If your destination is off trail, take the most direct route possible, as in leaving the trail in a perpendicular manner.
- Obey all rules and regulations for the trail on which you'll be hiking. Many trails are closed to certain uses, and kiosks at the trailhead will outline the rules.
- Avoid disturbing wildlife, period.
- Never roll rocks or logs downhill. You never know what—or who—is below you.

Canine First Aid

Dogs make lousy patients. Not only can't they tell you where it hurts, but they'll troop on forever with an injury, just because the sights and smells in the outdoors are so delicious. But with a height that's right about grass level, and a penchant for keeping their noses to the ground, dogs can run into all sorts of things that can cause injury.

Grasses. Sharp grasses can cut your dog's snout and poke his or her eyes. The worst is foxtail, a sharp seed that, left untreated, can burrow into the skin and cause infections. Make sure you watch your dog for signs such as vigorous head shaking, pawing at the snout, or constant sneezing. Remove any seeds you find with your fingers or with tweezers.

Scrapes and cuts. Scrapes, cuts, and punctures happen. If not serious, wash the cut with water and apply a Betadine solution. Don't close a puncture wound, as this could cause more serious infection. It's better to keep a puncture wound open, covered with a gauze square, until you can get to your vet.

Pad injuries. Pad injuries can be common if you haven't taken your dog out much. The pads can get abraded, cut, or blistered. It's best to clean them up with a Betadine solution and then to apply an antibiotic cream. I carry a tube of superglue, which can be applied to the pads to form a shield.

Water danger and CPR. Even the most water-loving dog can get in trouble and—without proper supervision—can drown. Creeks can be swift, waterfall pools deep, and most high-mountain lakes are ringed with rocks, making it difficult for a struggling animal to escape.

If your dog has taken in a lot of water and is struggling to breathe, pick him up by his hind legs so he hangs upside down, then have

Pay close attention to your dog's paws, pads, and claws while on the trail.

someone close the dog's mouth and blow into his nose several times to dispel the water and to get air to his lungs.

If your dog isn't breathing, begin CPR immediately. Lay your dog on his right side and check his pulse by placing your fingertips on the left side of his chest behind his elbow. If there's no pulse, clear your dog's airway, close his mouth, and blow into his nose until his lungs expand. Then push on his chest four times, depressing 1 to 2 inches. Repeat these steps about fifteen times per minute, until your dog regains consciousness, or for 5 minutes.

Soreness. Sore muscles can hit your dog as easily as they hit you. If, after a hard day of hiking, your dog is limping or lethargic—and you can't find an injury—it may be sore muscles. Your vet can prescribe a small amount of anti-inflammatory medication, but simple buffered aspirin works really well. Stay away from uncoated aspirin, since it tends to dissolve in the stomach and can cause some ailments. Buffered aspirin is designed to dissolve in the intestine, which won't cause any stomach issues.

With most anything, it pays to be observant. Watch how your dog is reacting, and check your pet often for injury. Look inside her ears, mouth, and between her toes for foreign objects or cuts.

And remember that even the friendliest, most loving pooch can snap when she is scared or in pain, so always apply a muzzle before treating a wound or injury.

What Goes in a Doggy First-Aid Kit?

Having a canine first-aid kit is essential, even if it has only the bare bones. For a comprehensive kit, though, carry the following items when heading into the wild with a canine companion:

Instruments
- Scissors/bandage scissors
- Toenail clippers
- Rectal thermometer (a healthy dog's temperature be should 101°F when taken rectally)

Cleansers and disinfectants
- 3 percent hydrogen peroxide
- Betadine
- Canine eyewash (available at any large pet-supply store).

Topical antibiotics and ointments (nonprescription)
- Calamine lotion
- Triple antibiotic ointment (Bacitracin, neomycin, or polymyxin)
- Baking soda (for bee stings)
- Vaseline
- Stop-bleeding powder

Medications (nonprescription)
- Enteric-coated aspirin or Bufferin
- Imodium A-D
- Pepto-Bismol

Dressings and bandages
- Gauze pads (4 inches square)
- Gauze roll
- Nonstick pads
- Adhesive tape (1-inch and 2-inch rolls)

Miscellaneous
- Muzzle
- Dog booties
- Any prescription medication your dog needs

For Extended Trips

Consult your vet about additional prescription medications or other supplies that might be needed in an emergency situation, including:
- Oral antibiotics
- Eye medications
- Ear medications
- Emetics (to induce vomiting)
- Pain medications and anti-inflammatories
- Suturing materials for large open wounds

Hydration

When hiking, you and your pet should be dogged about staying hydrated. In semiarid conditions, pack more water than you'll possibly need. A good rule to follow is 8 ounces of water for yourself—and for your dog—every 15 minutes, or about a liter an hour. Seems like a lot, doesn't it? Well, just a 2 percent loss of fluids in a 150-pound person equals 3 pounds, according to the good folks at Camelbak, makers of hydration systems;

and that means a loss of energy. It's worse for your dog, since he will literally play until dropping.

Dehydration can set in quickly, which can lead to heat exhaustion and heatstroke, for both you and your dog.

Learn to identify heat exhaustion and heatstroke in your dog. If your dog starts to pant excessively and the insides of her ears are bright red, these are warning signs to stop and have a drink (or a swim, if there's a water source nearby). If your dog exhibits weakness, staggers, or faints, these are the signs of heatstroke, a very serious condition that requires immediate attention: it's imperative to douse your dog with cool water or let her sit in a lake or mountain stream.

When hiking, I usually do not treat the water my dogs drink. *Giardia lamblia*, a protozoal parasite, is common in all lakes and streams in the West. It attacks the host's intestinal tract and can lead to weight loss, vomiting, diarrhea, and lack of appetite. While nasty in humans, giardia tends not to infect dogs as often. Estimates in some regions say that 70 percent of the dog population has giardia present in their systems, but the dogs don't get the symptoms. If you have any concerns, by all means, treat your dog's water with a good filter. Nowadays, filters that screen out giardia and other nasties can be purchased for less than $50.

Always remember to wash your hands before eating or preparing food in the backcountry. This is especially important after petting or otherwise handling your dog, because you never know what he or she could have come into contact with (or perhaps rolled in) along the trail.

Pack with Care

When planning a backcountry adventure, or just a simple day hike, be prepared. Bring the right gear and bring plenty of it, for you and your dog.

For the backcountry, I don't pack a stitch of cotton clothing, relying instead on synthetic fabrics that wick moisture away from my body and that help me stay warm, even in a downpour. To this I add lightweight raingear and plenty of synthetic socks. Dry—and clean—socks are golden on the trail.

So are a broad-brimmed hat and stocking cap. The brimmed hat is there to keep the sun from beating you down; the stocking cap is useful for evening use, since you lose most of your body heat through your noggin.

You shouldn't neglect your dog's comfort. If going on an overnight trip, you'll need to bring a blanket or thermal pad for your dog to sleep on, since dogs can lose body heat to the ground just as easily as humans can. In a pinch, large trash bags can be fashioned into cheap raingear, for both you and your dog.

The Mountaineers Ten Essentials: A Systems Approach

1. Navigation (map and compass)
2. Sun protection (sunglasses and sunscreen)
3. Insulation (extra clothing)
4. Illumination (headlamp or flashlight)
5. First-aid supplies
6. Fire (firestarter and matches/lighter)
7. Repair kit and tools (including knife)
8. Nutrition (extra food)
9. Hydration (extra water)
10. Emergency shelter

The Mountaineers Ten Essentials are a must, but here are the slightly modified ten essentials I bring for myself:

1. **Extra clothing.** This means more clothing than you expect to wear; always plan for the worst weather. If you get injured or lost, you won't be moving around to generate heat, so be prepared. And always layer. It's much easier to take off clothing than it is to put on what you don't have.

2. **Extra food.** If you have leftovers after an uneventful trip, you've planned well. But if you get lost or injured, that extra food can make the difference between comfort and disaster. Good choices include ramen noodles, oatmeal, and trail mix. Each is minimal in weight but packs a punch in carbohydrates and fat.

3. **Water filter.** I can't stress enough the need to stay hydrated. Carrying a water filter means you can "tank up" on water, whether from a mountain stream or lake.

4. **Knife or multipurpose tool.** A one-thousand-and-one-uses item: for everything from whittling kindling for a warming fire to first-aid applications and gutting a fish to fixing a pack or pair of boots with handy pliers.

5. **First-aid kit.** First, take an American Red Cross or Boy Scout first-aid training class. Then be sure to pack a first-aid kit on every outing. By all means, share some of the components of your doggie first-aid kit.

6. **Map and compass.** Take a course in map and compass reading. Then pack a U.S. Geological Survey (USGS) map of the area you plan to visit and a quality compass. I know a lot of people are switching to Global Positioning System units, since many have come down in price to under $100. But a compass doesn't run on batteries that can fail—and I think it's important to continue to use the underappreciated skill of navigation by map and compass.

7. **Emergency firestarter and matches.** Normally, I carry both a Zippo lighter (always remembering to refill before a trip) and matches in a waterproof container. Nothing beats a warming fire on a cold evening, not just for comfort but for the calming effect it has on people (and on dogs, of course). Candles and firestarter tape are good options for lighting wet wood, and a battery and steel wool (touch the wool to both ends of the battery) makes a fast, ferocious light. Just be sure to carry the steel wool and battery in separate, waterproof containers.

8. **Sunglasses.** I can't live without a good pair of sunglasses. I also have polarized lenses, so I can see the fish I'm trying to catch.

9. **Duct tape.** You can repair just about anything—including using it to close a wound—with duct tape. I wrap extra tape around a plastic water bottle to use as needed.

10. **Fishing rod and tackle.** I love to fish, just for the pure recreation of it. But in a pinch, I can feed myself if I'm stuck in the backcountry for an extra day.

Those are your essentials. You should also have the Ten Canine Essentials for your dog:

1. **Obedience training.** Before you set foot on a trail, make sure your dog is trained and can be trusted to behave when faced with other hikers, other dogs, wildlife, and an assortment of strange scents and sights in the backcountry.

2. **Doggie backpack.** Your dog should carry his own gear.

3. **First-aid kit.** (See "What Goes in a Doggy First-Aid Kit?" earlier in this section.)

4. **Dog food and trail treats.** You should bring more food than your dog normally consumes since he will be burning more calories than normal, and if you do end up having to spend an extra night out there, you need to keep the pup fed, too. Trail treats serve the same purpose for the dog as they do for you—quick energy and a pick-me-up during a strenuous day of hiking.

5. **Water and water bowl.** Don't count on there being water along the trail for your dog. Pack enough extra water to meet all of your dog's drinking needs.

6. **Leash and collar, or harness.** Even if your dog is absolutely trained to voice commands and stays at heel without a leash, sometimes leashes are required by law or just by common courtesy, so you should have one handy at all times.

7. **Insect repellent.** Be aware that some animals, and some people, have strong negative reactions to DEET-based repellents. So, before leaving home, dab a little DEET-based repellent on a patch of your dog's fur to see if he reacts to it. Look for signs of drowsiness, lethargy, and/or nausea. Restrict repellent applications to those places your dog can't lick; the back of the neck and around the ears (staying well clear of the eyes and inner ears) are where mosquitoes will be looking for exposed skin to bite.

8. **ID tags and picture identification.** Your dog should always wear ID tags, and I'd heartily recommend microchipping your dog as well. To do this, a vet injects a tiny encoded microchip under the skin between your dog's shoulders. If your dog ever gets lost and is picked up by animal control, or is taken to a vet's office, a quick pass over the dog's back with a hand scanner will reveal the chip and allow for quick identification. Microchipping is so prevalent that virtually every vet and animal shelter automatically scans every unknown dog they come in contact with to check for chips. The picture identification should go in your pack. If your dog gets lost, you can use the picture to make flyers and handbills to post in the surrounding communities.

9. **Dog booties.** These can be used to protect your dog's feet from rough ground or harsh vegetation. They are also great at keeping bandages secure if your dog damages his pads.

10. **Compact roll of plastic bags and trowel.** You'll need the bags to clean up after your dog on popular trails. When conditions warrant, you can use the trowel to take care of your dog's waste. Dig a small hole 6–8 inches deep in the forest duff, deposit the dog waste, and fill in the hole.

Obstacles, Wild Animals, and Weather

Being outdoors on a new trail can lead to sensory overload for your dog. Even the most well-mannered pooch can become a handful. It's just one of many obstacles awaiting hikers and their furry friends. But with preparation you can cut the odds so that the following won't be an issue.

Poison Oak

Poison oak is the itch that keeps on giving, especially if you hike with dogs. The oil that causes the itch, urushiol, can crystallize and linger in pet fur for weeks—and can continue to infect you every time you pet your pooch. (Your dog can also transfer the oils to pet beds and couch fabrics, as I discovered in my bachelor days.)

Poison oak grows as a deciduous shrub up to 30 inches high. It has triple leaves that are similar in shape to oak leaves and have smooth hair underneath. The plant is dark green, but the leaves can be bright red. The berries start out white, but turn brown.

In Northern California, poison oak is abundant on trails below 4000 feet (the plant doesn't grow above that elevation). Most people subscribe to the "Leaves of three, let it be" motto; however, most dogs don't, and go charging off into the shrub with abandon.

As a general rule, if you don't get the urushiol off your skin within 30 minutes of contact, you're likely to burst out in a nasty rash. There are many over over-the-counter products that you can use, but I've found that a cool-water wash with a good soap such as dish detergent cuts the oil and helps remove it from your skin. Cold or cool water is preferred because it keeps the oil from spreading to other parts of your body. Another solution, when washing isn't an option, is to wipe down any exposed skin with a rag and rubbing alcohol. This also helps cut and remove the oil. If you suspect that your dogs have romped through poison oak, rinse them off

Being prepared on the trail, even if it is in an urban area, is key to having a good hike with your dog.

in a stream or lake where permissible and bathe them with a good dog shampoo when you get home.

And wouldn't you know it? Most dogs are immune to the itch.

Mosquitoes and Ticks

These two pests are the bane of both man and beast. While mosquito and tick bites will leave both welts and scratchy spots, each bite can carry much more.

Mosquitoes. There are more than two hundred different species of mosquito in the United States, and the insect is the most common carrier, or vector, of disease in the world. Bites can cause severe reactions in dogs, but the most pressing problem today is the threat of the West Nile virus.

The virus was first reported in Uganda in 1937 and has spread rapidly to all temperate regions of the world. Since 1999, there have been more than 30,000 reported cases of West Nile Virus across forty-eight states. During this same time, there has been a very small number of reported cases of dogs contracting the disease, according to the Centers for Disease Control and Prevention.

Still, prevention for both you and your pet is paramount in the back-country. Most people infected by the West Nile virus show no symptoms. About 20 percent develop flu-like symptoms, and in some cases the infection can lead to encephalitis or meningitis.

Worse than West Nile for dogs, thirty species of mosquito carry heart-worm larvae. This is a deadly problem in dogs. One bite from a carrier mosquito can deliver millions of microfilaria, or young worms, that travel through the bloodstream and clog the heart.

It's best to pack insect repellent containing DEET. Just another reminder: apply a little to your dog's fur to make sure she doesn't have a reaction, and always avoid getting it near your pet's eyes.

Ticks. Ick. These little pests can carry Lyme disease, Rocky Mountain spotted fever, and a few other potentially fatal diseases. Some diseases and symptoms to watch out for in dogs include:

- Babesiosis: lethargy, weakness, pale gums, appetite loss
- Ehrlichiosis: muscle aches, high fever (most dogs have a core body temperature of 101 to 102 degrees)
- Lyme disease: swollen joints, fever, poor appetite, vomiting (some dogs will show no symptoms)
- Tick paralysis: odd gait from uncoordinated back legs, unsteadiness, gradual paralysis

Ticks also are a chore to remove if you or your dog is bitten. Ticks range in size from a sesame seed to a fingernail, once engorged with blood.

If you take your dog on hikes regularly, you should check him daily. If you find a tick attached, use a fine-pointed pair of tweezers and grasp the tick at the head, but don't squeeze. Use a slow and steady motion and pull the tick's head straight out from the skin, then clean the wound with soap and water.

There are all sorts of topical and chewable products available from your veterinarian to combat these tiny pests. Find out which products might be right for your pet, and use them.

Rattlesnakes

Many hikes in this book will take you through some prime rattlesnake habitat, so always be careful where you walk, especially when stepping over logs or rocks. This is another good reason to always have control of your pooch, as a curious, sniffing dog nose is a prime target for a nasty bite.

Bears and Mountain Lions

It's estimated that there are between 25,000 and 30,000 American black bears in California. Mountain lion populations are harder to track, since little is known about the cougar's comeback in the state (they are federally protected). Current estimates, derived from hunters and road kills, range from 10,000 to 50,000 across the United States and 4000 to 6000 in California alone.

Bears. Cases of bear attacks on humans are rare; however, there were two reported attacks in 2003, according to the California Department of Fish and Game (DFG). Black bears tend to shy away from human and dog contact and will generally flee if they spot you in time. With that said, bears are the Mr. Magoo of the forest; they have poor eyesight. What they can do is smell—extraordinarily well—and hear.

Dogs can be a blessing and a curse when it comes to bears. A leashed dog, or one that is under strict voice command, can alert you to the presence of a bear. A dog running loose, however, may give chase, which may cause a bear to turn and defend itself. In writing this book, I've seen more bears in six months than in the previous eight years of living in Northern California. Go figure. Each encounter ended as soon as it started, by following these guidelines:

- Hike with a group and during daylight hours (bears are more active in the evening and early morning).
- Keep your dog on a leash.
- Be aware of your surroundings and watch for bear signs. Footprints, claw marks on trees, and scat are all signs that a bear has passed your way.
- Talk or sing while on the trail. If bears can hear you coming, they'll likely hightail it the other way.
- Leave the hair spray, cologne, hand creams, scented soaps, and other stinky products at home. Use unscented products, and avoid anything that makes you smell like a huge, tasty treat.

If you're camping overnight in the backcountry, make sure you know the proper way to hang or store food while in camp. Sloppy backpackers make for educated—and bothersome—bears. Some general guidelines include:

- Never clean fish within 100 feet of camp.
- Store all food, including dog food, in designated stuff sacks; hang them overnight and when you leave camp for a day hike. Suspend food bags at least 12 feet off the ground and 8–10 feet from the nearest tree trunk, or use a bear-proof canister to store food. The National Park Service posts great tips on how to hang food at www.nps.gov/olym/planyourvisit/wilderness-food -storage.htm.
- Don't eat, or feed your dog, in your tent. Spilled food or food odors will permeate the tent fabric and serve as a beacon to a bear's nose.

Mountain lions. Chances are, you'll never see a mountain lion in the wild. In eight years, I've been lucky to catch a streak of gold twice—and I still can't be sure if it was a cougar. However, they will see you. These are solitary hunters that normally prey on big game, like deer, bighorn sheep, and elk.

Generally, mountain lions are calm, quiet, and elusive. They are most commonly found in areas with plentiful prey and adequate cover. Because such conditions exist in mountain subdivisions and urban fringes, the number of mountain lion/human interactions has increased.

Surprisingly, there has been little research done on how to avoid an attack by a mountain lion. The following suggestions, provided by the DFG, are based on studies of leopard, tiger, and, lastly, mountain lion attacks:

- Don't hike alone: go in groups, with adults supervising children.
- Keep children and dogs close to you: observations of captured wild mountain lions reveal that the animals seem especially drawn to children. Keep children within your sight at all times.
- Don't approach a lion: most mountain lions will try to avoid a confrontation. Give them a way to escape.
- Don't run from a lion: running may stimulate a mountain lion's instinct to chase. Instead, stand and face the animal. Make eye contact. If you have small children with you, pick them up if possible so they don't panic and run. Although it may be awkward,

Always be aware of potential obstacles and hazards on the trail, but don't forget to stop and take in the beautiful sights you'll encounter too.

pick them up without bending over or turning away from the mountain lion.

- Don't crouch or bend over: in Nepal, a researcher studying tigers and leopards watched the big cats kill cattle and domestic water buffalo while ignoring humans standing nearby. He surmised that a human standing up is just not the right shape for a cat's prey. On the other hand, a person squatting or bending over looks a lot like a four-legged animal. If you're in mountain lion country, avoid squatting, crouching, or bending over.

- Do all you can to appear larger: raise your arms; open your jacket if you're wearing one. Again, pick up small children. Throw stones, branches, or whatever you can reach without crouching or turning your back. Wave your arms slowly and speak firmly in a loud voice. The idea is to convince the mountain lion that you're not prey and that you may be a danger to it.

- Fight back if attacked: a hiker in Southern California used a rock to fend off a mountain lion that was attacking his son. Others have fought back successfully with sticks, caps, jackets, garden tools, and their bare hands. Since a mountain lion usually tries to bite the head or neck, try to remain standing and face the attacking animal.

Weather

Yes, everyone talks about it, people try to forecast it, but let's face it, weather just might be the biggest threat to man and beast in the back-country. Northern California weather is notoriously finicky, and mountain weather can change in a matter of minutes.

In the summer months, thunderstorms can come up quickly and produce heavy rains and, more importantly, lightning. A sudden rain squall can drop temperatures 15 to 20 degrees in minutes. Always remember to pack raingear and to dress in layers (please, please, please avoid cotton) to avoid hypothermia, a cooling of the body's core temperature.

According to the National Oceanic and Atmospheric Administration (NOAA), lightning originates at 15,000 to 25,000 feet above sea level as raindrops are swept upward and turn to ice. Most cloud-to-cloud lightning takes place in this region of ice and water. The charges then move down as if on steps and eventually encounter something on the ground—like a tall tree, or metal tower—that provides a good connection. Here are some guidelines for lightning safety:

- Lightning can strike as much as 10 miles away from the rain area of a thunderstorm. If you can hear thunder, you're within striking distance. Seek shelter immediately. Use the 30-6 rule: When you see lightning, count the time until you hear thunder. If that time is 30 seconds or less, the thunderstorm is within 6 miles of you and is dangerous.
- Be the lowest point. Lightning hits the tallest object. In the mountains if you are above tree line, you are the highest object around. Quickly get below tree line and get into a grove of small trees. Don't be the second tallest object during a lightning storm! Crouch down if you are in an exposed area.
- If you can't get to a shelter, stay away from trees. Crouch in the open, keeping twice as far away from a tree as it is tall.
- Get out of the water. It's a great conductor of electricity. Stay off the beach and out of small boats or canoes. Don't stand in puddles of water, even if you're wearing rubber boots.
- Avoid metal! Drop metal-framed backpacks, and stay away from clotheslines, fences, exposed sheds, and electrically conductive elevated objects.
- Move several yards away from other people. Don't huddle in a group.

Expect that Mother Nature will try to throw you a curve ball each and every time you venture outdoors. Come prepared, pack your raingear, and call ahead and get the latest forecast for the area you plan to visit. People also can use a NOAA weather radio (a radio set to tune into one of the national weather frequencies), which costs between $30 and $75.

How to Use This Book

Trail guides are hardly an exact science. What was true of a trail last summer might not be the case next summer. No guide can provide all the details of a trail or stay current with constantly changing conditions and administrative rules. Before heading out on any adventure, it's best to call ahead to the land management agency to get the latest trail report—and make sure the trail is open to you and your dog.

With each hike in this guide, you'll find round-trip or one-way mileage, hiking time, difficulty rating, high point, elevation gain, best times to hike, water availability, regulations for dogs, USGS or other mapping resources, contact information, and directions to the trailhead and a trail description.

Round-trip or one-way miles and hiking time. I can hike a mile in about 20 minutes, which is the estimate I used in determining time and distance in this guide. I also tried to factor in time for steep grades and rough tread. You might find that my estimates are too low, or too high. Apply them as needed to help you plan a trip.

Difficulty. Each hike in this book is labeled with one or a combination of three difficulty ratings:

- Easy: Short, lower-intensity hikes with mostly flat and rolling terrain and a relatively even trail surface
- Moderate: Long, more intense hikes with terrain ranging from short steep sections to rolling terrain with potential for uneven, rocky sections of trail
- Strenuous: Long or very intense hikes with sustained steep climbs and descents; rocky, loose, uneven sections of trail; and difficult-to-navigate obstacles.

While I've done my best to describe each hike's difficulty level, ratings are highly subjective and everyone will have different fitness levels and abilities. When in doubt, talk with an official familiar with the trail or someone who has hiked it before.

Paul keeps his eyes on the prize of Mount Eddy.

Elevation gain. The elevation gain is the total feet in elevation gained from the trailhead to the end of the hike. Thus, elevation gain combined with distance will give you a good indication of the overall difficulty of a hike.

Best hiking time. This also is subjective, and the season suggested here is meant as a guide, not as an absolute. I like to hike some trails in spring, when there's still snow on the ground. Others prefer not to be cold—in any instance. Many high-mountain trails might not be passable until July. Use the contact information to get the latest trail report.

Many of the trails—and I always indicate which—can be hiked year-round, with or without snowshoes.

Water. When you head out for a hike, always bring water for your dog and yourself. In addition, bring a purifier so you can pump water from a suitable source along the way if necessary. I have indicated suitable water sources for each hike. When in doubt, always plan on bringing your own.

Regulations. This is where you'll find out exactly what is allowed for your dog on each hike, whether he or she must be leashed or can be allowed to roam off leash under strict voice control.

Maps. While some USGS maps haven't been updated since the 1970s, I believe USGS maps are still the best to carry. I use the 7.5-minute series, which are available nearly everywhere, including online at http://ngmdb .usgs.gov/ or at www.topozone.com.

How the Trails Were Selected

With nineteen national forests comprising 20 million acres in California, the choices are nearly overwhelming. Factor in BLM lands, regional parks, and state lands, and you'd have a book that could go on forever.

This book isn't meant to be a complete resource for all the trails in Northern California, nor is it a guide to the best of them. My goal was to present a sampling of what is available, from the wilds of far Northern California to the easy day hikes of the Bay Area's regional park and preserve system. I sought to include day hikes and overnighters. I tried to stay away from those trails that are used heavily, since some people just don't like sharing the trail with dogs.

I tried for a mix of trails that would appeal to humans and dogs. Water features, places with awe-inspiring views, and simple places where a dog might run free are high on my list of "musts."

I avoided steep, rocky places where possible, and most waterfalls. I tried to find places where the reward is a pond, lake, or a gentle stream—I've yet to meet a dog that didn't love to swim.

Some of the trails were selected for their gentleness, to get those newbies with dogs out and about. I've tried to list a few trails that will appeal to summer hikers and that can double as snowshoe hikes in the winter.

With all this in mind, I came up with eighty-three hikes from my experiences on trails located around the San Francisco Bay Area, Sacramento, Tahoe, and Redding. Certainly, enjoy them all—but don't limit yourself to just these eighty-three. Find what works for you and your dog, and continue to expand your appreciation for the wonderful wilds of Northern California.

Keep Our Open Spaces Open: Get Involved

I wrote this book in hopes of sharing my love of the outdoors with other dog owners. The dogs and I have traveled far and wide in search of adventure, enjoying a simple day hike along a mountain stream as well as all-out backpacking treks into some of California's more rugged public lands.

The trails exist for our enjoyment, and for the enjoyment of future generations. Use the trails often, but always remember to protect them as well. Be careful with your actions, so no one can complain that dogs cause damage to our trails.

Also, be aware of what is happening to our public lands. Stay informed and stay involved. It might be as simple as contacting your representative, urging them to support wilderness protection, or even asking them to allow dogs in new regional parks and open spaces. For more information on open space issues, contact the following groups:

California Wilderness Coalition
PO Box 11094
Oakland, CA 94611
Phone: (510) 451-1450
Fax: (510) 451-1445
info@calwild.org
www.calwild.org

The Mountaineers
7700 Sand Point Way NE
Seattle, WA 98115
(206) 521-6001
www.mountaineers.org

—Thom Gabrukiewicz, author of the first edition

A Note About Safety

Safety is an important concern in all outdoor activities. No guidebook can alert you to every hazard or anticipate the limitations of every reader. Therefore, the descriptions of roads, trails, routes, and natural features in this book are not representations that a particular place or excursion will be safe for your party. When you follow any of the routes described in this book, you assume responsibility for your own safety. Under normal conditions, such excursions require the usual attention to traffic, road and trail conditions, weather, terrain, the capabilities of your party, and other factors. Keeping informed on current conditions and exercising common sense are the keys to a safe, enjoyable outing.

—The Mountaineers Books

PART 2

The Trails

SAN FRANCISCO BAY AREA

SAN FRANCISCO AND SOUTH BAY

1. Golden Gate Promenade

Round-trip: 6 miles
Hiking time: 2–3 hours
Difficulty: Easy
High point: 175 feet
Elevation gain: 150 feet
Best hiking time: Year-round
Water: Best to bring your own
Regulations: Dogs must be leashed except in the signed area on the beach where they are allowed off leash
Map: USGS San Francisco North
Contact: Presidio Visitor Center, (415) 561-4323

Getting there: From U.S. Highway 101 on the south side of the Golden Gate Bridge, take the Marina Boulevard exit and head south toward Fisherman's Wharf. Parking lots are available off Marina Boulevard at Fort Mason, Marina Green, Crissy Field, and near the St. Francis Yacht Club. The route below begins at Marina Green.

Okay, okay, this trek leads you past a lot of what people come to San Francisco for in the first place. But hey, who says we can't be hikers and sightseers?

This paved trail heads along the shoreline of San Francisco Bay from Marina Green to Fort Point and the southern footings of the Golden

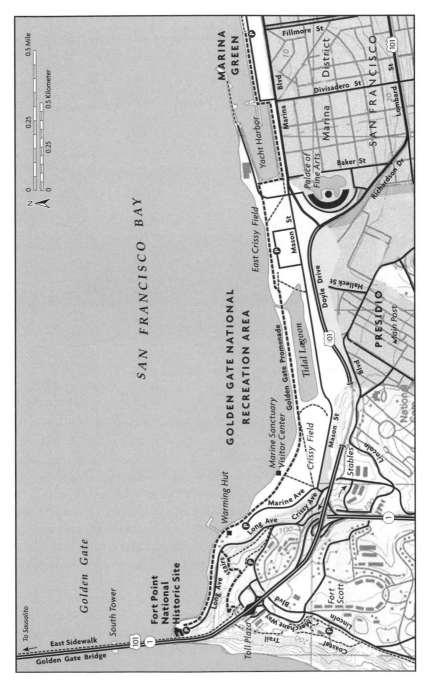

Both dogs and people enjoy strolling along the Promenade.

Gate Bridge. Along the way, you'll see the sights, like the San Francisco skyline, Alcatraz, Tiburon, San Francisco Bay, and of course, the brick-red bridge that just might be the most photographed landmark in the Bay Area—the Golden Gate.

This is a leisurely hike where you can socialize with other dog lovers (be sure to ask before introducing your pooch to other leashed pets) and people-watch to your heart's content. Be sure to pack a jacket so you don't get caught out by the gusty, cool breezes, significant temperature drops, fog, and rain that can roll in unexpectedly along the bay.

The entire length of the promenade is hip and artsy. In the morning, and again in the evening, recreational joggers fill the trail, and during the day you'll pass people painting, playing drums, or making sand sculptures, and others who will likely be fishing, in-line skating, and riding mountain bikes.

After passing Marina Green, a large grassy area where you'll likely see fanciful kite fliers, head toward Crissy Field, where the first aircraft to this field landed in preparation for coastal defense in the 1920s. Soon, you'll reach Fort Point, where the U.S. Army seeded the bay around the Golden Gate with mines in World War II.

After a short climb through a garden setting, Battery East comes into view, where five gigantic guns once protected the bay entrance, way back in 1870. Go through the tunnel and look down on Fort Point proper, where the red-brick buildings were designed to mount 126 huge muzzle-loaded cannons (but nary a one was actually fired).

Continue on underneath the Golden Gate, hang out, then reverse your tracks to head back to Marina Green and the maze of people doing their things.

2. Inspiration Point

Round-trip: 2-mile loop
Hiking time: 1.5 hours
Difficulty: Easy
High point: 365 feet
Elevation gain: 432 feet
Best hiking time: Year-round
Water: Bring your own, for you and your dog
Regulations: Dogs must be leashed
Map: USGS San Francisco North
Contact: Presidio Visitor Center, (415) 561-4323

Getting there: Driving north on State Route 1 in San Francisco, turn east (right) onto Lake Street, drive 0.7 mile, and turn left onto Arguello Boulevard. Follow this road 0.2 mile, turn right to stay on Arguello, and pass through the Arguello Gate into the Presidio. In another 0.2 mile turn right into the parking lot for Inspiration Point.

Driving south on SR 1, turn west (right) on Lake Street, drive one block, and turn left onto 14th Avenue. Take the next left onto California Street, drive 0.8 mile, turn left on Arguello Boulevard, and follow the same route to the trailhead.

Inspiration Point in San Francisco's Presidio is a great jumping-off place for a couple miles of scenic and relaxed hiking. This historic former military post and now national park offers much in the way of views and meandering trails.

Take the Ecology Trail down a set of stairs near the south end of the

Inspiration Point parking lot, and go left on the signed trail at the bottom. Within just a few steps you'll pass a serpentine grassland restoration project on your right. Continue along the well-graded and level trail as it passes beautiful grasslands on either side, then works its way across the hillside toward a tall stand of redwood trees.

Go left at the next junction to remain on the Ecology Trail as it descends through the darkening forest. As you near the 0.5-mile mark, you'll come to a clearing with a wooden bench. Continue downhill on the well-worn main path about 100 yards, bearing left at the junction to stay on the signed Ecology Trail.

Leave the Ecology Trail at the next junction, heading left on an

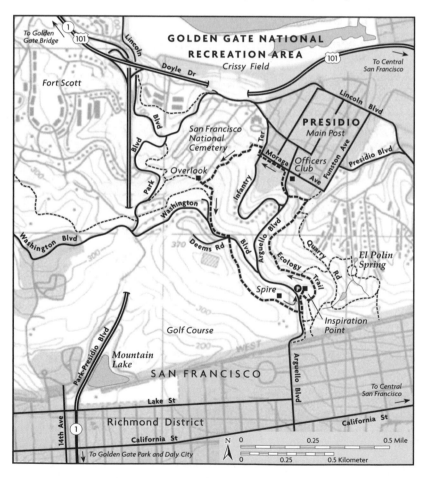

The Spire sculpture juts toward the sky near the top of the hill above Inspiration Point.

unsigned trail through a clearing and up a brick pathway to the sidewalk on the southeast side of Arguello Boulevard.

Cross the road and take the sidewalk downhill to the right. Very soon, you'll come to the junction with Moraga Avenue. Straight ahead is the Presidio's Main Post where you can see the old cannons and flags of this historic military post.

Go left on Moraga, and at almost 1 mile turn right on Infantry Terrace. Take the stairs on the left side of the road, and ascend toward the Presidio Chapel. At the top of the stairs is a good view of the Golden Gate Bridge through the trees to the north. Turn left to skirt the southeastern side of the chapel and take the unsigned trail, which climbs through the forest of eucalyptus and brambles up the hillside above.

At an unsigned junction, take the trail to the right. Stay on this path and ignore any smaller trails that split off to either side. At another unsigned junction, go right again and continue to climb through the forest with pleasant sandy soil underfoot.

At the top of the climb you'll reach the overlook for the San Francisco National Cemetery. Here you'll find benches where you can grab a short rest while taking in the view of the cemetery with its white cross grave markers, as well as the Golden Gate and Marin Headlands beyond. The cemetery, officially dedicated in 1884, was the first of its kind on the West Coast.

Continue to the paved path beyond the overlook and turn left. Go left at the next junction on the trail signed ARGUELLO GATE 0.7 MILE AND INSPIRATION POINT 0.6 MILE. The trail skirts the left side of a parking lot and continues along Washington Boulevard. You are now hiking along a portion of the Bay Area Ridge Trail.

At nearly 1.5 miles the trail crosses Washington Boulevard and Deems Road, continues to climb, and splits into three; take the unsigned middle trail. At the next junction take the unsigned trail to the left, which heads directly toward the giant jutting sculpture *Spire*.

The trail now descends gently toward a crosswalk at Arguello Boulevard just before Finley Road. Cross the road and go left on the trail on the other side. Within another 100 yards you'll find yourself back at Inspiration Point and your car.

3. Mount Davidson Park

Round-trip: 1-mile loop
Hiking time: 1 hour
Difficulty: Easy
High point: 927 feet
Elevation gain: 359 feet
Best hiking time: Year-round
Water: Bring your own, for you and your dog
Regulations: Dogs must be leashed
Map: USGS San Francisco South
Contact: San Francisco Recreation & Parks Department,
    (415) 831-2700

Getting there: Traveling north on State Route 1 in San Francisco, merge right onto Junipero Serra Boulevard and drive 1.7 miles to a multiple-road junction. Bear right onto Portola Drive, continue 0.9 mile, and turn right onto Rex Avenue. Take the next right onto Juanita Way, left on Lansdale Avenue, and another left onto Dalewood Way. Drive 0.3 mile on Dalewood and park on the street before the bus stop.

Traveling south on SR 1 (19th Avenue), north of SR 35 (Sloat Boulevard), turn left onto Sloat and drive 0.2 mile to the same multiple-road junction. Bear left onto Portola Drive and follow the same directions as above.

Mount Davidson is the highest point in San Francisco at 927 feet. Its peak is also home to a giant concrete 103-foot cross, which stands as a memorial to the 1.5 million victims of the genocide of Armenians at the hands of the Ottoman Turks between 1915 and 1923. A short and easy hike, it is one you shouldn't miss as it affords amazing panoramic views of the city of San Francisco, the bay, and, on a clear day, the jutting point of Mount Diablo off in the distance to the east.

Many unmarked trails crisscross the park, and while a fire road provides a straightforward direct ascent to the top, I prefer a less direct approach trail, which corkscrews its way around the mountain up to the top. This route gives you more mileage, exposes more views, and highlights the stark contrasts in the plant life you wouldn't get if you hiked the direct route.

The rolling, grassy side of Mount Davidson offers up some stunning views of the city.

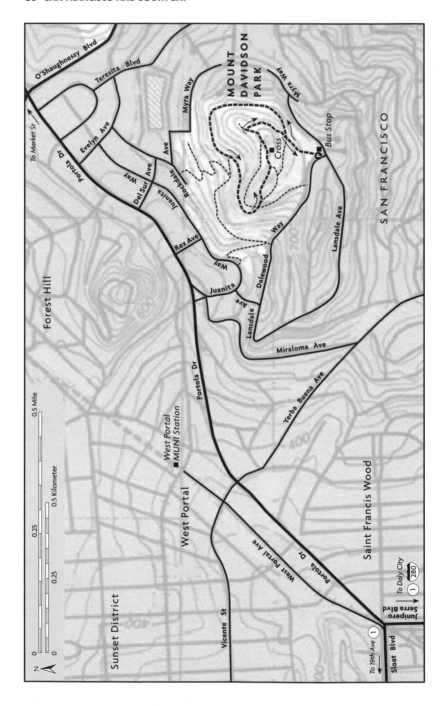

From the parking area, embark on the main trail as it climbs steadily toward the summit. Very soon you'll come to a junction; take the smaller, well-traveled trail to the right. This trail passes close to an erosion-control fence and traverses the rocky grassland that dominates the eastern flank of the mountain. Along this section of trail you'll get your first good views of the city and the bay below.

Ignore the several small "goat" trails that split off to either side, and continue your traverse. As you work your way around the north side of the hill to the western slope, the plant life changes from dry grassland to lush coastal forest. Soon after this transition, at 0.4 mile bear left at an unsigned junction where a side trail (shown on the map) heads northwest.

Within another couple hundred yards from the junction, the trail crosses a fire road and climbs a flight of steps. At the top of the steps, take the trail that splits off to the left, climbing another set of steps to a large clearing. Follow the trail through this large clearing to the southeast, and after another short climb you'll find yourself at the top of the hill, standing near the dramatic concrete cross. After a quiet moment of contemplation, make your way across the clearing to the official hilltop and the vista beyond. The best views of the area can be taken in here.

When you are done gazing at the views and snapping pictures, follow the stepped trail down the hill, which runs northeast toward another lesser hilltop vista point, and take the rocky trail immediately to the right. Very soon you'll find yourself back at the first junction you encountered.

4. Glen Canyon Park

Round-trip: 1-mile loop or more
Hiking time: 30 minutes–1 hour
Difficulty: Easy
High point: 383 feet
Elevation gain: 237 feet
Best hiking time: Year-round
Water: Bring your own, for you and your dog
Regulations: Dogs must be leashed
Map: USGS San Francisco South
Contact: San Francisco Recreation & Parks Department,
(415) 831-2700

Getting there: From Interstate 280 north in San Francisco, exit onto San Jose Avenue (exit 52) and turn right onto Rousseau Street. Take your next right onto Bosworth Street to cross under I-280. In 0.7 mile, turn right to stay on Bosworth and park in the small lot before the gate.

From I-280 south in San Francisco, exit at Monterey Boulevard (exit 52) and take a sharp right onto Monterey. In less than 0.1 mile turn left onto Diamond Street. After one block, turn left onto Bosworth Street and follow the same directions above to the parking area.

Man and beast have proven their ability to adapt to all kinds of living situations, but sometimes the environments we live in wear on us. A

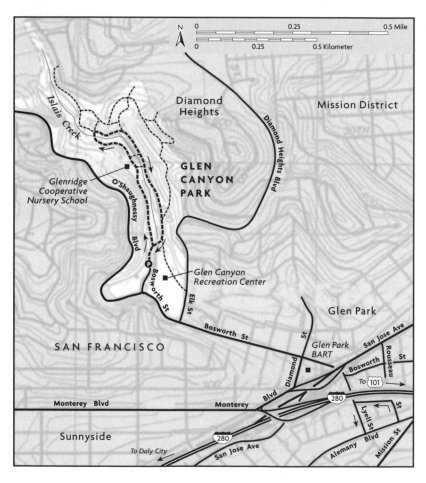

Glen Canyon's steep walls are crisscrossed with paths and peppered with trees.

great way to regain our sanity is to go outside and take a quiet stroll in nature with our faithful dogs, in a place like Glen Canyon Park, a lovely little canyon of open space around Islais Creek.

Glen Canyon Recreation Center near the base of the canyon is home to basketball and tennis courts, a baseball diamond, and playground. Beyond, up the canyon, is a loop of hiking and walking trails that skirt each side of the creek and put you in touch with lovely views, a lot of plant life, as well as some dramatic rock ledges and cliffs.

The park is popular with local hikers and dog walkers, as many trails connect to the park from the neighborhoods on either side. Starting your hike from the parking area, pass the gate and walk up the path past the recreation center. Here the trail splits to follow both sides of the creek. Take the trail on left side of the creek, which heads north through a grove of eucalyptus trees.

In less than 0.5 mile, pass the Glenridge Cooperative Nursery School and continue up the trail, which draws nearer to the creek and becomes dark and tunnel-like as it travels through brambles and underbrush. As you draw nearer to the creek, the water makes the ground very soft and muddy in places, so be sure to watch your step. This area is dog heaven with many places to sniff around and explore.

Soon the trail crosses the creek and heads back down the canyon on the other side. Several small side trails in this area offer places to explore and extend your hike. A side trail to the left climbs up to a landing where you can scramble up to the top of a huge outcrop for a nice view of the park below. Other trails, some quite steep, take off from this area up the north end and east side of the canyon, presenting opportunities for more exercise and views of the city. You and your pooch could easily stay in the park longer and both get an intense workout on these steeper trails. Just be careful around the rock ledges.

As you get back onto the main trail, it passes over a marshy creekside meadow via a raised walkway and continues back down the creek toward the recreation center. When you are ready to pack it in for the day, continue down this trail and make your way back to your car.

5. McLaren Park

Round-trip: 1.2-mile loop or more
Hiking time: 1 hour
Difficulty: Easy
High point: 468 feet
Elevation gain: 284 feet
Best hiking time: Year-round
Water: Bring your own, for you and your dog
Regulations: Surrounding the reservoir there is a large signed area where dogs are allowed off leash; elsewhere in the park, dogs must be leashed
Map: USGS San Francisco South
Contact: San Francisco Recreation & Parks Department, (415) 831-2700

Getting there: From Mission Street south of Interstate 280 in San Francisco, drive south and turn left (east) onto Persia Avenue. In 0.8 mile Persia becomes Mansell Street. Stay on Mansell for 0.4 mile and turn left onto John F. Shelley Drive. Continue another 0.4 mile and park at the lot on the right overlooking the reservoir.

In addition to being one of the largest parks in the city of San Francisco at over 300 hilly acres, McLaren Park has several features that make it a perfect destination for people who want to get outdoors with their dogs. The park has a huge area designated for off-leash play, complete with a man-made lake where dogs can splash around, make friends, play, and fetch.

The park attracts scores of dog owners and professional dog walkers every day. If your beast isn't friendly or properly socialized, it is best to

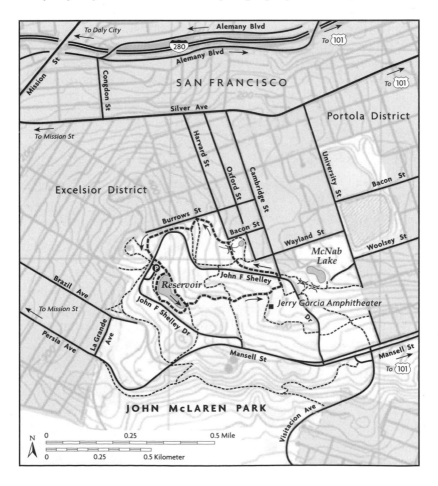

keep him or her on a leash to prevent conflicts. At McLaren you will be approached by a lot of unleashed dogs, so be in control of Fido at all times.

The options for hikes in the park are seemingly endless and the trails are unmarked, so you can put together whatever length and difficulty loop you'd like.

A loop I favor begins at the lot overlooking the reservoir. Take the trail at the north end of the lot with stairs down to the lake. I normally choose to walk first and play later, because I have found that a well-exercised dog is more manageable when it comes time to romp and play with other dogs.

Walk around either side of the reservoir and take the dirt trail at the far end, which leads downhill. The trail rolls through a few grassy meadows before it reaches a clearing with a tall stand of trees on the right. The trail here splits off in several directions with a smaller trail to the left and larger, worn trails to the middle and right. Take the well-worn middle trail down the hill, and soon you'll skirt and pass by the north side of

The reservoir at McLaren Park is a great place to meet and play with other dogs.

Jerry Garcia Amphitheater. This is a good place to releash your dog, as you'll soon leave the off-leash zone.

At just under the 0.5-mile mark you'll reach a junction with a paved path and turn left. At the next junction turn left again. This path will shortly deliver you to John F. Shelley Drive just across from its intersection with Cambridge Street. Cross the street and pick up the paved path to the left off Cambridge, which heads back uphill to the west, paralleling the road.

At the next junction, take a right and walk north across a wooden bridge over a lush marsh. Turn left at the next junction and climb up the rough asphalt trail as it hugs the north edge of the park.

Near the 1-mile mark you'll pass a fountain, turn south briefly, and then continue along the north border of the park. Pass a basketball court and bear left at the next junction. Then cross back over John F. Shelley Drive and find the parking lot just beyond. Now you can enjoy some playtime at the reservoir, or just call it a day.

6. Fort Funston Sunset Trail

Round-trip: 1.5-mile loop
Hiking time: 1 hour
Difficulty: Easy
High point: 180 feet
Elevation gain: Negligible
Best hiking time: Fall and winter (to avoid heavy fog); hikable year-round
Water: From fountains
Regulations: Dogs are allowed off leash but must be under strict voice control at all times; stay out of the 12-acre habitat protection area, signed closed
Map: USGS San Francisco South
Contact: Golden Gate National Recreation Area, (415) 561-4700

Getting there: From near Daly City, take Interstate 280 to State Route 1 in San Bruno. Turn west and drive 1 mile to SR 35/Skyline Boulevard. Turn right (north) onto SR 35 and drive 5 miles, where you'll bear left and pass Lake Merced. Turn left at Fort Funston and park for free.

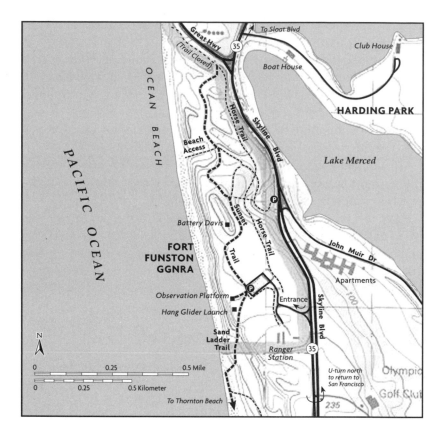

From San Francisco, take Geary Boulevard west until it dead-ends at the ocean near the Cliff House Restaurant. Turn left onto the Great Highway and drive 1 mile to the parking area.

If they built an amusement park just for dogs, it would look like Fort Funston. I mean, this Golden Gate National Recreation Area (GGNRA) park puts the fun in Funston. Dog owners are actually encouraged to take their dogs off leash for frolicking with the seemingly hundreds of other dogs that scamper along the park's paved Sunset Trail. There are plenty of places to stop and sniff, areas to chase balls, and plenty of warm sand to roll in.

The Fort Funston Dog Walkers promote good stewardship of the area (as well as assuring that the area stays dog-friendly) by providing plastic bags to police your pooch, as well as policing the area themselves.

Here, you'll also see people hang gliding off the cliff (there's a launching area just south of the parking area), as well as history buffs who come to visit the remnants of Battery Richmond P. Davis, which was completed in the early 1900s. The battery, which included two state-of-the-art 16-inch guns that each had a range of 25 miles, featured 10 feet of reinforced concrete topped by 20 feet of earth, which made it nearly impossible to see from the air. The battery was dismantled in 1948, but you can still wander around the fortified concrete structure.

This trail is best in fall and winter, when the fog clears and a walk at dusk will bring goose bumps—not from the chilled Pacific air, but from the sight of the sun sinking into the ocean.

Pick up the Sunset Trail near the viewing area for the hang gliders and go north. It meanders through the coastal bluffs (signs warn against getting too close) for 0.75 mile to the park's boundary. Return to your car the way you came.

You can also drop down to Ocean Beach, where you'll likely see a variety of dog breeds happily chasing balls and retrieving driftwood from the surf. To get to the beach, walk south from the parking area and look for the Sand Ladder Trail toward the edge of the bluff.

Hikers and dogs should not stray too close to the crumbly cliff.

7. Ocean Beach Esplanade

Round-trip: 6 miles
Hiking time: 3 hours
Difficulty: Easy
High point: 150 feet
Elevation gain: 150 feet
Best hiking time: Fall and winter (to avoid heavy fog); hikable year-round
Water: From fountains, but bring some of your own
Regulations: Dogs must be leashed on the paved trail; on the beach dogs must be under their owner's control at all times either on leash or under strict voice command
Map: USGS San Francisco South
Contact: Golden Gate National Recreation Area, (415) 561-4700

Getting there: From near Daly City, take Interstate 280 to State Route 1 in San Bruno. Turn west and drive 1 mile to SR 35/Skyline Boulevard. Turn right (north) onto SR 35 and drive 5 miles, where you'll bear left onto Great Highway. Drive north for 4 miles. Just past the Cliff House Restaurant, the road curves right. You'll take a quick left into the Lands End Lookout Visitor Center parking lot.

From San Francisco, take Geary Boulevard west until it becomes Point Lobos Avenue. Turn right into the Lands End Lookout Visitor Center parking lot before you reach the Cliff House Restaurant.

This expanse of beach is popular with many a group, from surfers who tackle the rough surf (the undertow here is tremendous; swimming is not allowed in the frigid waters), to runners passing over the hard-packed sand when the tide is low, to dogs and their owners out for a little exercise.

Ocean Beach features sand, surf, a paved trail, and the chance to explore Fort Funston (Hike 6) and Thornton Beach. Since there's the option of a paved trail, as well as the sandy expanse, you can create treks of variable length. The beach stretches from Seal Rocks near the Cliff House south to Fort Funston.

On the paved trail, please leash your dog and keep strict control, as this is a popular stop for tourists as well as locals. You used to be able to

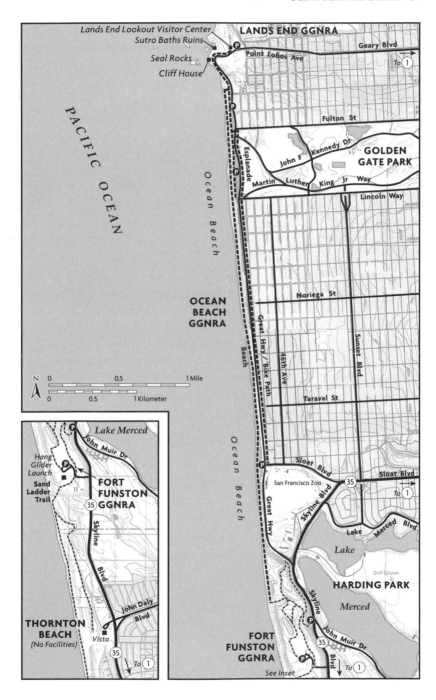

LANDS END GGNRA

Lands End Lookout Visitor Center

Sutro Baths Ruins

Seal Rocks

Cliff House

Geary Blvd

To 1

Point Lobos Ave

Fulton St

PACIFIC OCEAN

Esplanade

John F Kennedy Dr

GOLDEN GATE PARK

Martin Luther King Jr Way

Lincoln Way

Ocean Beach

OCEAN BEACH GGNRA

Noriega St

Great Hwy / Bike Path

46th Ave

Sunset Blvd

Taraval St

N

0   0.5   1 Mile

0   0.5   1 Kilometer

Ocean Beach

Sloat Blvd

Sloat Blvd

To 1

San Francisco Zoo

35

Great Hwy

Skyline Blvd

Lake Merced Blvd

Lake

Golf Course

Merced

HARDING PARK

Lake Merced

John Muir Dr

Hang Glider Launch

Sand Ladder Trail

FORT FUNSTON GGNRA

35

Skyline Blvd

Skyline Blvd

John Muir Dr

35

Blvd

To 1

John Daly Blvd

THORNTON BEACH
(No Facilities)

Vista

35

To 1

FORT FUNSTON GGNRA

See Inset

The Ocean Beach Esplanade is wide, inviting, and cooled by sea breezes.

take your dog off leash on the beach, but no more. The rangers and park police are enforcing the leash law on Ocean Beach.

Amble along the beach to the Esplanade's terminus at Fort Funston and watch people beachcombing for shells and bits of glass polished by wave action.

8. Sweeney Ridge

Round-trip: 4.2 miles
Hiking time: 3 hours
Difficulty: Moderate
High point: 1250 feet
Elevation gain: 550 feet
Best hiking time: Year-round
Water: Bring your own, for you and your dog
Regulations: Dogs must be leashed
Map: USGS San Francisco South
Contact: Golden Gate National Recreation Area, (415) 561-4700

Getting there: From the San Francisco Bay Bridge, take Interstate 80 to U.S. Highway 101 south to I-280 south. Take the Pacifica/State Route 1 exit and then get off at Skyline Boulevard south, signed for SR 35. Past the Skyline College entrance, about 4 miles, turn right on Sneath Lane and drive it through the neighborhood until its end. The parking area is on the right past the gate.

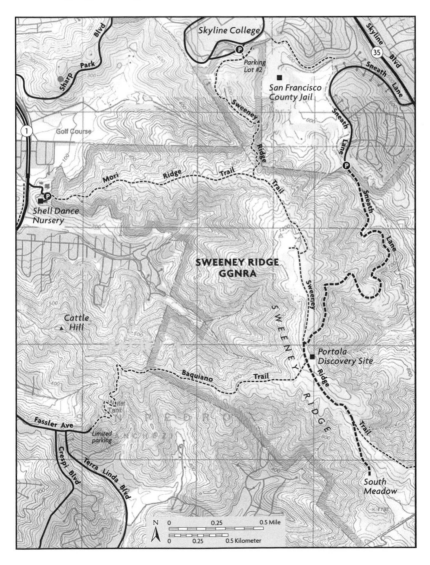

I don't live in the Bay Area; if I did, I'd take the dogs on this hike as many times as I could.

Sweeney Ridge is the dividing point between Pacifica and San Bruno, about 10 miles south of San Francisco proper. As a hiker (and outdoor-writer type) said about this trek, "No matter how long you've lived in the Bay Area, there's always a chance to make it new again."

The ridge, which includes the busy I-280/US 101 corridor and San Francisco International Airport, rises 1250 feet above the din, offering 360-degree views and something much better—some solitude from the very urban setting below. Protected as part of the Golden Gate National Recreation Area in 1984, there are trails here that will help you leave civilization, for a little while.

This hike starts with 550 feet of climbing, which isn't all bad, especially if the dogs have been in the car for any length of time. The views start on your left as you climb, with San Andreas Lake coming into focus, then Crystal Springs. While there are four access points total to this area, this trek brings you up the ridge directly to the Portola Discovery Site.

The view from atop Sweeney Ridge, where wildlife abounds in an urban setting

In 1769, an expedition led by Don Gaspar de Portola was charged with finding an overland route to Monterey Bay. The Spanish party left Mexico with sixty-four men and two hundred horses, including one scout, José Francisco Ortega. Ortega climbed the ridge near the group's camp (in the Linda Mar area of Pacifica today) and said he saw "an enormous area of the sea, or estuary, which shot inland as far as the eye could see." He became the first European to see San Francisco Bay.

On the ridge, you'll stand directly on that historic spot, now dedicated with a monument to Carl McCarthy, who helped secure public ownership of the area. The views here are just stunning, with the Bay Area and San Pedro Mountain, Montara Mountain, Mori Ridge, the Crystal Springs watershed, Mount Diablo, and the Mount Hamilton range.

It's easy to stop here, but walk a little farther, just 10 minutes. As you continue south on the ridge, look for a side trail off to the right (it's not signed). Make the right, and in 5 minutes you'll arrive at an overlook of what is known as South Meadow—a fantastic wildlife habitat where deer, rabbits, quail, and raptors make their home—along with a stunning view of the ocean.

Once you've had your fill, reverse course back to your car, back to humanity.

9. Rockaway Point

Round-trip: 2.6 miles
Hiking time: 1–2 hours
Difficulty: Easy
High point: 150 feet
Elevation gain: 150 feet
Best hiking time: Year-round
Water: Bring your own
Regulations: Dogs must be leashed
Map: USGS Montara Mountain
Contact: Pacifica Parks and Recreation Division, (650) 738-7381

Getting there: Drive to the south end of the community of Pacifica on State Route 1 and park for free in the large paved lot signed for San Pedro Beach, about a block north of Linda Mar Boulevard.

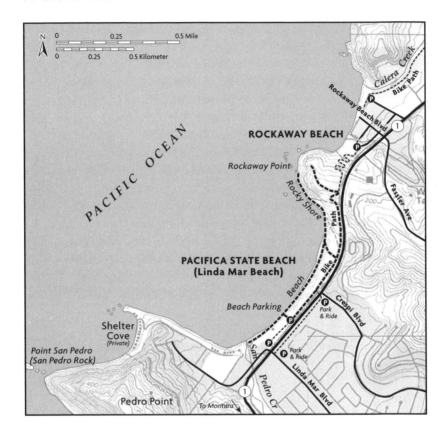

The first thing you'll notice on this hike is how many people pack the middle of Pacifica State Beach. Walk all the way up the beach to near Rockaway Point or along the paved recreation and bike trail, and you'll have a much greater chance to find a bit of solitude.

The beach is popular with surfers who jam the area to check out the waves. But those knowledgeable of Pacifica seek out the block-shaped Rockaway Point—said to hum with magical vibrations—where you can sit and get a great view of the Pacific Ocean. Be careful and abide by any trail closure signs, as this area, like many others along the rocky ocean cliffs, is susceptible to dangerous erosion conditions.

Start this hike from the parking lot and head north. This stretch of beach features hard-packed cocoa-colored sand, and if your dogs are like mine, they'll want to romp with you, chasing the frothy white surf—then running from the next incoming wave. San Pedro Beach to the south is nearly level, and where the low sand dunes rise to meet the sprawl near SR 1, ice plants bloom in a variety of colors in the spring.

Be sure to look to the southeast at Montara Mountain, which is shrouded by cloud cover for much of the year. A few Monterey cypress trees grow here, but not to the magnificent size they do elsewhere along the coast due to the pounding this area gets from the brisk sea breezes.

Hiking north you'll reach the bluff of Rockaway Point in a little under a mile, where you'll get the best view of San Pedro Rock to the south, which rises from the sea like volcanic lumps. Here, you'll find your first spur trail that will cross a gulch and lead into an area of sea stacks, where you can explore at low tide. Go a bit farther, about halfway around Rockaway Point, for great views of the impressive sea stacks, which seem to frame Montara Mountain.

Looking toward Point San Pedro along the Pacific Coast

From here, retrace your steps to the northern edge of the beach at about 1.2 miles and find another trail that leads up Rockaway Point. The summit is actually a sloping field that allows for exploration and fantastic 360-degree views of the area. Come in the spring, and the area will be ablaze in wildflowers.

Once you're finished exploring, just retrace your steps back to your car.

10. Gray Whale Cove

Round-trip: 4 miles
Hiking time: 2 hours
Difficulty: Easy to moderate
High point: 100 feet
Elevation gain: 150 feet
Best hiking time: Year-round
Water: Bring your own
Regulations: Dogs must be leashed
Map: USGS Montara Mountain
Contact: McNee Ranch State Park Ranger Office, (650) 726-8819

Paul takes in the ocean views.

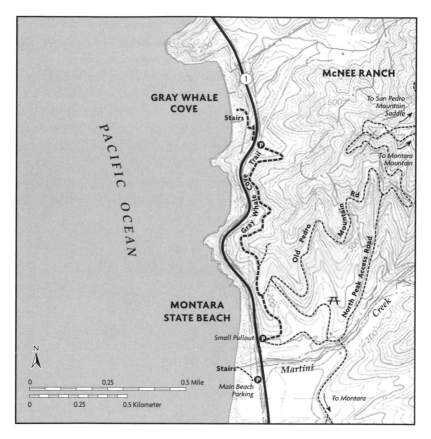

Getting there: Drive south on State Route 1 past the community of Pacifica to just north of Montara State Beach, some 10 miles north of Half Moon Bay. Park at the small pullout with an unsigned gate on the east side of the highway where you can park for free; if it's packed with surfers heading to the beach, you can also access the trail from the free parking area to the south at Montara State Beach.

This hike takes in the rugged Pacific coastline, where every view becomes a study of how the surf pounds the land. While the waves crash, you'll be pleasantly above it all, where the views give you a feeling of being perched on a lookout of a sailing ship—the wind constantly in your face. The trail stays near winding SR 1, but it never seems to detract from the view. Don't forget to bring your camera, as there are plenty of chances to take new and better shots of the sand, surf, and cliffs.

One note of caution: if you opt to take the wooden stairs down to Gray Whale Cove, the beach is clothing-optional. Gawkers are not welcome here, so stay on the trail to get arguably better views.

Gray Whale Cove Trail is mostly flat and, through its numerous twists and turns, you'll likely see waves of coffeeberry, monkey flower, and lizard's tail shrubs and coyote brush. As you work your way north, near the mid-point of the hike, a spur trail climbs steeply for some 200 yards to a welcoming knoll that offers great views of Montara Mountain and the blue Pacific.

Back on the main trail, you'll continue north and drop gently for a bit to the Gray Whale Cove parking area, which signals the point where you'll turn back to your own vehicle.

11. Montara Beach to North Peak

Round-trip: 8.6 miles
Hiking time: 4–5 hours
Difficulty: Strenuous
High point: 1840 feet
Elevation gain: 1740 feet
Best hiking time: Year-round
Water: Bring your own
Regulations: Dogs must be leashed
Map: USGS Montara Mountain
Contact: McNee Ranch State Park Ranger Office, (650) 726-8819; Half Moon Bay State Beach, (650) 726-8820

Getting there: From San Francisco, take State Route 1 south 17 miles through Pacifica. Continue south, past Devils Slide and down to the base of the hill. Look for a small pullout on the left. The trail access point is at a yellow gate with a state park property sign on it; do not block the gate. If the area is full, try parking at the lot on the west side of SR 1 at Montara State Beach.

Wildflowers on the way up to North Peak

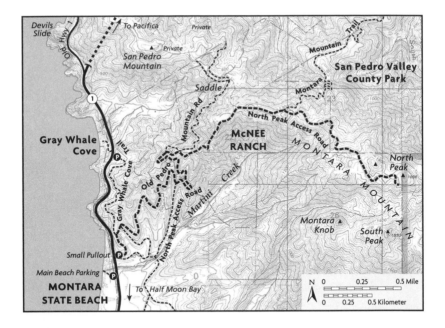

I'll admit it: I have a sick fascination with peak bagging. It's not my fault, you see. I have a border collie, and it's the only way I can get her to behave in the car. Tire her out so she'll actually sleep on the way home.

This trail actually started in 1879 when, according to the city of Pacifica, settlers pushed a dirt trail up from the coastline over San Pedro Mountain. Gaining 1740 feet in a very short stretch, this hike is for people who love a challenge, with a great payoff of spectacular views.

One note of caution: fog and wind pound the area at certain times of the year, so get a dependable weather report before venturing out, and always pack raingear just in case.

To start, go past the yellow gate and bear left through the coastal grasslands on an old fire road. The first few steps really don't inspire (you'll hear constant traffic noise from SR 1), but stick with it. As you continue and rise to the first ridge, you'll be able to see how the trail tracks up the spine of this coastal mountain. Sure, it's a brutal grade, but you'll be pleased with yourself for reaching the top.

The trail cuts through plenty of coffeeberry and poison oak, so be sure to stay on the path. You'll likely be passed by mountain bikers, so keep your dog leashed to avoid causing an accident.

Once you top out, you'll have spectacular views of the ocean, Mount

Diablo, Sweeney Ridge (Hike 8), and the San Francisco Bay. After you've had your fill of the views—and you've filled the tanks with some water and snacks—it's time to head back down the old fire road to your car.

12. Pulgas Ridge

Round-trip: 2.5-mile loop
Hiking time: 1.5 hours
Difficulty: Moderate
High point: 670 feet
Elevation gain: 400 feet
Best hiking time: September through June; hikable year-round
Water: Bring your own
Regulations: Dogs must be leashed on all trails except the Hassler
    Loop Trail and area it encircles
Maps: USGS Woodside; or online at www.openspace.org
Contact: Midpeninsula Regional Open Space District,
    (650) 691-1200

Getting there: From Interstate 280 in San Mateo County, take the Edgewood exit and drive 1 mile east, then turn left onto Crestview Drive (just before the entrance to Edgewood Park). Almost immediately, take a left onto Edmonds Road. After just over 0.1 mile, find the trailhead on the right side of the road.

In the Bay Area, you'll hear a lot of rants about this 293-acre preserve. This former tuberculosis sanitarium owned by the city of San Francisco was transformed into an open space preserve in 1983 and the buildings were torn down in 1985.

The squawking comes from people who don't care for dogs. See, Pulgas Ridge has a huge open space where dogs are allowed to be off leash (meanwhile, mountain bikers and horses aren't allowed in the preserve, which is another story). Trouble is, many people have adopted this off-leash policy for the trails, and that is against the rules. Stay out of the fray by putting your pooch on the leash on the short, 1.5-mile level hike to the dog-friendly open space.

The Pulgas Ridge Open Space Preserve is a well-maintained, quaint little park where you'll get to schmooze with other dog owners. Due to diligent work in the past decade by the Midpeninsula Regional Open Space District, there are now seven wonderful trails in the preserve.

Start this trek—signed CORDILLERAS TRAIL—at the kiosk. It cuts through private land, so stay on the trail. After 0.4 mile, at a signed junction, continue uphill on Cordilleras Trail. After just a few feet, you'll pick up the Polly Geraci Trail, where you'll turn left. In the spring, this area of trail is alive with ferns, poison oak, Indian warrior, milkmaids, and columbine. You'll likely see and hear deer crashing through the underbrush, under a canopy of buckeye, coast live oak, bay laurel, and madrone.

At 1.4 miles, the trail ends at a signed junction with the Hassler Trail. Here, you'll make a left and enter a thicket of eucalyptus. This paved trail heads downhill and, in good weather, offers the best views toward the

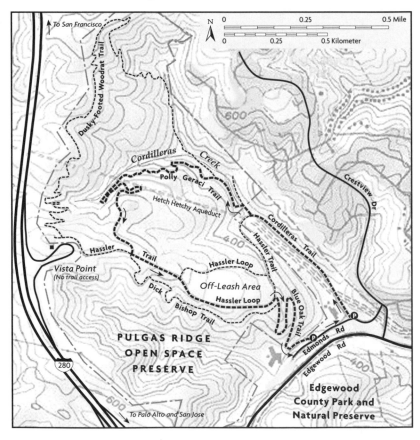

Paul surveys the off-leash area for potential playmates.

Santa Cruz Mountains. The trail splits at the off-leash area that includes and is encircled by the Hassler Loop Trail at 1.5 miles. Be sure to see who is hanging out, and bring a Frisbee or ball to share.

Back on the trail, bear right at the split to enjoy better views on your way back to the entrance. At 1.9 miles, you'll hit the Blue Oak Trail, which runs out at 2.3 miles, where the trail puts you back on Edmonds Road. Turn left and walk back to the trailhead.

13. Arastradero Preserve

Round-trip: 3.8-mile loop
Hiking time: 2–3 hours
Difficulty: Moderate
High point: 650 feet
Elevation gain: 400 feet
Best hiking time: Year-round
Water: From spigot in the parking area or bring your own
Regulations: Dogs must be leashed and are not allowed in the water; no swimming
Map: USGS Palo Alto
Contact: City of Palo Alto, (650) 329-2423

Buddy and Thunder enjoy a quiet stroll along the trail in the Arastradero Preserve.

Getting there: From Interstate 280 in Santa Clara County, exit at Page Mill Road and drive west about 0.3 mile. Turn right onto Arastradero Road, continue about 0.5 mile, and turn right into the parking lot.

With rolling grasslands, oak savannas, and a pretty little lake with fish in it, this slice of heaven is comparatively underused by most Bay Area residents. But that doesn't mean you should skip the Arastradero Preserve. The trails are mostly flat and wide and can accommodate mountain bikers, horse riders, hikers, and dog walkers. The destination here is Arastradero Lake, a little man-made lake that has all the charm of its natural cousins.

From the parking lot, you'll strike out on the signed Gateway Trail, where at less than 0.25 mile you'll cross Arastradero Road and be in the preserve proper on the Juan Bautista de Anza Trail. Watch for quail, deer, bobcat, and coyote. Besides the abundance of poison oak, also look for wild rose (the blooms are fantastic in the fall), willow, coast live oak, monkey flower, snowberry, and blackberry (which makes for great snacking in the summer).

The trail crosses a creek at a bridge, then meets up with signed Meadowlark Trail at about 0.4 mile. Here, the trail climbs slightly, then dips down toward the lake. In spring, the hills closer to the lake will be covered with California poppy, as well as buttercup, lupine, bluedick, and tomcat clover. Just before 0.6 mile at a signed junction, a bridge leads left just before the lake, but stay straight. About 0.1 mile farther on, bear left at a signed junction (where the pump house stands) and you'll find yourself on Arastradero Creek Trail.

Along this trail, there are a few spots where you can get to the water's edge, but watch out for the poison oak. Fishing is open on the lake year-round, and all state Department of Fish and Game rules apply. There is no swimming here.

At 0.7 mile, you'll come to another spur, but continue straight along Arastradero Creek; you'll notice that the trail parallels the creek, but the water is blocked by a thicket of vegetation. At 1.3 miles, the trail reaches the Woodrat Trail; turn right. The route climbs through the grasslands,

making an easy zigzag through the stands of poison oak. At 1.7 miles, you'll reach a T junction, where you'll turn left. At 1.8 miles, come to another T junction, where you'll turn right to reach Vista Point. This trail passes a picnic area in a grove of olive trees, and makes for a nice stop about 0.1 mile from the junction. At Vista Point, be sure to take a gander at the giant valley oaks here, which make for a stark photograph at sunset.

After your break, retrace your steps to the junction and take a left onto the Meadowlark Trail. Bear left at the next junction and continue on the Meadowlark Trail, which descends toward the Juan Bautista de Anza Trail and the parking area.

14. Coal Mine Ridge

Round-trip: 4.2-mile loop
Hiking time: 2.5–3 hours
Difficulty: Moderate
High point: 883 feet
Elevation gain: 895 feet
Best hiking time: Year-round
Water: Bring your own, for you and your dog
Regulations: Dogs must be leashed
Maps: USGS Mindego Hill; a trail map can be printed and additional trail information found under the "Trails" link at www.pvranch.org
Contact: Portola Valley Town Hall, (650) 851-1700

Getting there: From Interstate 280 in San Mateo County, take the exit for Alpine Road (exit 22) south toward Portola Valley. Drive 3.8 miles south on Alpine Road and park in the dirt parking area on the right just before the intersection with Willowbrook Drive.

On first glance at the town of Portola Valley on the San Mateo peninsula south of San Francisco, you'd never guess at the fantastic system of trails tucked away and woven through the hills southwest of the city. The Coal Mine Ridge trails are on land owned by the Portola Valley Homeowners Association who generously open these volunteer-maintained trails for

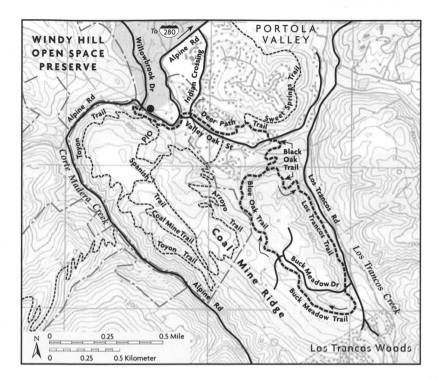

public enjoyment. As you enjoy all that Coal Mine Ridge has to offer, be sure you and your dog are respectful guests.

The jumping-off point for the trail is Alpine Road just south of its intersection with Willowbrook Drive. The trail climbs gently through a series of switchback corners and levels out as you pass a junction with the Toyon Trail and, a few steps later, the Old Spanish Trail, both of which split off to the right.

Stay straight on the Alpine Trail and descend slightly to parallel Alpine Road. At the next junction, take the trail to the right, signed TO DEER PATH TRAIL. After a short jaunt up a sidewalk, cross Indian Crossing Road and climb the single-track ribbon of Deer Path Trail on the other side.

At 0.5 mile ignore the junction with the Bay Laurel Trail to the right, and stay straight on Deer Path Trail as it climbs up a rolling hill peppered with oaks. After dropping steeply down the other side, Deer Path Trail comes out onto Valley Oak Street; cross the road and go left on the paved path along the opposite side. In 50 yards, take the signed Black Oak Trail into the forest to right, crossing a wooden bridge over a seasonal creek.

Exploring moss-covered boulders along the Black Oak Trail at Coal Mine Ridge.

The trail meanders through a lush forest between private residences before climbing the steep mountainside.

Near the 1-mile mark you'll reach a junction with the Blue Oak Trail straight ahead. Stay on the Black Oak Trail by making the switchback turn to the left. Huge beds of ferns and oaks with moss-covered trunks treat your senses as you climb higher and then gradually descend back toward the valley floor. At 1.5 miles you reach another junction; take the unsigned Los Trancos Trail to the right. You'll pass through a small meadow and then under a huge stand of bay laurel trees and begin a steep climb. As you climb, you'll parallel Los Trancos Road to your left, crossing a wooden bridge.

Cross Buck Meadow Drive at 2 miles and continue up the Los Trancos Trail. Where the trail reaches a gravel road, bear right, following the sign TO SUNRISE TRAIL. Sunrise splits off to the left, but continue straight at this junction and follow the signs for Buck Meadow Trail. About 50 yards after the trail turns to concrete, go right at the junction onto the Buck Meadow Trail.

The trail meanders through a meadow surrounded by large homes (fringing the Los Trancos Woods subdivision). At just over 2.5 miles, cross Buck Meadow Drive, reach the top of the climb, and take the signed Blue Oak Trail, which descends a steep canyon between homes.

In less than half a mile you'll find yourself back at a familiar junction with the Black Oak Trail. Head left back down the hill, and retrace your earlier steps back to Deer Path Trail, Alpine Trail, and the parking area.

15. Stile Ranch Trail

Round-trip: 2.7-mile loop
Hiking time: 1.5 hours
Difficulty: Moderate
High point: 728 feet
Elevation gain: 489 feet
Best hiking time: Year-round
Water: Bring your own, for you and your dog
Regulations: Dogs must be leashed
Maps: USGS Santa Teresa Hills; Santa Teresa County Park trail map available at trailhead kiosk
Contact: County of Santa Clara Parks and Recreation Department, (408) 355-2200

Getting there: From U.S. Highway 101 north of the San Jose International Airport, take State Route 87/Guadelupe Parkway south for 9.1 miles. Take SR 85 north (exit 1B) toward Mountain View, and in 0.9 mile take the exit for Almaden Expressway (exit 6). Turn south onto Almaden Expressway and drive 5.1 miles. Turn right on Harry Road, drive 0.1 mile, then go left onto McKean Road. After 1.3 miles take Fortini Road to the left. In 0.6 mile turn left onto San Vincente Avenue and park in the dirt lot at the trailhead on the right.

The South Bay Area ecosystems are so diverse that within a matter of minutes you can go from walking along the beach to hiking through a dense lush redwood forest to trekking across the rolling, rock-encrusted hills of the inland ranges. An example of the latter is the Stile Ranch Trail, part of Santa Teresa County Park south of San Jose, a great place to explore with dogs.

Orange moss on the rocks along the Stile Ranch Trail adds to an already interesting visual.

The picturesque trail, created in the early 1990s thanks to a land grant from IBM, which has a facility near the trail, features sparse foliage and embedded rocks interspersed with stands of oak, manzanita, and bay laurel. The trail is popular with mountain bikers and hikers year-round as well as those in search of wildflowers in the spring and early summer.

Embark from the trailhead and within 50 yards pass the Fortini Trail, which splits off to the right. The Stile Ranch Trail climbs relentlessly up a switchback-riddled hillside for the first 0.7 mile, topping out near a bay laurel tree where you'll get a great view of the valleys below and see jets landing and taking off from San Jose International Airport to the north. Looking northwest you'll get a peek of the dark green IBM building perched at the top of another rolling hill.

The trail continues downhill and then climbs up again to another hilltop vista at 1.2 miles. Many of the interestingly shaped rocks along the trail are painted with swaths of brilliant reddish-orange lichen, providing a beautiful contrast to the muted browns and greens that otherwise dominate the landscape.

At 1.5 miles you'll reach an unsigned fork in the trail and bear right. In 100 yards turn right onto the signed Mine Trail. Another rocky climb and quick descent brings you to a junction with the Fortini Trail, which you'll take to the right.

The trail now rolls you along, alternating between an old fire road surface and single-track. At just under 2 miles you'll come to a large oak tree that sprawls over a pretty little bend in Santa Teresa Creek and offers a great spot to take a quick rest and let your pup get a drink.

Soon after, go right at the trail junction signed FORTINI TRAIL–STILE RANCH ENTRANCE 0.5 MILE. As you near the trailhead, you'll pass a gnarled sprawling manzanita on the right of the trail and soon find yourself back at the Stile Ranch–Fortini Trail junction. Hang a left here and walk another 50 yards back down to your car at the trailhead.

16. Saint Josephs Hill Open Space Preserve

Round-trip: 3.2-mile loop
Hiking time: 1.5–2 hours
Difficulty: Moderate
High point: 1253 feet
Elevation gain: 823 feet
Best hiking time: Year-round
Water: Bring your own, for you and your dog
Regulations: Dogs must be leashed
Maps: USGS Los Gatos; Lexington Reservoir County Park map available at parking area; Saint Josephs Hill Open Space Preserve map available at trailside kiosk or online at www.openspace.org/preserves
Contact: Midpeninsula Regional Open Space District field office, (650) 691-1200; Lexington Reservoir Park, (408) 356-2729

The trek along the smooth fire road of the Jones Trail (Robin Fator)

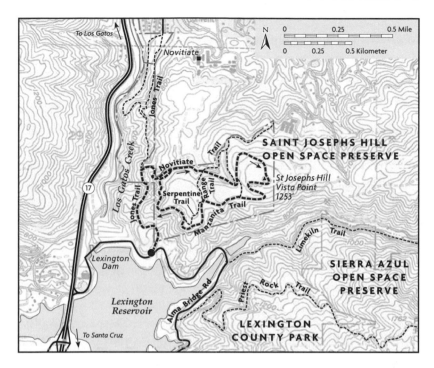

Getting there: From San Jose, take State Route 17 toward Santa Cruz. Go 3 miles past Los Gatos, take the Bear Creek Road/Alma Bridge Road exit, cross over the highway overpass, and get back on SR 17 north. Stay in the right lane and take the next exit for Alma Bridge Road to the right. Drive another 0.5 mile across Lexington Dam and park in the lot on the right.

From Santa Cruz, take the Alma Bridge Road exit from SR 17 and follow the same directions.

Great views, wide-open spaces, and excellent trail surfaces are the name of the game in this recreation area just a few miles out of the big-city congestion of Los Gatos of Silicon Valley. You are sure to have a great time with your dog on the short fire road loops that can be linked together around Lexington Reservoir and Saint Josephs Hill. This loop gives a great taste of what the preserve has to offer.

What there isn't a whole lot of on this hike is shade, so be sure you are prepared with sunscreen, a hat, and plenty of water for you and your dog. Even on a mild, cloudy day, you can both end up dehydrated if you go unprepared.

Begin your trek at the trailhead for the Jones Trail, just across the road from the parking lot. This short, steep climb levels off considerably before you reach the 0.5-mile mark. Here a kiosk provides more information on the area, as well as printed trail maps that are quite handy for navigating the many junctions.

Take a right at the first junction at 0.5 mile and follow the signs for the Novitate Trail. Continue to work your way along this trail, staying straight at the next junction, which comes in less than another half mile.

Leave the Novitiate Trail at the junction at just under 1 mile and take the middle trail, signed MANZANITA TRAIL TO HILLTOP VISTA. The climb steepens here as you push on toward the top of Saint Josephs Hill. Ignore the smaller connecting trails that shoot off the main trail, and circle your way around until you reach the top at 1.5 miles.

At the top, rest on the small bench and take in the views of sprawling city to the north and the reservoir and forested Santa Cruz Mountains to the south. Often the mountains are shrouded with clouds or peppered with wisps of fog, which adds to the surreal scene.

When you are ready to leave the hilltop, follow the Manzanita Trail as it winds down the south side of Saint Josephs Hill. As you descend, take in the many massive sprawling manzanita trees along the trail and look for the green serpentine rock formations in the area of the Serpentine Trail, which splits off just before the 2-mile mark and reenters shortly thereafter.

After several of these small trail junctions, the Manzanita Trail brings you back to the Novitiate Trail at 2.5 miles. From this point, finishing your hike is an easy downhill jaunt back the way you came on the Novitiate Trail, the Jones Trail, and finally down the steep hill to the parking area.

17. Pipeline Road Trail

Round-trip: 6 miles
Hiking time: 2.5 hours
Difficulty: Moderate
High point: 621 feet
Elevation gain: 1134 feet
Best hiking time: Year-round
Water: At the Environmental Education Center and Bookshop, or
   bring your own

Regulations: Dogs must be leashed

Maps: USGS Felton; printable park trail map available online at www.virtualparks.org/parks

Contact: Henry Cowell Redwoods State Park Nature Center, (831) 335-7077

Getting there: From San Jose, take State Route 17 toward Santa Cruz. Once you reach Scotts Valley, take Mount Hermon Road west toward Felton for 3.5 miles and turn right on Graham Hill Road. After 0.1 mile turn left on SR 9, go 0.5 mile south through Felton, and look for the park entrance on the left.

From Santa Cruz, go 6 miles north on SR 9 and look for the park entrance on the right.

Have you have ever wished you could spend a few hours hiking with your dog on the forest moon of Endor from the movie *Star Wars: Episode VI, The Return of the Jedi*? If so, you owe it to yourself to take a trip to Henry Cowell Redwoods State Park in the hills north of Santa Cruz and do the Pipeline Road hike. This area is so full of massive redwoods and so awe-inspiringly lush and green that after your hike your eyes may actually hurt a little from beauty overload.

Bindy and Boulee lead their owner up to the vista near the midway point on the Pipeline Road Trail.

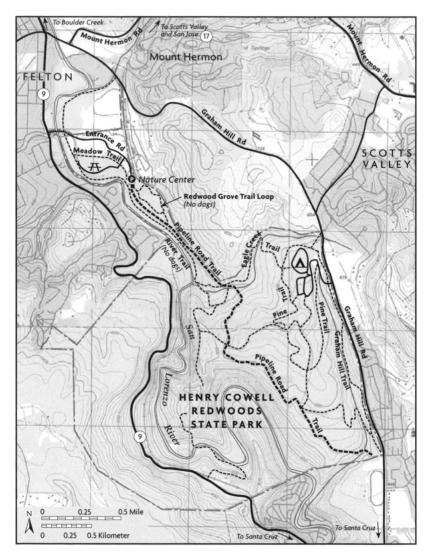

From the main parking lot, head south toward the Nature Center and the entrance to the Redwood Grove Trail loop. Unfortunately, dogs are not allowed on this loop. Turn right on the service road just before the center, and after about 50 yards look for the yellow water spigot and the sign for Pipeline Road to the left.

From its start, Pipeline Road meanders along the picturesque San Lorenzo River for more than 0.5 mile before cutting a diagonal path across the park toward its terminus at Graham Hill Road to the southeast. Stick to the paved road and enjoy the many photo opportunities along this section of the trail. Each bend in the river presents lovely new views, and the trees, mosses, and downed leaves provide a visual feast.

You may even catch a glimpse of a horse and rider at full gallop on the equestrian- and hiker-only River Trail, which runs on the narrow swath of land between Pipeline and the river. If it has rained recently, keep an eye out for the huge neon-yellow banana slugs that often can be found creeping through the leaves and moist duff along the road.

Once the road turns away from the river, wind your way up a ridge and top out near the 1.5-mile mark. The views at the top are worth the climb. This hike gets a moderate rating, mostly due to the steep sections and overall round-trip distance if you decide to do the whole thing. Of course, as an out-and-back, it gives you the option of turning around if you run out of time or energy.

From the top, continue on the mostly downhill trek through the park to Graham Hill Road, take a nice rest, and then retrace your steps back to the parking area.

Dogs are allowed on three trails in the park, so make sure you consult a map, talk to park officials before you embark on your trek, and abide by all rules and signs. In addition to Pipeline Road, you can also hike here with your dog on the Meadow and Graham Hill trails (Hike 18).

18. Graham Hill Trail

Round-trip: 2.6 miles
Hiking time: 1–1.5 hours
Difficulty: Easy
High point: 649 feet
Elevation gain: 340 feet
Best hiking time: Year-round
Water: Bring your own, for you and your dog
Regulations: Dogs must be leashed
Maps: USGS Felton; printable park trail map available online at
     www.virtualparks.org/parks
Contact: Henry Cowell Redwoods State Park Nature Center,
     (831) 335-7077

Getting there: From San Jose, take State Route 17 toward Santa Cruz. Once you reach Scotts Valley, take Mount Hermon Road west toward Felton for 3.5 miles and turn left on Graham Hill Road. Drive 3.7 miles toward Santa Cruz and park in the dirt lot on the right side of the road signed South Boundary Henry Cowell Redwoods State Park.

From SR 1 in Santa Cruz, go north on Ocean Street, which soon becomes Graham Hill Road, for 2.1 miles and park at the South Boundary dirt lot on the left, described above.

The Graham Hill Trail along the eastern edge of Henry Cowell Redwoods State Park offers a nice contrast to the park's Pipeline Road Trail (Hike 17). Whereas Pipeline is just what one would expect from Henry Cowell,

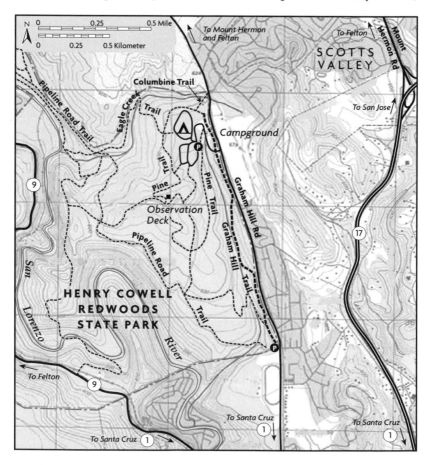

There are many places along Graham Hill Trail where you can stop and gaze into the interior of the park.

namely, a long hilly trek through lush redwood forest, the Graham Hill Trail throws a changeup—an easily accessible, relatively short and flat walk through moss-covered oak trees, small saplings, and underbrush, interspersed with the occasional grassy meadow.

The only real drawback to this trail is the fact that you will hear a fair amount of road noise due to its close proximity to Graham Hill Road. However, its ease of accessibility and fantastic sandy trail surface easily make up for any road noise present.

The trail begins at the park's southeastern boundary off Graham Hill Road and goes just beyond Henry Cowell Redwoods State Park Campground to the north. Whereas the interior of the park is dark and shady, full of giant redwoods and—in the case of Pipeline Road Trail—paved trail, this edge of Henry Cowell is characterized by more sunshine and a sandy trail surface that is also very easy on human and canine feet.

The signed trail begins near the south end of the parking lot and works its way immediately north past the lot and through a grove of oak trees. Nearly everywhere you look, you'll see brilliant shades of green. Poison oak grows thick in the underbrush, so be sure to keep yourself and your dog on the path. Just in case, I'd recommend having some soap and water available when you get back to the car to wash with as soon as possible after your hike.

As you continue winding along the trail, in less than a mile you'll enter a small but lovely meadow that runs alongside between the trail and road. Even with the noise of passing cars, from time to time I still found it possible to lose myself to the sights, sounds, and smells of nature as I trekked along and gazed into the more dense interior of the park.

At 1.2 miles, cross the access road to the park campground and continue on the signed Graham Hill Trail to the Pine Trail straight ahead. Very soon after that you'll reach the end of the Graham Hill Trail and the turnaround point for this hike. The Pine Trail, on which dogs are not allowed, continues straight ahead and to the left. From here, retrace your steps back down the trail and to your car.

19. Anthony Chabot Loop

Round-trip: 8.6-mile loop
Hiking time: 3–5 hours
Difficulty: Moderate
High point: 500 feet
Elevation gain: 500 feet
Best hiking time: Year-round
Water: At the trailhead
Regulations: Dogs must be leashed in developed areas and under strict voice control in undeveloped areas; obey all signs and see the website for definitions and additional restrictions; no swimming is allowed in Lake Chabot
Map: USGS Las Trampas Ridge
Contact: East Bay Regional Park District, (888) EBPARKS (327-2757), option 3, extension 4502; check www.ebparks.org for the latest trail information

Getting there: From Interstate 580 just south of Oakland, take the Estudillo Avenue exit and go east for 0.2 mile. Turn right onto Lake Chabot Road, drive 2.6 miles, and park for free on the road just before the turnoff to the marina. You can pay to park inside the park. Also note that it's $2 to bring your dog in (but the nice ranger will give your pooch a treat).

This trek takes you along the hidden bays and coves of 315-acre Lake Chabot; plenty of stairways lead to the water's edge where you can cast a line or just admire the view. The lake was completed in 1875 but was closed to visitors for ninety-one years. Then, on one weekend in 1966, the lake opened to some 30,000 anglers eager to cast a line in the still, blue waters (the lake has bass, trout, crappie, bluegill, and carp).

This 5065-acre park is an open space among the development of Oakland and San Leandro. You'll pass the busy marina, where anglers in rented boats and people looking for a little pleasure paddle out for a cruise. Indeed, for both the first and last mile, you'll run into crowds of people—bicyclists, anglers, joggers, and families pushing strollers. But

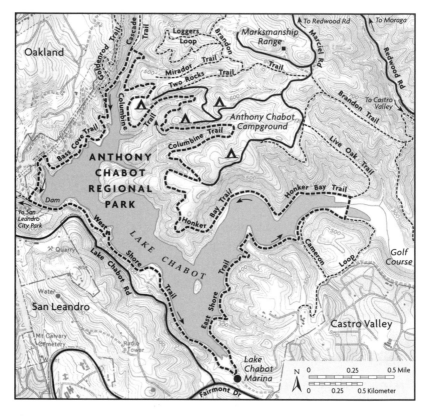

the more you hike, the fewer people you'll see. Lake Chabot also currently serves as an emergency water supply, so swimming isn't allowed.

You'll begin on the paved East Shore Trail, which takes you past the aforementioned staircases. The vegetation here is a mixed salad, with poppy and wild radish in the spring and cow parsnip and creambush later on. This is a pleasant, level stroll, under the cover of bay laurel and oak. At 1.9 miles, you'll reach the tip of Honker Bay, where you'll cross a small footbridge and come to an area that's free of cover. Soon, you'll enter a eucalyptus grove, as the Honker Bay Trail hugs the shoreline.

At 3.4 miles, bear left at a junction and head to the Anthony Chabot Campground. (Chabot was the pioneering businessman who created Lake Chabot by constructing an earthen dam.) You'll climb from the lake into the surrounding forest on the Columbine Trail. This is the most isolated part of the trek, which crosses canyons where seasonal streams burble with water in the winter.

Views abound along the Anthony Chabot Loop.

Turn left at the signed Bass Cove Trail at 4.8 miles. It'll take you south and past an area where ducks and geese squawk incessantly. You'll find fantastic views of the lake here, framed by bay laurel, buckeye, and coast live oak.

At 6.8 miles, you'll turn left onto the paved West Shore Trail where you'll spend the next almost 2 miles in shaded comfort on this level path. The trail leads past the marina and into the parking area.

20. Bort Meadow

Round-trip: 5.4-mile loop
Hiking time: 3 hours
Difficulty: Moderate
High point: 1200 feet
Elevation gain: 1000 feet
Best hiking time: September through June; hikable year-round
Water: Bring plenty of your own
Regulations: Dogs must be leashed in developed areas and under
    strict voice control in undeveloped areas; obey all signs and see
    the website for definitions and additional restrictions
Map: USGS Las Trampas Ridge
Contact: East Bay Regional Park District, (888) EBPARKS (327-2757),
    option 3, extension 4502; check www.ebparks.org for the latest
    trail information

Getting there: From State Route 24 in Alameda County, exit onto SR 13 south. Drive about 4 miles to Redwood Road. Turn left onto Redwood and drive uphill about 0.5 mile to the junction with Skyline Boulevard. Stay in the left lane, and continue straight on Redwood about 4.3 miles to the trailhead on the right side of the road.

From westbound Interstate 580 in Alameda County, take the Castro Valley exit to Castro Valley Boulevard. Turn left on Castro Valley Boulevard, then right on Redwood Road. Drive north about 6 miles to the trailhead on the left side of the road.

It's hard to imagine that a place so wild and so rugged exists so close to the hustle and bustle of downtown Oakland. But Bort Meadow is a magical place where you can pretend you're a Wild West settler seeking fame and fortune.

This hike features a lush grassland ringed by redwoods and eucalyptus, where you're bound to see an abundance of wildlife, including quail, bobcat, deer, coyote, and a number of raptors circling above. This hike can get very hot in the summer, so it's best to stick to visits from September through June. In spring, you'll have the chance to walk through an expanse of wildflowers.

Start by descending a paved road from the Bort Meadow Staging Area, where at 0.1 mile you'll come to a sign that announces three trails. Take the left trail, the Grass Valley Trail. This multiuse trail (be sure to yield to the frequent mountain bikers and horses) is nearly flat and somewhat curvy. This is actually part of the East Bay Skyline National Recreation Trail, as well as the Bay Area Ridge Trail.

At just over 1 mile, you'll reach a signed junction, where the Redtail Trail bears left. Stay on the Grass Valley Trail as this dirt path winds downhill and the grasslands give way to towering groves of eucalyptus and even taller redwoods. At 1.5 miles, the trail reaches a stone bridge, where you'll want to go left and uphill. Turn right and cross Grass Valley Creek (a good water stop for the dogs when it's flowing), and pass the signed Cascade Trail to the left and start hoofing it up Jackson Grade.

This old fire road offers some shaded relief, and after a short climb to the ridgeline it ends. Pick up the signed Goldenrod Trail and continue climbing. The trail actually nears Skyline Boulevard and stays close to the road, where you'll first gaze out at the buildings of the equestrian center at 3.6 miles. Turn left to stay on the Goldenrod Trail, just before

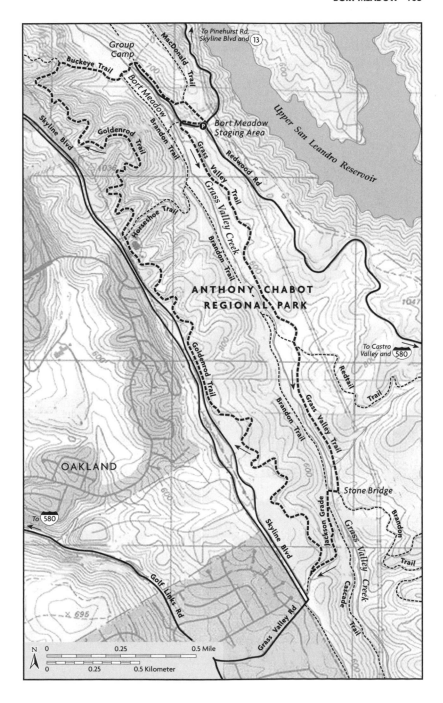

To Pinehurst Rd,
Skyline Blvd and 13

Group
Camp

MacDonald Trail

Buckeye Trail

Bort Meadow

Brandon Trail

Skyline Blvd

Goldenrod Trail

Bort Meadow
Staging Area

Upper San Leandro Reservoir

Grass Valley Trail

Redwood Rd

Grass Valley Creek

Horseshoe Trail

Brandon Trail

ANTHONY CHABOT
REGIONAL PARK

1047

To Castro
Valley and 580

Goldenrod Trail

Redtail Trail

OAKLAND

Brandon Trail

Grass Valley Trail

To 580

Stone Bridge

Brandon

Jackson Grade

Grass Valley Creek

Trail

Golf Links Rd

Skyline Blvd

Cascade Trail

695

Grass Valley Rd

N
0   0.25   0.5 Mile
0   0.25   0.5 Kilometer

Eucalyptus trees tower over Bort Meadow.

the gated trail crosses into the equestrian center (if the vegetation is tall, it might make it hard to see the signpost).

At 3.75 miles, the trail leads right toward the Horseshoe Trail, which drops down to the valley and meets up with the Brandon Trail. But you'll be staying on the Goldenrod Trail. At 4.4 miles, the trail seems to end as it meets a service road. Bear right, and walk the asphalt past the water tank. You'll hook up with the trail again at 4.5 miles. At 4.7 miles, you'll pick up the Buckeye Trail, just before the Goldenrod Trail heads uphill. Take the right onto Buckeye, and you'll find yourself on a fantastically secluded trail along the creek, where you'll pass a bench inviting you to sit for a bit.

Shortly after passing the bench, the trail crosses a second bridge and ends at 5 miles, at the edge of Bort Meadow. Cross this grassy area and look for a junction near the pit toilets. You can walk the paved road, but instead take the trail marked HORSES OK/NO BIKES to the right of the gate.

At 5.3 miles the trail splits; bear left and continue uphill. At the top of the hill, this trail ends and you'll pick up the MacDonald Trail at 5.4 miles. Turn right and walk a few steps back to the parking area.

21. West Ridge Loop

Round-trip: 3.7-mile loop
Hiking time: 4 hours
Difficulty: Moderate
High point: 1385 feet
Elevation gain: 85 feet
Best hiking time: September through May
Water: From a parking-lot faucet; or bring your own
Regulations: Dogs must be leashed in developed areas and under strict voice control in undeveloped areas; obey all signs and see the website for definitions and additional restrictions
Map: USGS Oakland East
Contact: East Bay Regional Park District, (888) EBPARKS (327-2757), option 3, extension 4553; check www.ebparks.org for the latest trail information

Getting there: From State Route 24 in Alameda County, exit SR 13 south. After about 3 miles, exit at Joaquín Miller Road. At the foot of the exit ramp, make a left, then take the next left and go straight onto Joaquín Miller. Drive uphill about 1 mile, then turn left onto Skyline Boulevard (there's a brown parks sign before the turn, and a traffic light). Drive about 3 miles (past the Chabot Space and Science Center), then turn right into the parking lot.

From SR 24 in Contra Costa County, exit at Fish Ranch Road (if you're driving eastbound on SR 24, it's the first exit after the tunnel, then stay in the right lane). Drive uphill on Fish Ranch Road about 1 mile, then turn right onto Grizzly Peak Boulevard. Drive 2.4 miles, then turn left onto Skyline Boulevard, drive 2 miles, and turn left into the parking lot.

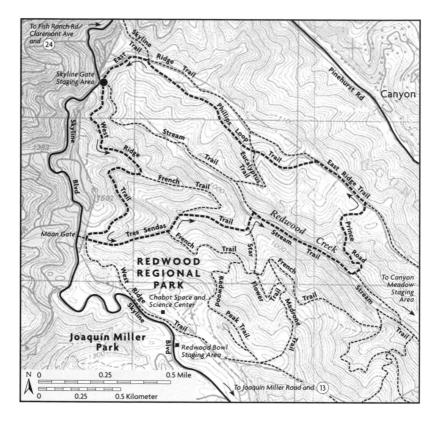

On the drive up, you'll have plenty of opportunity to gaze out on the East Bay, if you can see past all the home construction. But once you reach the large parking area announcing the Redwood Regional Park, breathe a sigh of relief, as you'll soon lose yourself in a forest of redwoods.

Yep, big ol' redwoods, here in the East Bay. Strange, but true. This is a park with a variety of trail choices—all open to leashed dogs—but taking the West Ridge Trail–East Ridge Trail route gets you into the wild the quickest, and it's the prettiest option (in my humble opinion).

To start, walk to the south corner of the parking lot, where you can tank up at a faucet, and look for the signed West Ridge Trail. This wide dirt path gets a lot of use, where on clear days you'll be able to see Mount Diablo. At 0.5 mile, you'll come to a signed trailhead for the French Trail; stay on the West Ridge Trail. At 1 mile, turn left onto the Tres Sendas Trail, which is closed to cyclists and offers the chance to get the dogs off leash. You'll be walking in the shade of the redwoods and through a mix of bay laurel and hazelnut. In the wetter months, this area can get slick, since the trail crosses a seasonal stream a couple of times. At 1.4 miles, Tres Sendas crosses the French Trail, but you'll stay on Tres Sendas (Spanish for "Three Paths.") At 1.7 miles, you'll come to the signed Star Flower Trail, but press on following Tres Sendas.

Just past this junction, you'll meet up with Redwood Creek, where wild trout still spawn. Follow the path as it crosses the creek and joins with the Stream Trail; bear right (bear left and the trail takes you back to the trailhead for a shorter hike).

At 2.2 miles, you'll reach the junction with Prince Road; turn left onto it. This trail heads a bit uphill, where you'll find a bench on which to rest. But the climb doesn't really last that long, as at 2.4 miles the trail ends at a junction with the East Ridge Trail where you'll turn left.

At 2.7 miles, the East Ridge Trail meets up with the Phillips Loop Trail, where you have the option of returning to the parking area on the relatively flat East Ridge Trail, or you can choose some ups and downs along the Phillips Loop Trail. I like the Phillips option, since it ends at

Redwoods in Oakland? Yes, along the West Ridge Trail.

3.6 miles with the East Ridge Trail. At that junction, take the East Ridge Trail toward the parking area, noting that the Bay Area Ridge Trail/East Bay Skyline National Recreation Trail breaks off near here and heads north (this 31-mile trail runs from Wildcat Canyon Park near Richmond to Anthony Chabot Park near Castro Valley).

From the East Ridge/Phillips Loop junction, it's a short, level hike back to the parking area.

22. Sibley Volcanic Regional Preserve

Round-trip: 2.6-mile loop
Hiking time: 1.5 hours
Difficulty: Easy
High point: 1400 feet
Elevation gain: 100 feet
Best hiking time: Year-round
Water: At the trailhead
Regulations: Dogs must be leashed in developed areas and under strict voice control elsewhere; obey all signs and see the website for definitions and additional restrictions
Map: USGS Briones Valley
Contact: East Bay Regional Park District, (888) EBPARKS (327-2757), option 3, extension 4554; check www.ebparks.org for the latest trail information

Getting there: From State Route 24 in Alameda County, exit at Claremont Avenue. Drive 1.5 miles northeast on Claremont Avenue to a major intersection with Ashby Road. Continue straight through the light, and turn right to remain on Claremont Avenue (Claremont Boulevard veers left). You should see a brown parks sign for Tilden and Sibley parks, then pass the back of the Claremont Hotel on the right. Continue on Claremont about 2 miles to the intersection with Grizzly Peak Boulevard. Turn right and drive about 2.4 miles to the intersection with Skyline Boulevard. Turn left onto Skyline, and almost immediately, after 0.1 mile, turn left into the preserve entrance.

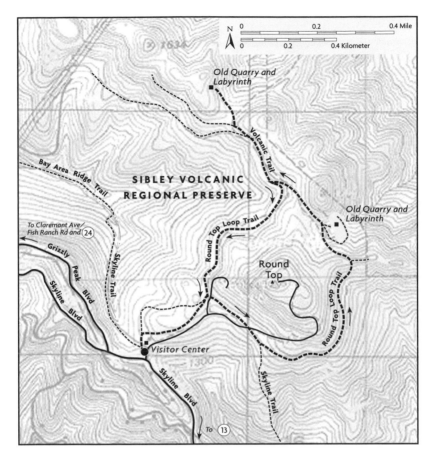

This is a complicated geological area, with volcanic dikes, mudflows, and lava flows. A eucalyptus forest covers most of the trails in this area, which has a violent past and a calm and comforting future.

The Sibley Volcanic Regional Preserve was one of three initial parks established by the East Bay Regional Park District, way back in 1936. Even farther back, about 10 million years ago, lava flowed through the area, spreading north toward Inspiration Point and southeast to Morgana. Eventually, weather eroded the hard volcanic rock, which is now open for all to see. At the unstaffed visitor center, be sure to pick up the brochure detailing a self-guided trek through this volcanic wonderland.

From the visitor center (where there are bathrooms and water fountains), turn left and continue on the paved road, where you'll gain views toward Redwood Regional Park (Hike 21) and the Huckleberry Preserve

Peaks surround the Sibley Volcanic Regional Preserve.

(where dogs are not allowed). After just 0.1 mile, the trail splits at an unsigned junction. Stay on the paved trail leading right. Here, you'll see bay laurel, Monterey pine, and coast live oak.

At 0.3 mile, you'll reach the signed junction with the Round Top Loop Trail; bear right onto this narrow trail. It stays nearly level, then gains elevation slightly, where you'll find a spur road at 0.3 mile. Stay with the Round Top Loop Trail. At 0.8 mile, the trail reaches a junction; walk toward a fenced viewpoint. Here you'll get to see the Round Top volcano.

Mining opened the area to basalt extraction, and in that time a labyrinth appeared at this viewpoint; there are now two labyrinths, one a bit farther on. These are not true mazes, but rather stone-lined paths, their origin a mystery (by some, attributed to visitors from other worlds). You'll find signs of someone lovingly caring for their upkeep, leaving small trinkets, coins, and other objects piled in the center of the labyrinths. They are bizarre places, worth exploring.

After the first labyrinth, head back to the junction and continue north on the signed Volcanic Trail. At 1.5 miles, you'll reach a junction where there is a water trough; bear right and you'll come to a second junction where you'll go right again. The second labyrinth is near here. When you're done exploring it, retrace your steps to the junction to regain the Round Top Loop Trail, at 1.9 miles.

At 2.3 miles, you'll reach a multiple-trail junction, where you started your loop around Round Top. Turn right to return to the parking area.

23. San Pablo Ridge Trail

Round-trip: 6-mile loop
Hiking time: 3 hours
Difficulty: Moderate
High point: 1057 feet
Elevation gain: 1200 feet
Best hiking time: Year-round; but pretty hot in the summer
Water: At the trailhead
Regulations: Dogs must be leashed in developed areas and under strict voice control elsewhere; obey all signs and see the website for definitions and additional restrictions
Map: USGS Richmond
Contact: East Bay Regional Park District, (888) EBPARKS (327-2757), option 3, extension 4567; check www.ebparks.org for the latest trail information

Getting there: From eastbound Interstate 80 in Contra Costa County, take the Solano exit. At the base of the ramp, turn left onto Amador

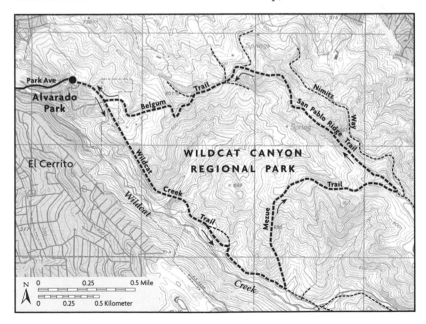

Avenue, drive 0.4 mile, and turn right onto McBryde Avenue. Move into the left lane, and after about 0.3 mile, at the stop sign, continue straight onto Park Avenue. Drive 0.1 mile, turn left into the park, and continue a short distance to the Alvarado Staging Area at the end of the road.

From westbound I-80 in Contra Costa County, exit at McBryde. Turn left (east) on McBryde and after crossing over the highway, get into the left lane of McBryde and proceed as above.

Okay, you're new to the Bay Area and wondering, "What is the wildest place I can get to where even the thought of civilization will melt away?" Try Wildcat Canyon Regional Park just east of Richmond. You'll be amazed how quickly you can get back into the grassy canyons, where deer, coyote, bobcat, and all manner of birds roam and flit around.

This park, now at 2430 acres, has a history to match its wildness. Here's what the East Bay Regional Park District has to say:

On a spring day in 1772 Pedro Fages, Fray Juan Crespi and a "small band of six Catalonian volunteers" entered a Native American village located near the mouth of Wildcat Creek. Although their search for a trade route north had been frustrated by the broad, swift waters of the Carquinez Straits, they found the native people to be welcoming. Fages traded glass beads for food and tools. In his diary he refers to his hosts as "peaceful heathens." These Native Americans did not practice agriculture since they were able to identify and gather a great variety of edible and medicinal plants. They hunted deer and elk and took fish, clams, mussels and oysters from the Bay.

In 1935 the East Bay Regional Park District acquired the southern part of Wildcat Canyon to create Charles Lee Tilden Regional Park. In 1952 the northern part was sold by East Bay Municipal Utility District to private interests. Standard Oil drilled exploratory wells there in 1966, but the results did not justify further drilling. In 1967 the Park District bought an initial 400 acres, and by 1976 the District owned enough land to form a 2,197-acre Regional Park.

This 6-mile loop takes you from a starting point at 180 feet to the top of San Pablo Ridge at 1057 feet. Start on the paved Wildcat Creek Trail, which climbs from the parking lot in an easy grade. At 2 miles, you'll meet up with the Mezue Trail, and take a left. After crossing a cattle gate, the trail begins to climb again, but the views will keep you going. As you continue to climb, you'll think the ridge is within reach, but the trail dips right and loses ground until it reaches the junction with the San Pablo Ridge Trail at 3.3 miles.

Turning left on San Pablo Ridge Trail, notice the hawks and turkey vultures that soar on the thermals. Finally, you'll reach the high point of the trek, a nifty spot to take a rest and drink some water (be sure to bring plenty for your dog, too).

At 4.5 miles, San Pablo Ridge Trail ends at a signed junction. Stay straight, where you'll find yourself on the Belgum Trail. This trail makes an easy sweep downhill, and you'll pass an old settlement (the palm trees look out of place). The Belgum Trail meets up with the Wildcat Creek Trail at 5.5 miles. Turn right and retrace this paved trail back to the parking area.

San Pablo Reservoir from San Pablo Ridge

24. Sobrante Ridge Trail

Round-trip: 2.5 miles
Hiking time: 1 hour
Difficulty: Easy
High point: 750 feet
Elevation gain: 330 feet
Best hiking time: Year-round
Water: At the trailhead
Regulations: Dogs must be leashed in developed areas and under strict voice control elsewhere; obey all signs and see the website for definitions and additional restrictions
Map: USGS Briones Valley
Contact: East Bay Regional Park District, (888) EBPARKS (327-2757), option 3, extension 4558; check www.ebparks.org for the latest trail information

Getting there: From Interstate 80 in Contra Costa County, exit at San Pablo Dam Road. Drive about 3.5 miles southeast on San Pablo Dam Road to the traffic light at Castro Ranch Road. Turn left and drive about 0.8 mile, then turn left (into a housing development) on Conestoga Way. Drive uphill about 0.3 mile, turn left onto Carriage Drive, drive about 0.2 mile, and then turn right onto Coach Drive. Take Coach Drive about 0.3 mile to the park entrance at the end of the cul-de-sac.

A new subdivision fills the valley below Sobrante Ridge.

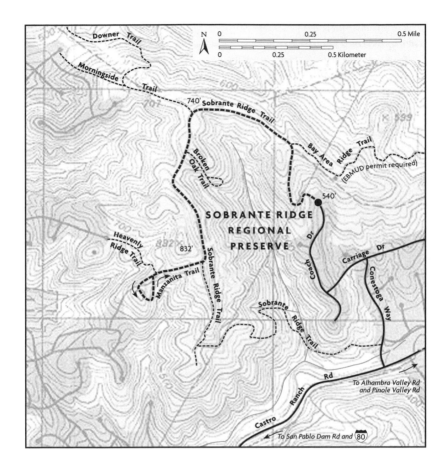

If there's one hike in the Bay Area that shows how important the East Bay Regional Park system is, this might be it. *Sobrante* in Spanish means "leftover," or "surplus," but this area is anything but a scrap of land. Nope, this is prime real estate, a 277-acre island wedged between look-alike housing developments (top the ridge, and that's all you can see).

The land provided a vital link for the East Bay Municipal Utility District's (EBMUD) watershed lands, as well as for the rest of the East Bay Regional Parks. A wide variety of animals, from raptors and songbirds to deer and coyote, use this land as a migration corridor. The botanical preserve is also the home of one of the last stands of Alameda manzanita, a rare and endangered chaparral plant. A miniature forest of manzanita clings to the grassy hillsides in soil so barren that nothing else grows.

The manzanita survives by sucking up moisture from the frequent fog that spills over the ridge.

Pick up the trail at the small parking area and start uphill (it's a leg stretcher), cross under the high-tension powerlines, and come to a gate at 0.2 mile. Go straight and find your first views, and not just of cookie-cutter housing developments. On a clear day, expect to see San Pablo Bay and Mount Diablo. The trail shrinks from a road to a footpath here, and in the summer it bakes hard; you'll likely see rattlesnakes sunning themselves. It's best to keep your dogs under control, lest they get poked in the nose by a disturbed rattler.

At 0.6 mile, you'll reach the junction with the Morningside Trail; stay on the Sobrante Ridge Trail, where you'll find yourself on part of the Bay Area Ridge Trail (when completed, the trail will circle San Francisco Bay). The trail continues south, to the first of the preserve's picnic tables. At 0.7 miles, you'll reach the junction with the Broken Oak Trail. Stay straight, where you'll dip into a forest of bay laurel and coast live oak (be sure to watch for bobcat footprints on the dusty trail).

At 1.1 miles, take a right onto Manzanita Trail, which drops sharply near the edge of a housing development. At 1.2 miles, just past a junction with the Heavenly Ridge Trail, the trail splits, but you'll stay to the right. Here, you'll get your first look at the Alameda manzanita, but they're still spread out among the coast live oaks. You'll soon reach a grove and an interpretive sign that explains the plight of the manzanita, where the plants literally crowd the trail.

The trail crests a hill, passes a giant madrone tree, and drops back down to a junction at 1.3 miles. From here, retrace your steps back down to the parking area.

25. Briones Crest

Round-trip: 5.6-mile loop
Hiking time: 3.5 hours
Difficulty: Moderate
High point: 1483 feet
Elevation gain: 1300 feet
Best hiking time: Spring; hikable year-round
Water: At the trailhead

Regulations: Dogs must be leashed in developed areas and under strict voice control elsewhere; obey all signs and see the website for definitions and additional restrictions

Maps: USGS Briones Valley; park map from kiosk

Contact: East Bay Regional Park District, (888) EBPARKS (327-2757), option 3, extension 4508; check www.ebparks.org for the latest trail information

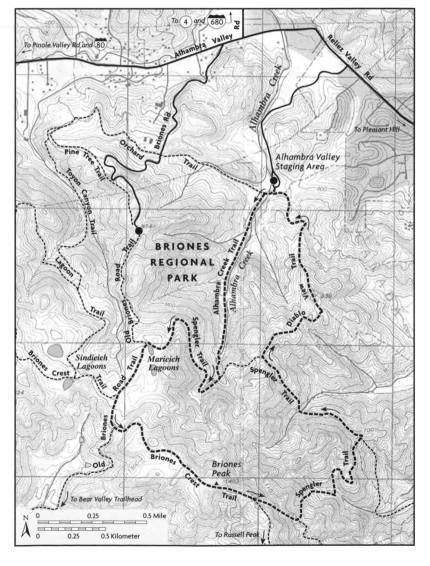

The trail toward Briones Crest is wide and inviting.

Getting there: From Interstate 680 north of Pleasant Hill, take State Route 4 west for 3 miles to the Alhambra Avenue exit. Turn south on Alhambra Avenue and drive 0.5 mile, where you'll bear right onto Alhambra Valley Road. Drive another mile to Reliez Valley Road. Turn left and follow Reliez Valley Road 0.5 mile to the park entrance (there are stables there). Turn right and drive 0.5 mile to the parking area. When the kiosk is staffed, usually on weekends and holidays, it costs $4 to park.

East Bay regulars rate this 5700-acre park as the best of the bunch in the East Bay Regional Park system. With places to hike, bike, and ride horses, it is no wonder this park gets a lot of use. Well, no one said you didn't have to conform; come on, join the crowds and see how this park's network of trails can take you to places where you'll swear no one else has stood.

There's a host of trail junctions on this loop, so it's best to pick up a free map at the kiosk in the parking lot and match it up with a good topo map.

From the gate near the information kiosk, start on the Alhambra Creek Trail. This is a typical East Bay trek—plenty of grasslands with valley oaks standing guard—but as you gain elevation on the Alhambra Creek Trail, you'll be greeted in the spring by the most dazzling wildflower display I've ever found. California poppies, buttercups, lupine, and clover cover the landscape.

At 1 mile, you'll come to the junction with the Spengler Trail, where you'll make a right and start climbing away from the creek. At 1.6 miles, you'll reach two treeless ponds (they're fenced off to keep the cattle out) called the Maricich Lagoons. Here, you'll turn left onto the Old Briones Road Trail. Climb gradually along more grassy knolls, then bear left onto Briones Crest Trail at 1.9 miles.

This stretch of trail takes you up to 1483-foot Briones Peak. It's a leg killer, gaining much elevation in just 2.5 miles. The sweat you spill is worth it, as this is the highest peak in the entire park and grants a panoramic view of the East Bay's rolling hillsides.

To complete the loop, turn left on the Spengler Trail, then take a right onto the Diablo View Trail, which you'll follow down to the parking area in another 1.1 miles.

26. Lafayette Ridge

Round-trip: 4.5 miles
Hiking time: 4 hours
Difficulty: Moderate
High point: 1400 feet
Elevation gain: 1300 feet
Best hiking time: Year-round
Water: Bring your own
Regulations: Dogs must be leashed in developed areas and under strict voice control elsewhere; obey all signs and see the website for definitions and additional restrictions; there is a $2 per dog fee
Map: USGS Briones Valley
Contact: East Bay Regional Park District, (888) EBPARKS (327-2757), option 3, extension 4508; check www.ebparks.org for the latest trail information

Getting there: From State Route 24 just west of Walnut Creek, take the Pleasant Hill Road exit. Drive north for about a mile and then make a U-turn at Reliez Valley Road. Double back on Pleasant Hill Road for 0.2 mile and park for free at the large Lafayette Staging Area. Parking is $3 per vehicle.

The 6002-acre Briones Regional Park has four major access points that lead to all sorts of trail loops. This hike is not one of those. This trek takes you from the parking area just off the road up Lafayette Ridge Trail to its terminus at the Russell Peak Trail, giving you the option to extend this trek all the way to Russell Peak and back.

I like this trip because it gets you into views quickly. From the ridge-line, you'll likely see hawks (notably, red-tailed hawks and the occasional golden eagle) and turkey vultures soaring, and jays and red-shouldered blackbirds will likely call to you from the scrub.

Pick up the trail past a gate and head up the grassy hillside (in spring it's awash with wild radish and mustard). This shadeless portion can bake you well-done in the summer, but it does offer great views of Mount Diablo and Las Trampas Ridge. Catch the wildflower explosion in the spring, when you'll see California poppy, chamomile, and fiddleneck in a showy display.

At 0.6 mile, you'll pass a boarded-up structure, an old farmhouse that must have been really something in its day. About 100 yards farther, there's an unsigned junction, but you'll want to continue on the Lafayette Ridge Trail, where you'll pass a grove of evergreen bay laurel and coast live oak. This stretch features the most strenuous climbing, but push on.

At 1 mile, pass a gate next to a grove of eucalyptus, wipe the sweat from your brow, and enjoy some level walking. The trail turns to single-track, just wide enough for one person to pass, and you'll enter a forest

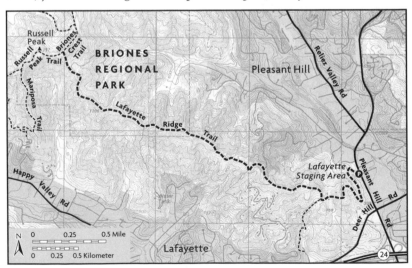

On the way to Lafayette Ridge, be on the lookout for hawks and soaring turkey vultures.

of coast live oak. After a rainstorm, try searching for bobcat, deer, and coyote tracks left behind in the soft mud.

You'll come to the end of the trail at 2.25 miles, where you can either push to the top of Russell Peak (in just more than 0.6 mile, making for a 5.8-mile round-trip), or take a breather on top of the ridge and retrace your steps back down to the trailhead.

27. Franklin Ridge

Round-trip: 3.4-mile loop
Hiking time: 3 hours
Difficulty: Moderate
High point: 650 feet
Elevation gain: 1200 feet
Best hiking time: Year-round
Water: Bring your own
Regulations: Dogs must be leashed in developed areas and under strict voice control elsewhere; obey all signs and see the website for definitions and additional restrictions
Map: USGS Benicia
Contact: East Bay Regional Park District, (888) EBPARKS (327-2757), option 3, extension 4514; check www.ebparks.org for the latest trail information

Getting there: From State Route 4 in Contra Costa County, exit at Alhambra Avenue. Drive north on Alhambra about 2 miles, then turn left (at a stop sign) onto Escobar Street. Drive about 0.1 mile, then turn right onto Talbart Street. Drive on Talbart (which becomes Carquinez Scenic Drive) about 0.3 mile, then turn left into the Nejedly Staging Area.

What, another hike through the rolling grasslands and oak-studded hillsides of the East Bay? Well, sure. Remember, you're in East Bay Regional Park District territory, where one park can look just like another. Still, open space is open space, and this park system is dog-friendly, so you might as well enjoy what they have to offer.

And this hike, on the east side of the Carquinez Strait Regional Shoreline near Martinez (where hiker extraordinaire John Muir is buried), offers something the others can't—exceptional views of the strait, which is the gateway to the San Joaquin Delta. You'll be hiking up and down and up and down, but there are enough benches and rest stops for gazing out onto the choppy, frothy, olive-brown waters of the strait. From the top of Franklin Ridge, you'll also see Mount Diablo and Mount Tamalpais, as well as ships passing under the Interstate 680 bridge.

The city of Martinez, where John Muir is buried, from Franklin Ridge

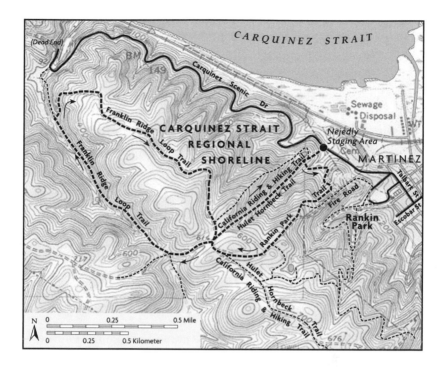

The trek starts with a choice of three trails, which are all pretty steep. You'll want to take the gated Rankin Park Trail, which starts next to a picnic table under an oak. The trail soon forks at a cattle gate, but stay to the left. Continue up Rankin Park Trail (you'll come to your first bench at 0.2 mile) and reach the California Riding and Hiking Trail-Hulet Hornbeck Trail at 0.7 mile; turn right.

This trail—open to hikers, mountain bikers, and horse riders—descends slightly to the junction with the Franklin Ridge Loop Trail at 0.8 mile. Turn left onto Franklin Ridge, where you'll gain access to views of Grizzly Bay, Suisun Bay, and the towns of Benicia and Martinez.

Continue clockwise, and at 1.75 miles a spur trail continues straight to link up with Carquinez Scenic Drive; veer right and continue on the Franklin Ridge Loop Trail. Here, you'll gain a lot of the elevation eventually lost, as this stretch rises through gnarled, but stately, oaks. At a little more than 1.9 miles, look for an unsigned trail that goes left. It leads to a bench with great views at 2 miles, making for a good lunch spot; but in summer the star thistle nearly takes over, and this plant can really do a number on your dog's nose.

Retrace your steps back to the Franklin Ridge Loop Trail and turn left. At 2.2 miles, you'll reach an unsigned junction, but stay straight. At 2.75 miles, there's another junction, but stay straight again. At nearly 3 miles, you'll reach the last dead-end trail junction, and yes, continue straight a few short steps until you get to the signed junction for the California Hiking and Riding Trail-Hulet Hornbeck Trail, where you'll turn left. At 3.4 miles, the trail ends at the gate of the parking lot.

28. Black Diamond Mines Regional Preserve

Round-trip: 3.3-mile loop
Hiking time: 2.5 hours
Difficulty: Moderate
High point: 1291 feet
Elevation gain: 1112 feet
Best hiking time: Year-round; may be hot in the summer months
Water: Bring your own, for you and your dog
Regulations: Dogs must be leashed in developed areas and under strict voice control elsewhere; obey all signs and see the website for definitions and additional restrictions
Maps: USGS Antioch South, USGS Clayton
Contact: East Bay Regional Park District, (888) EBPARKS (327-2757), option 3, extension 4506; check www.ebparks.org for the latest trail information

Getting there: From State Route 4 in Antioch, take the Somersville Road exit and drive south 2.5 miles to the park entrance. Pass the entrance and drive another 1.1 miles to the parking lot and trailhead for the Nortonville Trail.

Visiting this area today, it is hard to believe that it was once home to the largest coal-mining operation in California. What is now an open space preserve with more than 6000 acres of land crisscrossed with 65 miles of wonderful trails, was then a hotbed of mining activity, first with coal and then with underground sand mining from the 1850s well into the mid-1900s.

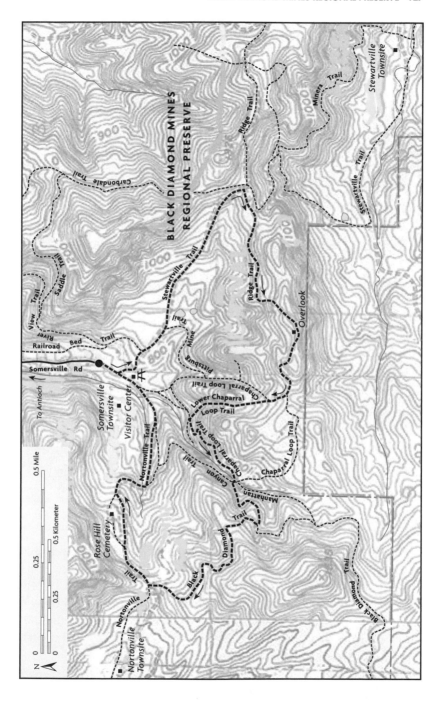

The Ridge Trail makes its way along a fence line offering views the valley below.

One of the greatest things about Black Diamond Mines Regional Preserve is that it is dog-friendly—dogs are allowed off leash under strict voice control on the trails. There aren't many places in the Bay Area where this is permitted, and being able to let your pooch romp along off leash is a nice treat. Keep in mind that you will meet other dogs on the trail here, so if your dog doesn't play well with others, keep him or her on a leash for the whole hike.

Go straight up the Nortonville Trail at the south end of the parking lot, and you'll quickly reach a trail junction. Go left on the signed Stewartville Trail, passing junctions with the Railroad Bed Trail and the Pittsburg Mine Trail. Continue to climb the Stewartville Trail's steady grade, which steepens as it approaches the saddle above. You'll work up a good sweat on this climb, reaching the saddle just past 0.5 mile.

At this junction take the signed Ridge Trail to the right before the gate and follow it around the contour of the hillside. Ignore the handful of smaller unsigned trails that split off to the right. The trail stays fairly level but steepens sharply at 1 mile and passes through another gate.

Huffing and puffing, you'll reach the top of the hill with a grand vista from atop the sandy bank on the left side of the trail. Here you can rest, take in fuel, and gaze down at the valley below. On a clear day you can see Mount Diablo.

The Ridge Trail takes a short jaunt downhill and terminates at a junction with the Chaparral Loop Trail. Go right on the signed Chaparral Loop Trail toward a large rocky outcropping. At the next junction go left on the signed Lower Chaparral Loop Trail. This trail descends a rocky creek bed, then levels off significantly and comes to another junction at 1.5 miles. Go left here on the signed Chaparral Loop Trail.

You'll climb gently through a tunnel of manzanita and scrub. As you near a wooden bridge, go right at the trail junction signed To MANHATTAN CANYON TRAIL. This trail climbs up a couple of sandy switchbacks and comes to yet another junction. Go right on the signed Manhattan Canyon Trail, then left almost immediately on the trail signed To BLACK DIAMOND TRAIL.

At 2 miles the trail levels off and you'll go right on the Black Diamond Trail, which climbs steeply, passes through another gate, and hugs the north side of the hill as it works its way northwest. The views here open up and you can look across the canyon.

At 2.5 miles go right at the junction on the signed Nortonville Trail, which passes by the picturesque Rose Hill Cemetery perched on the windswept hillside.

At 3 miles pass through another gate and just beyond on the right is the visitor center and picnic area. Turn left to continue on the Nortonville Trail, passing the junction with the Stewartville Trail, and descend the remaining few feet to your car.

29. Murietta Falls

Round-trip: 11.5 miles
Hiking time: 8 hours
Difficulty: Strenuous
High point: 3300 feet
Elevation gain: 3500 feet
Best hiking time: September through June
Water: Bring plenty of your own
Regulations: Dogs must be leashed in developed areas and under strict voice control elsewhere; dogs allowed only during the day; obey all signs and see the website for definitions and additional restrictions
Map: USGS Mendenhall Springs
Contact: East Bay Regional Park District, (888) EBPARKS (327-2757), option 3, extension 4547; check www.ebparks.org for the latest trail information

Getting there: From Interstate 580 in Livermore, take the North Livermore Avenue exit and turn right. Drive south for 3.5 miles (the road becomes Tesla Road) to Mines Road. Turn right on Mines Road and drive 3.5 miles to Del Valle Road. Continue on Del Valle Road for another 3 miles until you come to the Del Valle Regional Park entrance. Drive less than a mile to the dam at Del Valle Reservoir, cross it, turn right, and drive 0.5 mile to the Lichen Bark Picnic Area and Campground and the trailhead for the Ohlone Trail. Parking is $6 and a wilderness permit is $2, with a $2 fee for bringing your dog in.

Psssssst: wanna know where the tallest waterfall in the Bay Area is? Right at the end of this hike, that's where.

Murietta Falls plummets some 100 feet down slick, moss-covered granite and makes for a nifty spot to take a dip in the numerous small pools. The falls, located inside the Ohlone Regional Wilderness, are named for Joaquín Murietta, a noted outlaw who rode this area in the 1800s.

Quite frankly, there's no other destination like this one in the Bay Area. Hit it right—when the stream is free-flowing and the falls are a pounding fountain of froth—and you'll be rewarded. Hit it wrong—don't

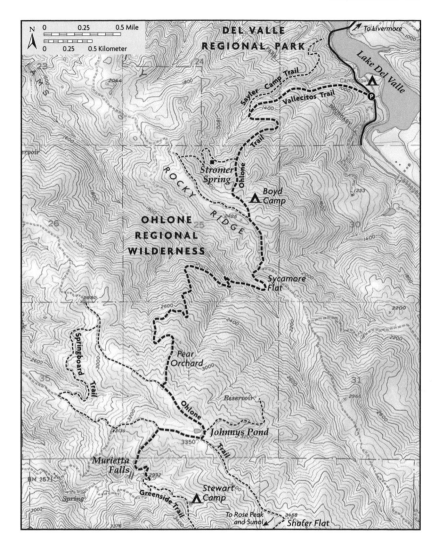

even try it in July, when the falls just trickle—and the only thing you'll get is a hardy workout.

Yep, this hike is a butt kicker. It's 5.75 miles one-way and sticks to a steep, rocky ridgeline that gains and loses elevation. In fact, on one stretch of the Ohlone Trail, you'll gain 1600 feet in 1.5 miles of hiking (it's truly the worst part). So be prepared.

But get this: it's one place in the Bay Area where you can actually take a decent backpacking trip (alas, sans dogs; the park is only open to pooches

Murietta Falls, early spring
(Marc Soares)

in the daylight hours). This is rugged country, where you have the chance to see bald eagles, mountain lions, coyotes, bobcats, deer, and a herd of majestic tule elk.

The route tops out on Rocky Ridge at 2.3 miles, drops 500 feet in 0.5 mile, and then climbs another 1200 feet to Wauhab Ridge. You'll reach Johnnys Pond at 4.7 miles. Turn right at the junction with Springboard Trail (marker 35); from here, it's a mile hike to the falls.

Trek along the ridge for 0.25 mile, then turn left onto the Greenside Trail, which will take you on a sharp descent to the gulch where the falls remain hidden. You can't really get a good look from this trail, so you'll need to find the unsigned path that takes you past the creek to actually get into the floor of the canyon, where the water flows down rocky points into a large pool.

Since this hike takes some time to complete (and you need to get your dog out before the sun sets), it's best not to linger too long at the falls. Just retrace your steps back out to the Ohlone Trail (the trail is very well marked) and remember to be careful as you make your way back down the rocky ridge.

30. South Beach Trail

Round-trip: 0.5–20 miles
Hiking time: 20 minutes–8 hours
Difficulty: Easy
High point: Sea level
Elevation gain: Negligible
Best hiking time: Year-round; low fog is common in summer
Water: From drinking fountain at the trailhead
Regulations: Dogs must be leashed; from December through April, during the elephant seal pupping and mating season, pets and humans are not allowed on the beach south of the South Beach parking lot; check www.nps.gov/pore/planyourvisit/pets .htm for the latest information regarding pets
Map: USGS Drakes Bay
Contact: Point Reyes National Seashore, (415) 464-5137

Getting there: From U.S. Highway 101 in Marin, take the Sir Francis Drake Boulevard exit and drive about 20 miles west to the town of Olema. Turn right on US 1 and drive a short distance to Bear Valley Road. Turn left on Bear Valley Road and drive 2 miles. Turn left on Sir Francis Drake Boulevard and drive 11.6 miles to the access turnoff for the South Beach parking lot to the right. Park for free near the bathrooms; several trails lead down to the beach.

Point Reyes National Seashore is a national treasure, where dogs are pretty much not allowed—except for South Beach, an untouched beachfront where people can bring their pets, so as long as there are no marine mammals on the beach.

This is one of those make-your-own-adventure hikes. Stay close to the parking area on the beach, pull out a blanket for a picnic, and take it easy. Roam the sandy hillsides that are covered with ice plants (blooms of yellow, orange, pink, purple, and red will amaze you).

Or, for the best hike, reach the beach and turn south for about a mile until you come to the sand dunes, stopping every so often to find out

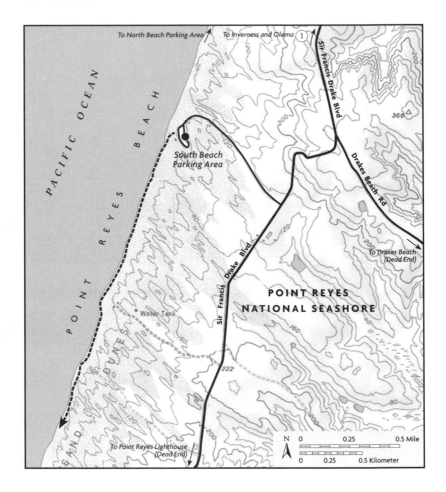

what the ocean has brought to shore. When we were there, we found bits of sand-blasted glass (an artist friend made me swear I'd look), shells, boat floats in several colors, and one big, dead cabazon, a deep ocean fish. You can even go as far as you'd like on the beach. Some days, it may be just you and your dog on this stretch, where the Pacific meets California.

A note about the water: don't go swimming, and watch for rogue waves. The area is known for its tremendous undertow, which will take even the strongest dog paddler under and out to sea, despite all attempts to swim back in.

Oh, and on your way in on Sir Francis Drake Boulevard, don't miss the chance to pick up some fresh oysters and talk about oyster farming at

Ice plants in a variety of colors cover the sandy hills at Point Reyes National Seashore.

Drake's Bay Family Farms (formerly Johnson's Oyster Company). You'll see the sign; the store is open from 8:30 AM to 4:30 PM every day.

31. Bolinas Ridge

Round-trip: Up to 11 miles
Hiking time: 4–6 hours
Difficulty: Moderate
High point: 1300 feet
Elevation gain: 1100 feet
Best hiking time: Year-round
Water: Bring your own
Regulations: Dogs must be leashed
Maps: USGS Iverness, USGS San Geronimo
Contact: Golden Gate National Recreation Area, (415) 464-5137

Grazing is allowed on Bolinas Ridge, so dog walkers need to be aware of the local bovine residents.

Getting there: From U.S. Highway 101 in San Rafael, take the Sir Francis Drake Boulevard exit and go west for 17 miles (3.4 miles past Samuel P. Taylor State Park's entrance). The trailhead is on the left side of the road.

Alternately, from the community of Olema on State Route 1, drive 1.1 miles east on Sir Francis Drake Boulevard to the trailhead, on the right.

If sweeping views and a certain amount of solitude are your idea of a weekend escape, the Bolinas Ridge Trail just might be your cup of tea. The trail is open to hikers, mountain bikers, and leashed dogs, of course.

The trail starts from a wooden gate and gains 700 feet in elevation in the first 2.5 miles, cutting through rough granite outcroppings as the wide and inviting path inches up the ridgeline. You'll come to your first spot to look around at a little over 0.5 mile. Look northwest for good views of

Tomales Bay and the Point Reyes peninsula. Look east to Barnabe Peak.

At 1.3 miles, you'll get to a signed trail junction for the Jewell Fire Road. Stay right on the Bolinas Ridge Trail. A little farther on, you'll come to a field from which you can see the dark forested Iverness Ridge as well as the Olema Valley. The trail gains its highest point nearly 5 miles into the trek, where eucalyptus trees stand guard.

But the best place to look around is at the junction with the Shafter Fire Road, where you can scramble up any knoll for great views of Iverness Ridge and the Pacific. From here, it's 0.5 mile to the left to reach Lagunitas Creek, where the dogs can cool off and you can get out of the sun and rest in a canopy of dense oak and bay laurel. After a rest, maybe a little lunch, just retrace your steps back to the trailhead.

A note of caution: the recreation area allows cattle grazing, so make sure to keep control of your dog, as cows can get downright nasty if harassed.

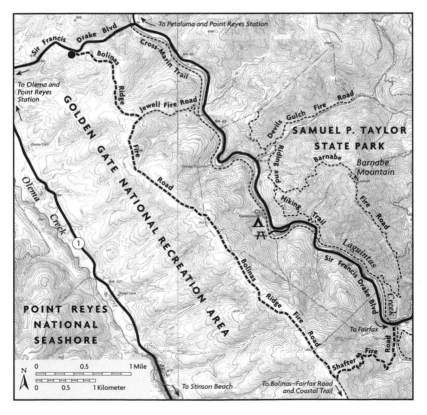

32. Indian Tree Open Space Preserve

Round-trip: 3.8-mile loop
Hiking time: 2 hours
Difficulty: Moderate
High point: 992 feet
Elevation gain: 751 feet
Best hiking time: Year-round
Water: Bring your own, for you and your dog
Regulations: Dogs must be leashed
Map: USGS San Geronimo
Contact: Marin County Open Space District, (415) 499-6405

Getting there: From U.S. Highway 101 in Novato, take the De Long Avenue exit and turn west onto De Long, which soon becomes Diablo Avenue. In 0.2 mile turn right onto Novato Boulevard, drive 1.1 miles, and go left onto Wilson Avenue. Drive 0.5 mile on Wilson, then turn right onto Vineyard Road. Continue on Vineyard for 2.2 miles and park along the road near the trailhead for the Upper Meadow Trail, on the southwest side of the road.

The trails at Indian Tree Open Space Preserve make for many great hikes, and due to the close proximity of other, more popular spots in the Bay Area, you may find more seclusion here. This loop hike can serve as an introduction to the area with the option to go farther if you have more time and desire to explore.

The Big Trees–Deer Camp hike is pure Northern California—you'll get huge sweeping views and walk through giant stands of madrones, California bay laurels, oaks, and redwoods, all interspersed with grassy meadows and huge beds of ferns, as you climb ever upward and take in one expansive view after another.

From the trailhead, follow the signed Upper Meadow Trail about 100 yards to the first junction and go left on the signed Big Trees Trail. The trail zigzags up a perfect grade through many switchbacks and one section

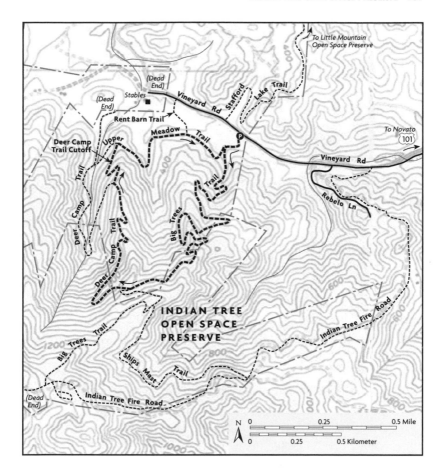

of varied foliage after another. You'll be on this gentle climb for about 2 miles, so settle in and enjoy the scenery.

As you climb you'll pass a beehive in the trunk of a large oak tree just off the trail. Signs warn you to be careful. When I passed in early 2012, it was cold and the bees were calm. If you or your dog are allergic to bee stings, come prepared and keep your pooch on a short lead.

In addition to frequent views of the rolling hills to the north, there are places along the trail where you'll see the exposed trunks of very large madrone trees, which look strangely beautiful when shedding their bark.

At 2 miles you'll come to a junction; go right on the Deer Camp Trail.

The Big Trees Trail takes a winding route up the mountain.

For a longer hike with the reward of a dramatic mountaintop vista, you could take a left and climb higher up the Big Trees Trail.

As you roll along the Deer Camp Trail, you'll begin to descend as you approach another trail junction; go right on the signed Deer Camp Trail Cutoff. Continue down to the next junction, at just over 3 miles, and go right on the Upper Meadow Trail. Continuing your descent, you'll soon cross a wooden bridge and exit the trees as the trail cuts a path through lush green grasslands.

Go through a gate, and near 3.5 miles pass a horse ranch on your left. As you round the next few bends, the trailhead comes into view and you may just be able to see your car across the meadows. Ignore a smaller trail splitting off to the left toward the ranch, and stay straight on Upper Meadow Trail.

After passing through another gate, you soon arrive at the junction with Big Trees Trail, completing the loop. A few more steps down the Upper Meadow Trail bring you back to the trailhead.

33. Roys Redwoods Trail

Round-trip: 3-mile loop
Hiking time: 2–3 hours
Difficulty: Easy
High point: 800 feet
Elevation gain: 500 feet
Best hiking time: Year-round
Water: Bring your own
Regulations: Dogs must be leashed
Map: USGS San Geronimo
Contact: Marin County Open Space District, (415) 507-2816

Getting there: From a few miles west of Fairfax on Sir Francis Drake Boulevard, turn north onto Nicasio Valley Road. Drive 0.4 mile and park for free on the side of the road, by the outhouses.

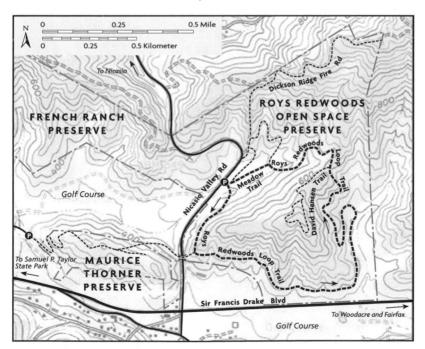

Coastal redwoods tower over a meadow in Roys Redwoods Open Space Preserve.

Here's a happy little trail that passes through a pleasant meadow, dives into a darkened forest of giant redwoods, and comes back out again. There's no destination here, just a carefree jaunt where you're likely to strike up any number of conversations with people who stop to walk this tiny strip of open space.

The Roys Redwoods Loop Trail starts near the outhouses, skirts the meadow below Nicasio Valley Road, and heads into the towering redwoods. As you enter this forest, you'll see bay laurel and madrone; ferns and poison oak rule the underbrush.

Soon the trail breaks from the forest and heads into a mix of grassland and sagebrush with stands of coast live oak. Stay left at the first junction as the trail begins to climb, alternating between rocky outcrops and pretty little meadows ablaze with wildflowers in the spring.

At the next junction, ignore the David Hansen Trail to the left and stay right, continuing on the Roys Redwoods Loop Trail. The trail now veers east, stays high for a bit, then drops back toward the meadow. Go left at the next junction on the Meadow Trail, which loops back into the redwoods. Here you'll be hard-pressed not to play a little hide-and-seek with the dogs as they sniff around the many delectable scents.

34. Cascade Falls Trail

Round-trip: 1.8 miles
Hiking time: 1 hour
Difficulty: Easy
High point: 400 feet
Elevation gain: Negligible
Best hiking time: Year-round
Water: From San Anselmo Creek; or bring your own
Regulations: Dogs must be leashed
Map: USGS Bolinas
Contact: Marin County Open Space District, (415) 499-6405

Getting there: From U.S. Highway 101 in San Rafael, take Sir Francis Drake Boulevard west to the town of Fairfax. Turn left onto Claus Drive, then make an immediate left onto Broadway, followed by an immediate

Paul tentatively peeks over the edge of the falls.

right onto Bolinas Road. Drive 0.3 mile to a three-way intersection, where you'll take the middle road (Cascade Drive) for 1.5 miles. Park near the gate to the Elliot Nature Preserve, but watch for the no parking signs in this residential area and be sure not to block any driveways.

It's not the most powerful waterfall you'll likely see in your life, more like a gurgling friend, a quiet spot to rest, relax, and step out of the rat race, if only for the hour it takes to wander though Cascade Canyon Open Space Preserve and the Elliot Nature Preserve. But make no mistake about it, happy Cascade Falls is worth the trip; indeed during my first trek there, numerous harried people asked if they were getting close to the falls, which tumble down San Anselmo Creek before it widens out and provides a couple of great dipping spots for the dogs.

The trail starts at a sign for the Elliott Nature Preserve. You'll want to ignore the unsigned fire road and trails to the left and stick to the signed High Water Trail, which hugs the rocky right side of the creek. As you near the 0.5-mile point, the trail widens and then passes a junction with the Cut Trail on the right.

At 0.5 mile, cross the creek on a wooden bridge and continue up the trail to the right (you'll now be on the creek's left side) going deeper into Cascade Canyon, where currant and madrone make up the cozy canopy.

Through the canyon, San Anselmo Creek will narrow, and the gurgling will start to echo off the cliff walls. You'll end up at Cascade Falls a little less than a mile from where you started. The falls are encased in a rocky, moss-covered grotto, where large boulders make a perfect spot to stop and contemplate your navel (hey, it's so peaceful that you really don't need to be thinking of anything).

After a few quiet moments, retrace your steps to your car, but be sure to reward your dog for waiting while you got a little Zen with a quick dip in San Anselmo Creek.

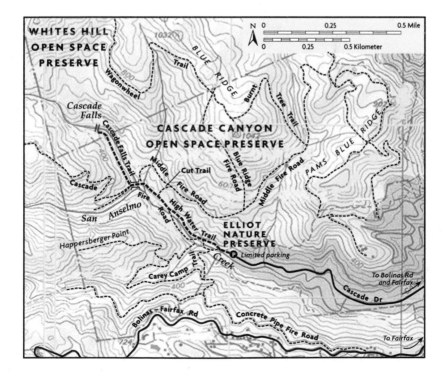

35. Cataract Falls and Laurel Dell

Round-trip: 2.5 miles
Hiking time: 1.5 hours
Difficulty: Strenuous
High point: 1670 feet
Elevation gain: 1030 feet
Best hiking time: Winter through spring; hikable year-round
Water: From Cataract Creek, or bring your own
Regulations: Dogs must be leashed
Map: USGS French Gulch
Contact: Marin Municipal Water District, Sky Oaks Ranger Station, (415) 945-1181

Cataract Creek is peaceful as it flows into Alpine Lake.

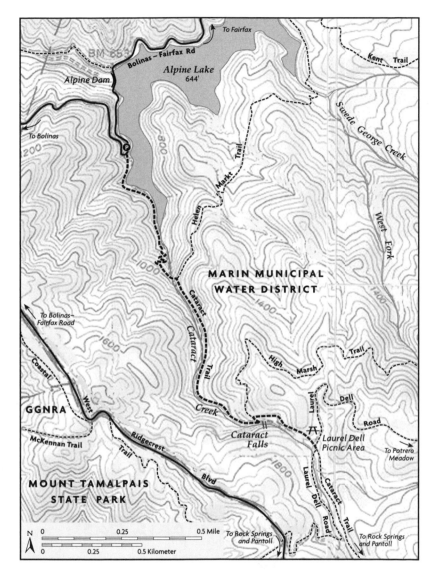

Getting there: From the Golden Gate Bridge, take U.S. Highway 101 north and turn west onto Sir Francis Drake Boulevard to Fairfax. Turn left on Claus Drive, make an immediate left onto Broadway, and turn right onto Bolinas–Fairfax Road. Drive 8.2 twisty miles to Alpine Dam, cross it, and look for the parking area just before a tight, right-hand hairpin turn. Park for free off the road; the trailhead starts on the other side of the road.

It's a gut-wrenching climb that makes sweat pour down your forehead, and even the stoutest dog will have his tongue extended fully, but Cataract Falls and the Laurel Dell Picnic Area are worth every pounding heartbeat. For Cataract Falls isn't just one falls, but a set of cascading waterfalls that rush down a wooded ravine on the slopes of Mount Tamalpais.

The sights and smells are worth the sweat equity you'll expend on this 750-foot climb. Besides, the picnic area is a welcomed pit stop where you can spread out a blanket and have a feast (go ahead and pack carbs, you'll burn them).

The signed trail starts to climb gently (where there are good spots to cast a line along the shores of Alpine Lake). The well-shaded trail offers a canopy of redwood, bigleaf maple, tan oak, and hazelnut. Don't be deceived. At a little more than 0.5 mile, where huckleberries and ferns are thick, you'll come to a trail junction (stay straight) where the climbing commences. The roar of the falls takes over as the water tumbles down the canyon. It's a restful beat to climb to, as you constantly come to new and higher steps cut into the canyon.

At 1.4 miles, a spur trail takes you to the best view of the falls, where water slips, slides, and cascades down slick boulders into inviting pools. During the wet months, Cataract Creek becomes a whitewater torrent, with foam and spray and a roar that can drown out conversation with someone standing right next to you.

A little ways up, you'll hit Laurel Dell, a wide, open spot surrounded by coast live oak, bigleaf maple, bay laurel, and Douglas fir. Stay as long as you like (remember that it might be tough to find a spot on the weekends), then retrace your steps back down to Alpine Dam. Or continue on a longer, steeper hike up Mount Tam (Hike 36).

36. Mount Tamalpais East Peak Trail

Round-trip: 13 miles (5.4 miles from Rock Springs Picnic Area)
Hiking time: 6–8 hours (3–4 hours from Rock Springs Picnic Area)
Difficulty: Strenuous
High point: 2571 feet
Elevation gain: 2300 feet (1500 feet from Rock Springs Picnic Area)

Best hiking time: Year-round

Water: Bring plenty of your own

Regulations: Dogs must be leashed

Maps: USGS San Rafael, USGS Bolinas

Contact: Marin Municipal Water District, (415) 945-1438; Mount Tamalpais State Park, (415) 388-2070

Getting there: From Sir Francis Drake Boulevard in Fairfax, turn southeast on Claus Drive. Take an immediate left onto Broadway and then an immediate right onto Bolinas–Fairfax Road. Drive 8.2 twisty miles, cross the Alpine Dam, and park for free at the hairpin turn. The signed trail begins on the left side of the road. (For a shorter hike, drive an additional 2.2 miles west on Bolinas–Fairfax Road and turn left on Ridgecrest Boulevard. Drive 3.8 miles southeast on Ridgecrest to the parking lot for the Rock Springs Picnic Area on the left.)

It's quite a hike to the top of Mount Tamalpais.

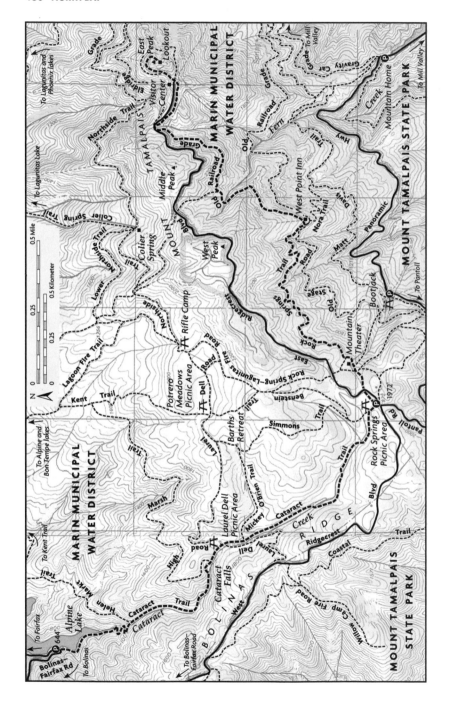

So the ranger says, "If you really want a nice hike up Mount Tam, try this route up Colier Springs Trail to the Northside Trail. Inspiration Point has some killer views and it's a good route to the top, not too strenuous."

Mount Tam, or Tamalpais, is the Bay Area's beloved "Sleeping Maiden." It towers 2571 feet above the congestion and development that is the Bay Area. The area is a breath of fresh air, an open space for the masses. On one side, there's the Marin Municipal Water District's 18,500-acre open space area. On the other is the 6300-acre Mount Tamalpais State Park.

Mount Tam is actually three peaks on one ridge, with East Peak being the tallest. I decided that the most direct route—the very one suggested by the nice ranger who gave my dog Trinity a dog biscuit—didn't fit my particular needs (to be honest, I couldn't find the trailhead among the myriad of trails in the open space). No, I started from the one trailhead I knew, from the base of Alpine Dam, past lovely Cataract Falls and a great pit stop at Laurel Dell Picnic Area (Hike 35).

This East Peak route is a heart-pounding assault through a dense forest of redwood, tan oak, bigleaf maple, and hazelnut. It's the one trail with about 2300 feet of climbing. (I am not kidding. The dam sits at 644 feet.) The trail gains 750 feet just to Cataract Falls, in just under 1.5 miles. It's also a trail that's dog-friendly (just be sure to keep your dog on a leash—it's the rule, not a suggestion). Be prepared to sweat. Pack plenty of water, a hearty lunch, and some dog treats. And don't forget a camera.

This trek has it all: pristine forest, a lake full of fish, a cascading falls (winter and spring), a great picnic area at an historic outdoor theater and inn, and jaw-dropping views of San Pablo and San Francisco bays. (Be sure to stay on the trails and fire roads; it's kinda like cheating if you hoof it up paved Ridgecrest Boulevard to the top.)

At least you'll have the option to rest at the pretty Laurel Dell Picnic Area, a large clearing with plenty of room to spread out. The area is framed by coast live oak, bay laurel, Douglas fir, and bigleaf maple.

From the picnic area, continue on the Cataract Trail 1.3 miles to Rock Springs Picnic Area. Be sure not to miss the Mountain Theater, a 3500-seat open amphitheater made of stone. To get there, cross Ridgecrest Boulevard and follow the signs to the theater, then rejoin the Rock Springs Trail. The trip up to East Peak also features a jaunt past West Point Inn at 4.5 miles. This is a neat stone lodge tucked in the forest, where you'll get great views of Angel Island and the Golden Gate Bridge.

Resume your trek to the top by finding the signed Old Railroad Grade Fire Road Trail and be sure to stop for a striking photo opportunity: Douglas fir in the foreground and Alcatraz Island, the Bay Bridge, and San Francisco's towering downtown in the background. The old dirt road stays fairly level through open chaparral until it reaches the Mount Tam visitor center. From the parking lot, hike the final 400 feet up a rocky trail to the terminus at East Peak.

There, take your pick of boulders, pop open a water bottle, and drink in the sweeping 360-degree views.

If this route sounds like too much for you and your dog to handle, a much shorter, but excellent option for making the summit of East Peak is to cut out the entire Cataract Falls–Rock Springs Picnic Area section of the hike, and simply start your journey at the parking lot at Rock Springs Picnic Area instead.

37. Dawn Falls Trail

Round-trip: 2 miles
Hiking time: 1.5 hours
Difficulty: Easy
High point: 437 feet
Elevation gain: 407 feet
Best hiking time: Year-round
Water: Bring your own, for you and your dog
Regulations: Dogs must be leashed
Map: USGS San Rafael
Contact: Marin County Open Space District, (415) 499-6405

Getting there: From U.S. Highway 101 in Corte Madera, take the exit for Tamalpais Drive toward Paradise Drive and go west on Tamalpais for 0.9 mile. After the road rounds a corner to the right, bear left onto Redwood Avenue and take the second right onto Corte Madera Avenue, which becomes Magnolia Avenue after 0.2 mile. In 0.3 mile turn left onto Madrone Avenue. After nearly a mile, Madrone becomes Water Way and dead-ends. The limited parking is confined to the outlined white spaces on the south side of the road. If they are all full, you may be able to find a place to park farther down Madrone.

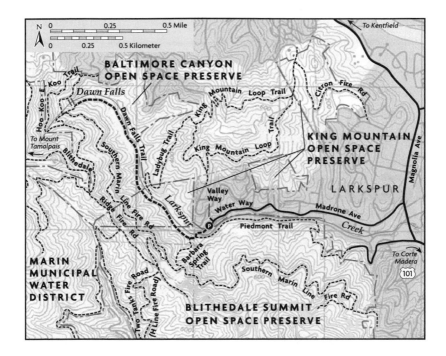

A dark canyon filled with redwoods, and a trail that culminates at a lovely little waterfall, all in a 2-mile round-trip? You are probably asking, "Where do I sign up?" The answer to that question is to head for Baltimore Canyon Preserve near Corte Madera in Marin County and take the hike to Dawn Falls.

Parking can be limited and somewhat difficult, and initially this hike is overlooked by large homes on the northern side of the creek, but you and your dog will soon pass these and lose yourselves in nature, even if just for a little while. With the waterfall, creek, redwoods, and other plant life, there is plenty of environmental eye candy in the canyon as well as an excellent trail to keep you and your pooch interested.

From its start the trail dips down toward the north side of Larkspur Creek, and a few steps later crosses the creek on a nice little bridge. After you cross, go right on the signed Dawn Falls Trail.

Almost immediately, pass a junction with the Barbara Spring Trail, which splits off to the left and climbs steeply up the hillside of the south canyon. Stay straight to continue on Dawn Falls Trail along the left side of the creek.

The canyon is mostly very dark, though it does open up from time to time to let rays of sunlight in through the green foliage along parts of the creek, especially as you get farther up toward the falls.

The trail surface is mostly rich loamy soil with the occasional protruding root or, as the trail winds nearer the creek, a few embedded rocks. It does get muddy here during the rainy season, so be aware of that and avoid this trail under those conditions or come prepared with the proper footwear.

At 0.5 mile you'll reach a junction with the Ladybug Trail, which heads right over a wooden bridge across Larkspur Creek. If you would like a longer hike, this trail can be taken out-and-back and/or linked up with other trails beyond to make a longer loop. Stay straight at this junction, continuing along the west side of the creek toward Dawn Falls.

The lovely Dawn Falls Trail meanders along Larkspur Creek.

You'll know you are very close to the falls when you reach a giant boulder on the right side of the trail and begin a short series of switchbacks gaining elevation and working farther up the canyon. In just under 1 mile you'll round a corner and reach Dawn Falls, which trickles or rushes (depending on the time of year and recent rainfall) over a rock ledge and then drops several feet to the rocks below.

There is a great view of the falls from the trail as well as some nice places to sit just beyond. You can also find a place to lounge near the top of the falls or on the opposite side of the creek. Once you've had your fill of the relaxing sounds of water splashing over rocks and had a chance to get rested and refueled, it is time to head back down the same route to your car.

38. Crane Creek Regional Park

Round-trip: 1-mile loop
Hiking time: Less than 1 hour
Difficulty: Easy
High point: 459 feet
Elevation gain: 123 feet
Best hiking time: Year-round
Water: Bring your own, for you and your dog
Regulations: Dogs must be leashed
Maps: USGS Cotati; park map also available online www.sonoma
-county.org/parks/pk_crane.htm
Contact: Sonoma County Regional Parks, (707) 823-7262

Getting there: From U.S. Highway 101 in Rhonert Park, take the exit for Rhonert Park Expressway. Turn east on the expressway and drive 2.4 miles to the junction with Petaluma Hill Road. Go right on Petaluma Hill Road for 1.2 miles and turn left on Roberts Ranch Road. After 1.3 miles the road becomes Pressley Road. Go 0.6 mile on Pressley Road and turn left into the signed Crane Creek Regional Park parking area.

This beautiful little park located in the vineyard-dotted hills of Sonoma County isn't a place to head if you are looking for an ambitious, leg-burning hike for you and your pup. Rather, this is a relaxing place to come when your only desire is to get away and enjoy a peaceful walk with your canine friend.

Crane Creek is home to several miles of trails as well as a disc golf course, so solitude in your wanderings isn't likely. Guaranteed, however, are views of lovely rolling hills with grazing livestock and vineyards, huge oak trees, and quite a wildflower show in the spring. There is a day-use fee of $6 per vehicle, so be prepared with cash or a check.

Many routes through the park can be taken, but a favorite is the Fiddleneck Trail, which begins to the left of the information kiosk at the trailhead. The trail climbs briefly and then comes to a junction. Go right to continue on the Fiddleneck Trail, which follows the ridge of a small hill and then heads down toward Crane Creek to the north.

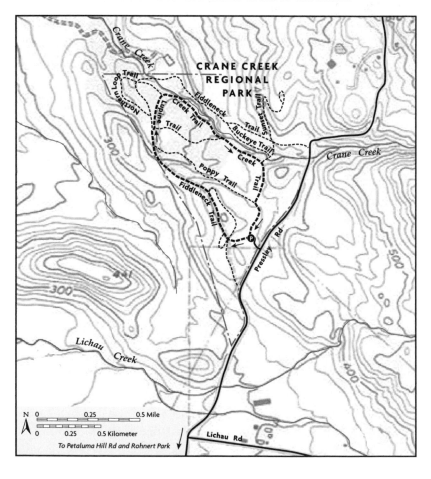

Paul gazes out over the rolling, green hills toward Rhonert Park to the west.

As you make your descent through a section of embedded rocks, the trail levels off. You'll pass the Poppy Trail on your right; remain straight on Fiddleneck. Soon you'll cross a usually dry seasonal creek bed and reach another junction; take the trail in the middle, signed LUPINE TRAIL.

Lupine will take you straight toward Crane Creek. On your right is a large open meadow punctuated with a few stands of oak trees. Wildflowers bloom here, and you'll be perfectly positioned to take in the show. At just over 0.5 mile, you'll reach a junction and take the Creek Trail to the right. This trail skirts the northern edge of the meadow, winding along Crane Creek to your left.

Another junction with the Lupine Trail comes in on the right, but stay left to remain on the Creek Trail. You'll pass an area on the creek with a picnic table and a junction with the Buckeye Trail to the left. Stay right to remain on the Creek Trail and continue to enjoy the views of the surroundings as you follow this trail back to the parking lot.

For other options in the park, the trail kiosk has a nicely detailed map with suggestions for alternate loops and mileages.

39. Pine Mountain Summit

Round-trip: 4.3 miles (5.8 miles with side trip to Carson Falls)
Hiking time: 3–5 hours
Difficulty: Strenuous
High point: 1762 feet
Elevation gain: 1100 feet
Best hiking time: Winter through spring; hikable year-round
Water: Bring your own
Regulations: Dogs must be leashed
Map: USGS Bolinas
Contact: Marin Municipal Water District, Sky Oaks Ranger Station,
    (415) 945-1181

Getting there: From Sir Francis Drake Boulevard in Fairfax, turn south-east on Claus Drive. Take an immediate left onto Broadway and an immediate right onto Bolinas–Fairfax Road. Drive 3.8 twisty miles to a parking turnout on the left. The signed trail starts across the road (watch for cars).

The rugged trail approaches the Pine Mountain Summit.

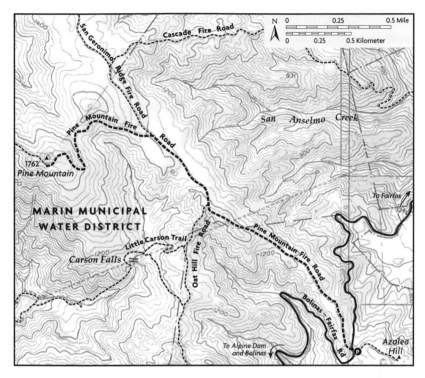

Another trek with 1100 feet of elevation gain? Hey, the whole idea is get out with your dog and get a little exercise. This trail, however, is more than just a sweaty excuse to get outdoors. Pine Mountain is a beautiful trek where a wide fire road winds its way up through low-growing chaparral—like chamise and ceanothus—coast live oaks, madrones, and twisted boulder outcroppings. If you hike this trail at certain times of the year (and certain times of the day), you might see only a couple of mountain bikers taking the challenge to get to the top; but the top is where you'll want to be, for sweeping views of Mount Diablo, San Pablo Bay, Alpine Lake, and Mount Tamalpais.

The first 0.5 mile starts out easily enough, slowly winding up from the parking lot and through a sea of boulders and bunchgrass. The climb then steepens, heads past some huge boulders, and hits a trail junction at 1 mile. For an optional side trip to Carson Falls, bear left onto signed Oat Hill Fire Road. In 0.2 mile, go right at the junction on the signed Little Carson Trail. Just 0.5 mile up this trail you'll reach the falls. They are powerful in the wet months, and since the trail has been rerouted in recent years it is a lot safer to get to them than it used to be. The falls is actually a series of five waterfalls that make up a cascade of water over rough serpentine. It's about 1.5 miles, round trip, to the falls and back from Pine Mountain Fire Road.

Continuing on up Pine Mountain Fire Road, you'll be amazed at the mix of chaparral and meadow the trail passes through. In spring, the hills become Technicolor with the blooming wildflowers, including lupine, wild iris, and California poppy. The trail actually levels out a bit as you reach a grassy plain, at about 1.4 miles. Here, you'll turn left and start the steep climb to dome-shaped Pine Mountain.

There are plenty of places to rest, out of the sea breezes that blow in. And be sure to get the camera ready, since you'll have views of the ocean and several ridges and lakes that make up the area.

40. Phoenix Lake

Round-trip: 4.2 miles
Hiking time: 3 hours
Difficulty: Easy to moderate
High point: 350 feet
Elevation gain: 200 feet
Best hiking time: Year-round
Water: At the trailhead and one bathroom stop
Regulations: Dogs must be leashed and are not allowed in the lake
Map: USGS San Rafael
Contact: Marin Municipal Water District, Sky Oaks Ranger Station, (415) 945-1181

Getting there: From U.S. Highway 101 in San Rafael, take the Sir Francis Drake Boulevard exit, drive west to the community of Ross, and turn left on Lagunitas Road. Drive 1.3 miles and park for free in a large parking lot at the end of the drive. You'll pick up the trail just past the bridge (just follow the other dogs).

If you have a dog who "loves to read the signs," gentle Phoenix Lake is the place to be. This 4.2-mile trip is a dog walker's heaven, where

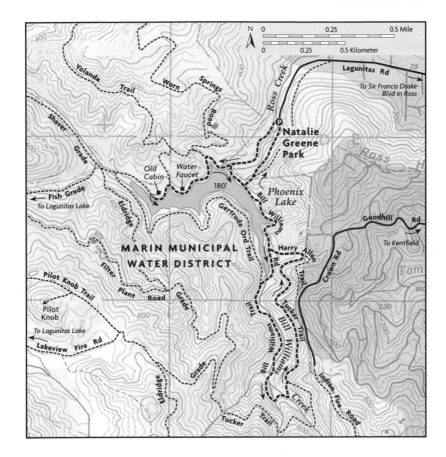

friendly people ask—often—if their dogs can meet your dogs. After a few minutes of sniffing (by dogs, of course), you'll be on your way until the next encounter.

Phoenix Lake was created in 1905 when the long-defunct Marin Water and Power Company built the dam, which created the reservoir. History has it that the dam was going to be put up over the old Shaver stagecoach line, cutting off the dairies from Ross Station so that the ranchers would have to make the more tedious run over the hills to Fairfax. There were some threats, some guns pulled, and in a compromise, a road was built across the dam and up the canyon. It's this road where the hike begins.

The Marin Municipal Water District now maintains the 25-acre lake, which has some good fishing for bass. In the fall, the leaves all turn

The sun sets on Trinity at Phoenix Lake.

orange and red, and in the spring wildflowers bloom all over. In between, manzanita—with its cool, mint-green leaves and mahogany-colored bark—and ferns make up the color palette.

The first part of the hike (going west on Bill Williams Road) takes you to an old redwood cabin, which was built by James and Janet Porteous for their coachman and which predates the reservoir by twelve years. The cabin is unique and was the only building left standing after a fire destroyed the Porteous estate in the 1920s. The building has been vacant for more than sixty years, but it was restored in 1989.

Doubling back to the east, past the trail to the parking area, Bill Williams Road takes hikers into a small canyon dotted with bay laurel, buckeye, and coast live oak. Pass a junction with the Harry Allen Trail and reach an area that opens up to a grassy swath and hugs Bill Williams Creek. Cross the creek and soon reach a junction with the Tucker Trail. Go left and follow Tucker Trail back along the creek. Go left on the Harry Allen Trail then turn right on Bill Williams Road and follow the signs back to the parking area.

Supposedly, Williams was a Confederate Army deserter who mined gold on the creek where his cabin stood. One of the big mysteries is that Williams hid all his treasure somewhere in the canyons, where it is said to remain today. Indeed, people tell stories that workers building the dam spent more time digging for the treasure than working on the project. However, the real treasure here is the hike itself.

41. Deer Island

Round-trip: 3-mile loop
Hiking time: 1 hour
Difficulty: Easy
High point: 250 feet
Elevation gain: 200 feet
Best hiking time: September through June
Water: Bring your own
Regulations: Dogs must be leashed and are not allowed in creeks
    or surrounding wetlands
Map: USGS Petaluma Point
Contact: Marin County Open Space District, (415) 507-2816

Getting there: Drive U.S. Highway 101 north 2.6 miles past State Route 37 and take the Atherton/San Marin exit. Go east on Atherton and after 1.8 miles, turn right on Olive Avenue, then left on Deer Island Lane. After 0.5 mile, you'll reach a gravel parking area, where you can park for free. The trail starts just past the trash can and wooden gate.

If you're not a local, you'll swear we're leading you along here. In a mix of new, grand estates, thirty-year-old ranch homes, and a strip mall, no way will you think there was any place around to enjoy a little open space in this built-up area north of San Francisco.

But the Deer Island Open Space Preserve is a little sliver of heaven. Joggers use the trail, as do hikers, horseback riders, and dog walkers. It really is an island that rises slightly above the surrounding wetlands. In the spring, when the oaks are leafing out and the grass is green, you'll have the added thrill of looking down at the bird life that will be searching for food in the flooded fields.

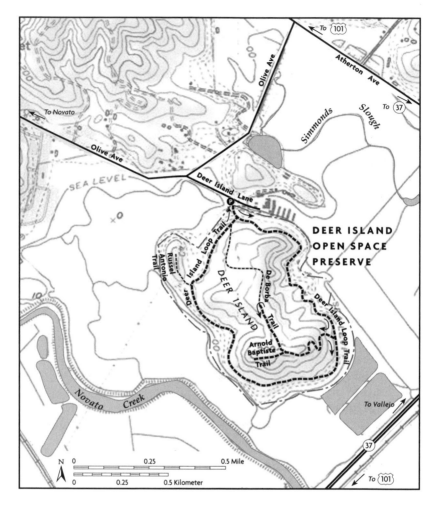

To start, go east on the packed-dirt trail and head directly into a hardwood forest of bay laurel and oak, where massive trees look as wide as
they are tall. After 0.5 mile, turn right and begin a 200-foot climb to the
signed De Borba Trail and the first of many sweeping vistas. As soon as
you reach the Deer Island Ridge, you'll bear left onto the Arnold Baptiste
Trail, which leads to a grassy knoll. This is the best place to stretch out
and have a snack.

Double back and continue to ridge-hike north on the De Borba Trail,
where you'll find a massive, moss-covered boulder. Here's where the

Oaks dot the Deer Island Open Space Preserve.

sweeping views get really good, with swanky developments in Novato, Mount Diablo, and San Pablo Bay in the distance.

To complete the Deer Island loop around the island's perimeter, backtrack a bit to the Deer Island Loop Trail where it meets the southeast end of the De Borba Trail (1.8 miles), and head south. This 1.2-mile trek passes by some historic old corrals and offers the best views of Novato Creek and the surrounding wetlands.

If time is short, continue north along the De Borba Trail instead of heading back to the ridgetop. The trail will drop back to the trailhead in about 0.25 mile to complete a shorter loop of 1.4 miles.

42. Mount Burdell

Round-trip: 6.2-mile loop
Hiking time: 3–5 hours
Difficulty: Moderate to strenuous
High point: 1550 feet
Elevation gain: 1400 feet
Best hiking time: Year-round
Water: Bring your own
Regulations: Dogs must be leashed
Maps: USGS Petaluma River, USGS Novato
Contact: Marin County Open Space District, (415) 499-6405

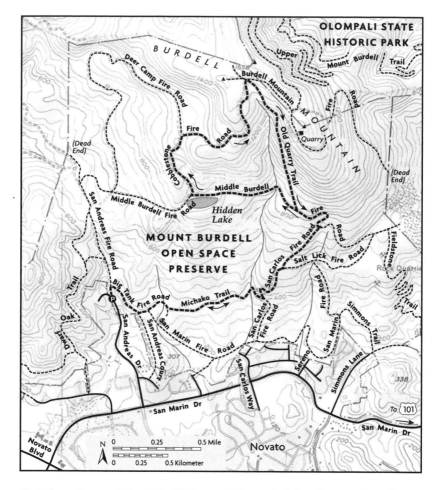

Getting there: Drive U.S. Highway 101 north 2.6 miles past State Route 37, take the Atherton/San Marin exit, and go west 2.1 miles on San Marin Drive to San Andreas Drive. Turn right on San Andreas Drive and drive 0.6 mile to the preserve's parking area on San Andreas Drive.

For 6000 years, the Miwok Indians had a village at the base of Mount Burdell, which they called Olompali. Food, namely acorns, was abundant, as was water as rains ran down from the ravines. But history changes things. This open space preserve—also once a part of the 8877-acre Olompali Ranch—takes hikers through the green-studded hills, past an old quarry where cobblestone was mined for the streets of San Francisco, and through canyons studded with oaks and bay laurel.

For students of geologic and ecological history, Mount Burdell was created some 12 million years ago when the ocean receded and lava forced its way past the Franciscan sandstone and serpentine. The lava gave way to bunchgrass, where live oak, scrub oak, and bay laurel landed. This oak savanna is typical of the Bay Area.

The preserve now sits wedged among housing developments and a few horse stables. The Marin County Open Space District began buying parcels in 1978 and made the last addition in 1994. The open space now includes 1558 acres of land where mountain bikers, horses, hikers, and dogs are most welcome.

Start at the trailhead on Big Tank Fire Road. At 0.5 mile, turn left onto signed, hiker-only Michako Trail (there's a cattle gate). Continue climbing and, eventually, you'll find yourself on the inviting San Carlos Fire Road that will snake its way up Mount Burdell's southern shoulder.

The rocky summit of Mount Burdell

At 1.6 miles, head left onto the signed Middle Burdell Fire Road past a lone buckeye tree and water troughs near Two Brick Spring, where you may find cows having a drink. Continue to climb up Middle Burdell Fire Road and stay left at the junction with Old Quarry Trail. You'll return to the fire road via Old Quarry Trail to complete this loop. You'll start to get sweeping views of the surrounding hillsides. The rock quarry appears to the north before the steep climb; carry on to the western knob at 2.9 miles.

To complete the loop portion of the trail, pass seasonal Hidden Lake on your left and promptly turn right onto Cobblestone Fire Road. After about 0.5 mile, stay straight on the fire road, ignoring the junction with Deer Camp Fire Road to the left. A mile later, turn right off Cobblestone onto the Old Quarry Trail. This trail brings you past the quarry and, after 0.5 mile of southeasterly travel, rejoins Middle Burdell Fire Road. From here, retrace your earlier steps back to the trailhead.

43. Waterfall Trail and Indian Valley

Round-trip: 3-mile loop (3.2 returning via Waterfall Trail)
Hiking time: 1.5 hours
Difficulty: Easy
High point: 600 feet
Elevation gain: 500 feet
Best hiking time: September through June
Water: Bring your own
Regulations: Dogs must be leashed; visitors are asked to keep their dogs out of the ponds
Map: USGS San Rafael
Contact: Marin County Open Space District, (415) 507-2816

Getting there: From U.S. Highway 101, take the Ignacio Boulevard exit that's located a couple of miles south of State Route 37. Go west on Ignacio Boulevard for 2.8 miles and enter the College of Marin campus, where you can park for free at the field house near the softball fields.

Pacheco Pond is a great place for dogs to take a swim.

The highlight of this hike is cattail-ringed Pacheco Pond, a quiet space where you and the dogs will have a wonderful time exploring—or simply taking a rest and having a snack. The closeness to the College of Marin makes the Indian Valley Open Space Preserve a popular place on weekends, but the farther back you go on the trails, among the bay laurel and live oak woods, the more solitude you'll find.

The trail, which is signed Pacheco Pond Fire Road, begins near left field of the first baseball diamond. After traveling on this trail for about 150 yards, swing left to continue on Pacheco Pond Fire Road, and you'll soon reach circular Pacheco Pond. This 3-acre pond is a great spot to sit and relax as you gaze at the resident duck population and other freshwater animals.

Back on the trail, a series of switchbacks takes you up the canyon, where shade from the mostly bay laurel forest is a welcome friend.

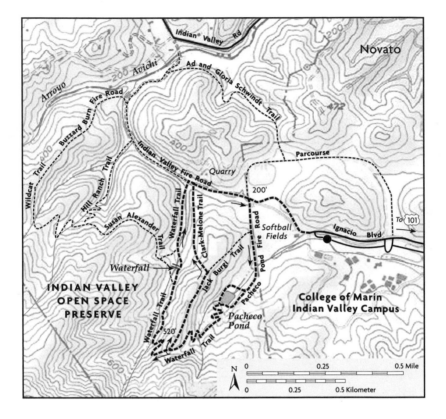

Soaproot (the plant is topped with white flower spikes in June) grows here in clusters, among the seasonal grasses that are tan by summer, only to come alive in greens in the fall.

At 1.1 miles, you'll get a great view of San Pablo Bay to the east, and 75 yards farther you'll reach a junction. If taking this trek in the wet months, continue straight on the Waterfall Trail another 0.5 mile to a slender falls. From the falls, it is another 0.25 mile on the Waterfall Trail to reach the Indian Valley Fire Road. During the dry months of the year, go right on the Jack Burgi Trail and head for the grassy hills to the north.

At 1.6 miles (having taken the Jack Burgi Trail), go left onto the signed Clark-Melone Trail, which heads down the canyon and soon comes to the Indian Valley Fire Road Trail near its junction with the Waterfall Trail. Turn right here and head straight for the trailhead and a quick, 3-mile loop.

44. Ring Mountain

Round-trip: 1.75-mile loop
Hiking time: 2 hours
Difficulty: Moderate
High point: 600 feet
Elevation gain: 600 feet
Best hiking time: Year-round
Water: Bring your own
Regulations: Dogs must be leashed
Maps: USGS San Quentin, USGS San Rafael
Contact: Marin County Open Space District, (415) 507-2816

Getting there: From San Francisco, take U.S. Highway 101 north to the Paradise Drive/Tamalpais Drive exit. Turn left off the freeway and make the first right onto San Clemente Drive, which turns into Paradise Drive. You can park for free on Paradise Drive, near the wooden gate trailhead, just past the Marin County Day School.

At a rocky outcrop along the Loop Trail you can look back down toward San Pablo.

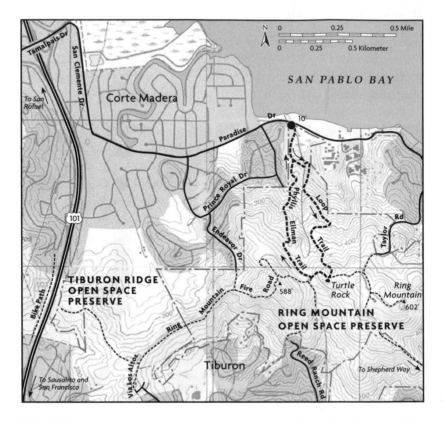

This 377-acre open space preserve encompasses the ridge between the towns of Corte Madera and Tiburon and has great views of San Francisco to the south and the ferries shuttling passengers across San Pablo Bay. It's a surprisingly happy space, one of my favorite hikes in all of the Bay Area.

Besides being an easy hike that gains 600 feet in elevation, there's a great granite rock outcropping at the top—pack your climbing shoes and chalk bag for a little bouldering while the dogs rest in the shade.

Start at the open space preserve sign and head up the single-track Loop Trail that crosses a bridge at Triangle Marsh; you'll reach a Nature Conservancy sign here that dedicates the area to the memory of Patricia Bucko-Stormer. Before the Nature Conservancy purchased the area, development of the surrounding hillsides threatened to consume it. The nonprofit organization, along with the Marin branch of the Native Plant Society, saved the area for everyone's enjoyment. Indeed, this marsh area is home to salt grass, salt pickle weed, poison oak, wildflowers, bay laurel, live oak, and rare plants like the Tiburon mariposa lily, Tiburon paintbrush, Tiburon buckwheat, Marin dwarf flax, and Oakland star tulip.

Just past the information kiosk that explains the history of the area, take the left trail at the split, through a series of Himalayan blackberry thickets that is the Loop Trail. At marker 4, about 0.3 mile in, you'll reach a crisscross of unmarked game trails. Continue right on the main trail; at marker 5, at about 0.5 mile, turn left and pass through a grassland.

At marker 8, you'll reach a shady little grove, where on a railroad tie the word "trail" is etched for everyone to see. At about 0.8 mile, turn right onto unsigned Champe Trail, named after the Nature Conservancy intern who laid out this course. It leads into a forest of bay laurel and, at 1 mile, crosses over the gravel ridge to Turtle Rock.

To get back down, take Ring Mountain Fire Road from Turtle Rock. At just past the 1-mile mark, take the signed Phyllis Ellman Trail and head up the hill and then back down to the trailhead.

45. Blithedale Ridge

Round-trip: 7-mile loop
Hiking time: 3–5 hours
Difficulty: Moderate to difficult
High point: 800 feet
Elevation gain: 900 feet
Best hiking time: Year-round
Water: Bring your own
Regulations: Dogs must be leashed
Map: USGS San Rafael
Contact: Marin County Open Space District, (415) 507-2816

Getting there: From U.S. Highway 101 in San Rafael, take the East Blithedale exit a few miles north of the Golden Gate Bridge and go west for 3 miles to Mill Valley. Turn right onto West Blithedale Avenue, drive 1.2 miles, and park for free where you can find a spot along the very narrow road near the gate to the Blithedale Summit Open Space Preserve.

This is a hike where you wouldn't expect it. Nestled in the developments and neighborhoods is a trek that features remote trails through a forest

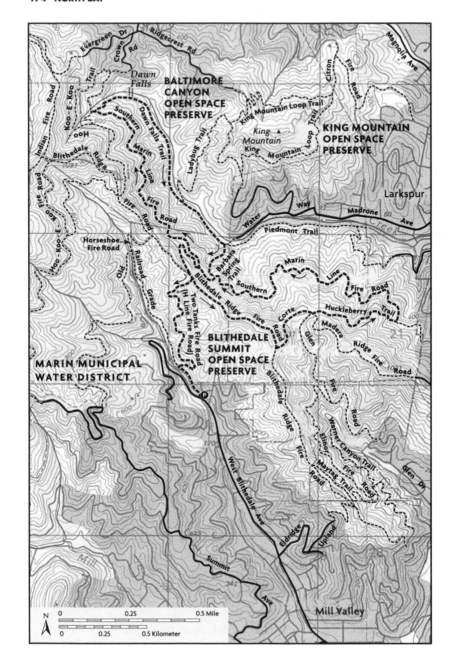

Evergreen Dr
Crown Rd
Ridgecrest Rd
Magnolia Ave
Dawn Falls
Koo-E-Koo Trail
Indian Fire Road
BALTIMORE CANYON OPEN SPACE PRESERVE
ooH
Southern
Dawn Falls Trail
Marin
Line
Fire
Road
Blithedale Ridge
Koo-Koo-E Fire Road
Ladybug Trail
King Mountain Loop Trail
King Mountain
King Mountain Loop Trail
Citron Fire Road
KING MOUNTAIN OPEN SPACE PRESERVE
Larkspur
Water Way
Madrone Ave
Creek
Piedmont Trail
Horseshoe Fire Road
Railroad Grade
Old
Barbara Spring Trail
Blithedale Ridge Fire Road
Two Tanks Fire Road
(H Line Fire Road)
Southern
Marin
Line
Fire Road
Huckleberry Trail
Corte
Madera
Glen
Ridge Fire Road
BLITHEDALE SUMMIT OPEN SPACE PRESERVE
MARIN MUNICIPAL WATER DISTRICT
Blithedale Ridge Fire Road
Water Canyon Trail
Elinor Fire Road
Maytag Trail
Glen Dr
P
West Blithedale Ave
Eldridge
Upland
Summit
Summit Ave
Mill Valley
Mill

N
0   0.25   0.5 Mile
0   0.25   0.5 Kilometer

of native trees—mixed hardwood and conifer and some redwoods too. Six trails lead into this open space, where Dawn Falls is a perfect destination if rains have fallen recently. Best yet, dogs are allowed on all six trails.

Start on the other side of the gate and go up on an old fire road called Two Tanks (H Line), which climbs from the trailhead along a babbling stream. Here, you'll be shaded under tan oaks, redwoods, and bigleaf maples. The climb continues after you turn right onto the Blithedale Ridge Fire Road at about 0.8 mile. From here, you'll walk another 0.5 mile and make a left on the Corte Madera Ridge Fire Road. After a short jaunt on the fire road, go left at the junction onto the signed Huckleberry Trail, which, as the name implies, heads through a thicket of evergreen huckleberries.

Hang another left onto Southern Marin Line Fire Road at 2.1 miles, which is thankfully level for another

A tiny brook greets visitors looking to hike Blithedale Ridge.

2 miles (you'll pass your return route, the Barbara Spring Trail). Through the peeling madrones, you'll catch some good views. At Dawn Falls Trail, take a right and after 0.25 mile, reach modest Dawn Falls at 4.3 miles in. The water flows peacefully 15 feet down granite slabs. For an alternate, shorter hike to Dawn Falls, see Hike 37.

Dawn Falls Trail continues along deeply shaded Baltimore Canyon to the Barbara Spring Trail, where you'll make a right, then turn right again to retrace a part of Southern Marin Line Fire Road before making a left onto a connector trail that links up to Blithedale Ridge Fire Road. Make a left at Blithedale Ridge Fire Road, then a right, which will take you back to the gate on Two Tanks (H Line) Fire Road.

46. Rodeo Lagoon

Round-trip: 1.7 miles
Hiking time: 1 hour
Difficulty: Easy
High point: 170 feet
Elevation gain: 170 feet
Best hiking time: Year-round
Water: At the trailhead
Regulations: Dogs must be leashed on the beach and under strict voice control elsewhere; dogs are not allowed in the lagoon
Map: USGS Point Bonita
Contact: Golden Gate National Recreation Area, Marin Headlands Visitor Center, (415) 331-1540

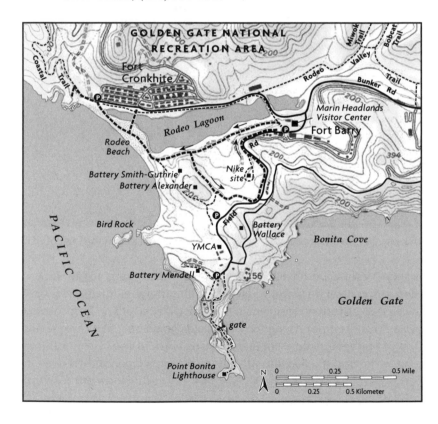

The fantastic views of Rodeo Lagoon, Rodeo Beach, and the Pacific Ocean are your reward for this short walk.

Getting there: From just north of the Golden Gate Bridge on U.S. Highway 101, take the Alexander Avenue exit and turn immediately left under the freeway. Follow the brown recreation signs for Marin Headlands and drive the twisty road (which has great views of the Golden Gate and San Francisco) about 2 miles, where you'll end up on Bunker Road. Park for free in the large lot at Fort Barry.

Getting here is half the fun. The Marin Headlands is 15 square miles of beaches, marshes, lagoons, and lush coastal hills that rise to spectacular views.

Wildlife lovers will enjoy this trek, since there's the chance to spot a number of raptor species, seabirds, marine mammals, and the occasional bobcat and mountain lion. History buffs will be pumped about the 150 years of military history, including bunkers, batteries, cannons, and in an extension of this hike, a trek past an old Nike missile site. Dog lovers like it, well, because it's a place where leashed dogs can stroll, too.

From the Civil War through the Cold War, the Marin Headlands— along with the Presidio across the Golden Gate Bridge—protected San Francisco Bay from invasion. The Marin Headlands served as a military base until the 1960s; now it hosts a network of mixed-use trails. This trip alongside Rodeo Lagoon is an easy warm-up for the nearby 6.6-mile Miwok and Bobcat Trails (Hike 47).

The hike's starting point, Fort Barry, was once a major post for military operations. After walking around the fort, cross the road and go up the hill to the trailhead. First, you'll head out toward a bluff overlook, where you'll see surfers catching waves on Rodeo Beach.

Then, you'll take the trail that hugs the south side of Rodeo Lagoon. The lagoon is a mixed freshwater/saltwater area that rises and falls with the seasons. Swelled by rainwater, the lagoon stays mostly brackish-brown, but make no mistake about it, the waterway is teeming with life. In fall, the endangered brown pelican is present, along with egrets, ducks, gulls, and herons.

It's easy to extend this hike to up to 4.5 miles, making a loop from the south side of the lagoon around the Nike missile site (now in a state of disrepair) and along Rodeo Beach.

47. Miwok and Bobcat Trails

Round-trip: 6.6-mile loop
Hiking time: 2–3 hours
Difficulty: Moderate to difficult
High point: 1050 feet
Elevation gain: 1250 feet
Best hiking time: Year-round
Water: At the trailhead
Regulations: Dogs must be leashed
Map: USGS Point Bonita
Contact: Golden Gate National Recreation Area, Marin Headlands
    Visitor Center, (415) 331-1540

Getting there: From just north of the Golden Gate Bridge on U.S. Highway 101, take the Alexander Avenue exit and turn immediately left under the freeway. Follow the brown recreation signs for Marin Headlands

The Miwok Trail is wide and inviting.

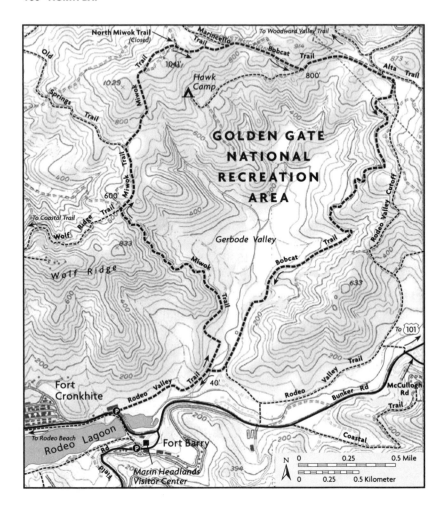

and drive the twisty road (which has great views of the Golden Gate and San Francisco) about 2 miles. Park for free in the large lot on the north side of Rodeo Lagoon.

This nearly circular trail takes hikers along a wide path up and down the pretty grasslands that make up the Marin Headlands. It's hard to imagine that for nearly 100 years, the area served as a military base of operations. In spring, the grassy hills are filled with wildflowers, including purplish-blue lupine and Creamsicle-orange California poppies.

The Miwok and Bobcat Trails will escort you around the U-shaped Gerbode Valley, which takes on many aspects during the year. Windswept grassy hills show their colors in spring with the aforementioned wildflower display, go brown in the summer heat, and when the clouds and fog descend, seem eerie and mysterious.

It's easy to extend this trek by using a number of connector trails (pick up a copy of the free Marin Headlands brochure from the visitor center), but this loop provides a decent workout for hikers and their canine friends. It also gets pretty solitary, and hikers will have a chance to see coyotes, bobcats, and even mountain lions (when we were last there, signs at the trailhead warned of sightings).

One note: as this is a national recreation area, the rangers are sticklers about dogs being on a leash at all times. Let's keep our dog-friendly spaces open and obey the rules. Also, this trek is used heavily by Bay Area horse enthusiasts, so be warned—you and your pooch will likely run into a few horseback riders.

The hike starts on the Rodeo Valley Trail, then you'll head northeast on the signed Miwok Trail. The trail follows a creek for a bit, then starts to climb up Wolf Ridge. Stay on the Miwok Trail and you'll reach a gap at 1.2 miles, where there's a trail junction. Go right and right again at the next junction.

Here's where the climbing comes in on this hike, as you ascend to the trek's high point just prior to reaching the Bobcat Trail turnoff and a gentle downhill. The views—when the clouds and fog are gone—are inspiring, with the Tennessee Valley to the northwest and the Gerbode Valley to the southeast.

Go right on the Bobcat Trail at 3.3 miles. Backpackers (backcountry permit required) can turn right at 4 miles to camp at Hawk Camp, but dog walkers will want to continue on the Bobcat Trail and take another right turn at 4.3 miles, where you'll drop steadily into the valley.

At 6.3 miles, turn right onto the signed Rodeo Valley Trail. Then take an immediate left back onto the Miwok Trail and return to the parking area.

48. Fort Baker

Round-trip: 2.5 miles
Hiking time: 2 hours
Difficulty: Moderate
High point: 600 feet
Elevation gain: 600 feet
Best hiking time: Year-round
Water: Bring your own
Regulations: Dogs must be leashed in developed areas; elsewhere dogs must be under their owner's control at all times, whether on a leash or under strict voice control; dogs are not allowed in the lagoon
Map: USGS San Francisco North
Contact: Golden Gate National Recreation Area, Marin Headlands Visitor Center, (415) 331-1540

Getting there: From San Francisco, drive north on U.S. Highway 101 and cross the Golden Gate Bridge; get in the right lane, and take the Vista Point exit to the Vista Point parking lot.

This hike is a quiet secret: a nifty drop from Vista Point on the north side of the Golden Gate Bridge to Fort Baker below. And completing the hike depends on the country's present threat level.

See, once the Office of Homeland Security's threat level is elevated, this trail is off-limits to hikers. But in that case you'll either have the option of crossing the Golden Gate—possibly the Bay Area's most frequented stroll—or of driving down to Fort Baker to wander among the historic buildings, as well as taking in the shoreline and maybe striking up a conversation with the U.S. Coast Guard crews stationed there.

Vista Point is like a mini United Nations, where people from across the globe come to gaze at the famous brick-red bridge and the San Francisco skyline. They stop to take pictures, maybe cross the bridge—you can go halfway to admire the view, turn back to the car, and you've gone 1.5 miles—but most people never think to take the short walk down to Fort Baker. A paved trail from the parking area loops under the northern footings of the Golden Gate, then works its way back around to the fort.

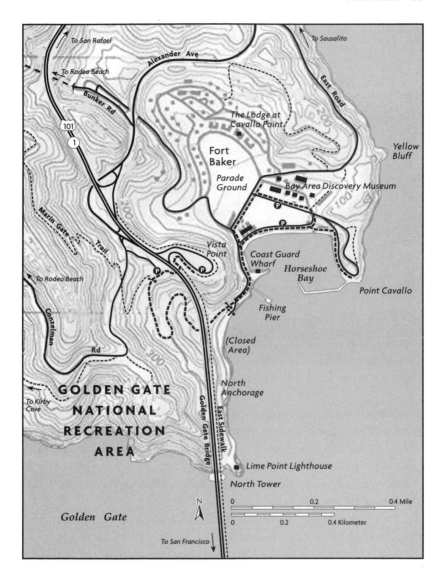

To San Rafael
To Sausalito
Alexander Ave
To Rodeo Beach
East Road
Bunker Rd
101
1
The Lodge at Cavallo Point
Yellow Bluff
Fort Baker
Parade Ground
Bay Area Discovery Museum
Marin Gate Trail
Vista Point
Coast Guard Wharf
Horseshoe Bay
Point Cavallo
To Rodeo Beach
Conzelman
Rd
Fishing Pier
(Closed Area)
To Kirby Cove
North Anchorage
GOLDEN GATE NATIONAL RECREATION AREA
Golden Gate Bridge
East Sidewalk
Lime Point Lighthouse
North Tower
N
0   0.2   0.4 Mile
0   0.2   0.4 Kilometer
Golden Gate
To San Francisco

The U.S. Army established Fort Baker in 1897 to support the many coastal batteries that were established on the northern side of the Golden Gate. According to Golden Gate National Recreational Area information, Fort Baker was a departure from earlier, western military forts. It represented a new, modern army, one where enlisted men and officers enjoyed a better standard of living.

The Golden Gate Bridge can be admired from all angles near Fort Baker.

Once you wind your way to the base of the Golden Gate (be sure to bring a camera for probably the best views of the bridge and the San Francisco skyline), take the road along the shore toward the Bay Area Discovery Museum (interesting displays; no dogs allowed). From a kiosk in the museum's main parking area, be sure to pick up the brochure for the new self-guided Fort Baker History Walk, and amble the 0.5-mile trail that makes nine stops through the fort. Dogs are welcome to come along, as long as they're leashed.

Once you've completed the loop, head out toward Horseshoe Bay to take in the salt breezes and see how the shore fishermen are doing. Then return to the north footing of the bridge and the moderately strenuous walk back up to the parking area.

SACRAMENTO, THE GOLD COUNTRY, AND TAHOE

49. South Yuba Independence Trail

Round-trip: 7 miles
Hiking time: 3 hours
Difficulty: Easy to moderate
High point: 1450 feet
Elevation gain: Negligible
Best hiking time: Year-round
Water: Bring your own
Regulations: Dogs must be leashed
Map: USGS Nevada City
Contact: South Yuba River State Park, Bridgeport Visitor Center and Ranger Station, (530) 432-2546

Getting there: From Nevada City, drive 5.5 miles north on State Route 49 and park in one of the turnouts near the trailhead, which is about 0.5 mile south of the Yuba River Bridge. If you reach the bridge, you've gone too far. Be careful walking across SR 49.

The mid-1850s in gold rush–crazy Nevada County brought engineering marvels of all kinds to extract the precious metal from the streambeds and canyon walls. The origin of the Independence Trail was an old miner's ditch once known as the Excelsior Canal. It was built in 1859 to carry water from the South Yuba River to hydraulic mining sites in Smartville, some 25 miles away. California legislators outlawed hydraulic mining in 1885, and the canal was used for irrigation until 1967.

According to the nonprofit hiking group Sequoya Challenge, Oakland Museum docent John Olmstead rediscovered the entire water system in 1975. And what a system. First, there was the ditch, which carried the water; then there was the berm, where the ditch-tender treaded to check the system and all the wooden flumes that bridged the ravines. Olmstead's wish was to answer a friend's lifelong dream: "Please find me a level wilderness trail where I can reach out and touch the wildflowers from my wheelchair."

North Fork of the American River (Marc Soares)

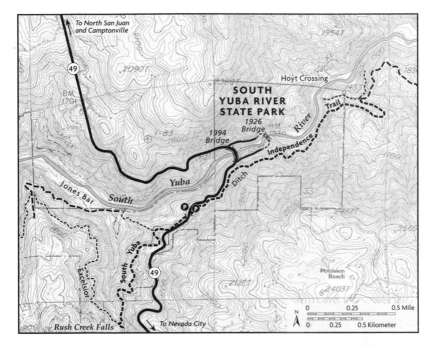

Don't think you can walk your dogs in a wilderness setting? This is the hike for you. The trail is gloriously flat, a fantastic walk that takes you through history. It rests inside South Yuba River State Park and is the very first wilderness trail in the country designed to be wheelchair accessible, according to Sequoya Challenge. The entire wheelchair loop is 7 miles.

Your car is parked midway along this trail, which runs west–east. Going west along the unmaintained portion, you'll find a fantastic waterfall just a mile from the trailhead. People and wheelchairs then can travel a switchback ramp from Flume 28 (520 feet long) to the sparkling waters of Rush Creek.

As you stroll along the western trail, you'll come upon a grand overlook of the South Yuba River. In spring, the overlook is covered in wildflowers. Come summer, the canyons switch to green, then dress up for autumn in red and gold hues.

Hike back and take a stroll along the eastern trail. You'll cross cliff-hanging flumes, take in more great views of the river and surrounding foothills, and have the opportunity to take a dip in several swimming holes that have been scooped out of the granite. The eastern side of the route is 2.5 miles of maintained trail.

Along the entire trail, you'll find picnic areas, restrooms, and even a camping area designed for disabled guests. This truly is a trail for all people—and their dogs too. Sequoya Challenge offers guided hikes for a small donation; call (530) 477-4788.

50. Bullards Bar Trail

Round-trip: Up to 14 miles
Hiking time: 7 hours
Difficulty: Easy to moderate
High point: 2243 feet
Elevation gain: Negligible
Best hiking time: Spring; hikable year-round
Water: From reservoir; or bring your own
Regulations: Dogs must be leashed
Maps: USGS Camptonville, USGS Challenge
Contact: Tahoe National Forest, North Yuba Ranger Station,
    (530) 288-3231

Getting there: From Nevada City, take State Route 49 North to Marysville Road (2 miles south of Camptonville) and turn left. Follow Marysville Road for 2.6 miles to the Dark Day turnoff. Turn right and drive down to the parking area above the boat ramp. Both the east and west trail sections can be accessed from here.

Dogs that like to swim will love the Bullards Bar Trail. Owners who like to swim, fish, and view wildflowers will love it just as much.

This easy trail follows the contours of New Bullards Bar Reservoir, a 4700-acre lake that offers 56 miles of shoreline wrapped by both the Plumas and Tahoe national forests. Most people hike this trail in spring, when temperatures are most comfortable, but this means greater opportunity for solitude as the summer wears on. One of the best features of this recreation area is that it's heavily wooded with huge ponderosa pine and Douglas fir, which means every campground site is shaded from the heat of the Sierra Nevada foothills summer. With the lake within easy reach for the entire 14-mile trip, there's always the chance to cool off. And you'll always get the feeling that you're the only one at this

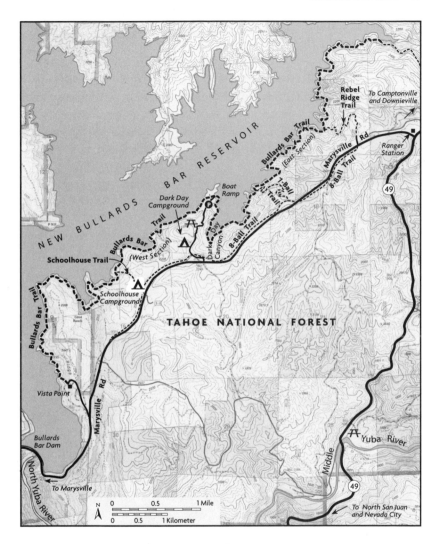

clear mountain lake, which doesn't get as much pressure as some other Northern California reservoirs.

But spring is prime here. During a spring storm, the dogs and I never had a raindrop touch us because of the dense forest covering. The underbrush is rife with wildflowers and giant ferns, which thrive under the canopy.

This hike starts at the Dark Day Campground, where you have the option to go east or west. You can also link up with the 23 other miles of trail in and around the recreation area, including Schoolhouse, 8-Ball, 7-Ball, and Rebel Ridge.

Don't be daunted by the 14-mile distance (if you do both sections). This in an uncomplicated trek with plenty of options. The trail is flat, wide, and inviting and always offers a great lake view. Most people take off east or west, take a splash in the water, stop at the vista point above the dam for the view, and maybe drop a line before heading back to the car. There's no hassle here, no pressure. Relax.

Lupine grows in abundance near New Bullards Bar Reservoir.

51. Codfish Creek Trail

Round-trip: 3.4 miles
Hiking time: 2 hours
Difficulty: Easy
High point: 950 feet
Elevation gain: 110 feet
Best hiking time: Spring through fall
Water: Best to bring your own
Regulations: Dogs must be leashed
Map: USGS Colfax
Contact: Auburn State Recreation Area, (530) 885-4527

Getting there: From Auburn, take Interstate 80 east to the second Weimar exit (Weimar Cross Roads) and turn right on Canyon Way. After about a mile, the road turns left and becomes Ponderosa Way. Drive to the parking area, on the right just before the bridge over the North Fork American River (6 miles south of Weimar). The trailhead is beyond the parking area. Note: Ponderosa Way is a rough road, made for high-clearance and four-wheel-drive vehicles. It can get treacherous in winter.

Granted, the Codfish Creek Trail takes a bit to get to, but the views are worth the trip. It's an easy trail, gaining just over 100 feet in a little more than 3 miles. In the springtime—the best time to go, really—the trail comes alive with several species of wildflowers and butterflies, which are attracted to flowers' sweet nectar. And of course, the terminus of this hike is a spectacular, 40-foot waterfall, which usually dries up in the summer.

An excellent brochure detailing the area's flora and fauna is available at a discovery marker located 0.25 mile from the trailhead across the sandy beach. The pamphlet was written and illustrated by Heather K. Mehl for her 2001 senior project at Colfax High School, according to the good folks at the Auburn State Recreation Area.

The trail begins at the north side of the bridge on Ponderosa Way and leads downstream on the sunny, exposed side of the canyon, following an old mining route along the North Fork American River. The river was mined extensively for gold well into the twentieth century. Along the trail, you'll be able to see the results of the dredge-mining operations:

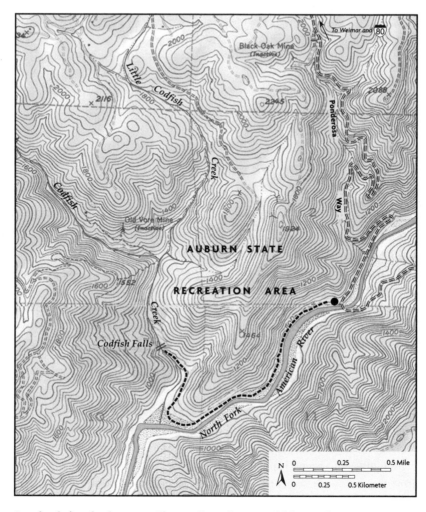

just look for the large, uniform piles of river cobble on the opposite side of the river.

The first mile is relatively flat, and there are plenty of side trails that lead to the water's edge so the dogs can cool off and get a drink. While at the river's edge, look for dippers (water ouzels)—a small, brownish-gray bird about the size of a robin, searching out a meal. They bob up and down, then dive suddenly below the water's surface. Mergansers—waterfowl that hunt fish—are also prevalent here. In spring, the males will be wearing their brilliant mating colors, then will transform in summer to a color closer to the female.

Gray pine at North Fork American River, early fall (Marc Soares)

This is also a classic trail to view the riparian habitat. Three species of oak can be found here, including canyon live oak, black oak, and interior live oak. You'll also find Pacific madrone and manzanita, which are sometimes mistaken for each other since they both have smooth, reddish-brown trunks. Known as one of the more exotic of the western hardwoods, Pacific madrone is distinguished by a very consistent salmon color, beautiful knot patterns, and a smooth grain. The wood is prized for exotic flooring, furniture, cabinetry, and picture frames, according to a woodworking craftsman I know. You'll also be treated to huge stands of ponderosa pine, gray pine (also known as foothill pine), and Douglas fir.

At 1.2 miles, the trail turns toward Codfish Creek and the falls. The trail cuts up to the right through the Codfish Creek canyon to the falls, a mere 0.5 mile away from the turnoff.

52. American River Parkway

One-way: Up to 23 miles
Hiking time: 30 minutes to all day
Difficulty: Easy
High point: 500 feet
Elevation gain: 300 feet
Best hiking time: Spring and fall; hikable year-round
Water: Along the trail from potable-water taps; or bring your own
Regulations: Dogs must be leashed
Maps: USGS Sacramento East, USGS Carmichael, USGS Citrus
    Heights, USGS Folsom
Contact: County of Sacramento, Parks and Recreation Division,
    (916) 875-6961

Getting there: The trail begins at Discovery Park in Old Sacramento, on the north side of the American River. From Interstate 5, take the Richards Boulevard exit and drive west to Jiboom Street. Turn right and follow the road to the park. There are other access points along U.S. Highway 50 as well. Each county park along the trail charges a fee to park, although no permit is required to hike. There is a parking fee at the Folsom Lake State Recreation Area.

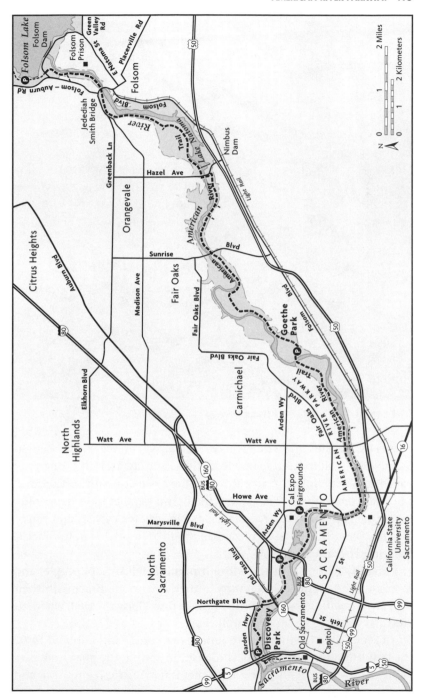

Oaks along the American River Parkway

Every city, it seems, has a trail where dog walkers can see and be seen. In Sacramento, that trail is the American River Parkway, a 23-mile (one-way) paved trail that links Sacramento with the towns of Rancho Cordova, Fair Oaks, and Folsom. There are actually two parallel trails happening here. One is the paved American River Parkway for cyclists and roller-bladers. Then there's the dirt Jedediah Smith Memorial Trail for horses, trail runners, and hikers.

Certainly no one does the entire trip in one fell swoop; people tend to enjoy short sections and return to their cars to continue with their busy lives. Evening seems to be the busiest time along the trail, when it's crowded with joggers and dog walkers.

The trail is a year-round destination, but spring and fall tend to be the best times for out-of-towners to visit. In spring, the grass and trees along the river are richly green, the water is flowing fresh and clear, and you'll have the chance to see American shad—in huge schools—complete their migration from the ocean into the river to spawn. Anglers revere this fish, since it packs a punch when caught on light tackle. In fall, the trees burst into reds, golds, and oranges.

The trail gets some 5 million visitors a year, so if you're looking for solitude, this isn't a trail for you. But it is a good hike to get your dogs socialized to group settings that include a lot of dogs. Remember to have good control of your pet, since not everyone will share in your dog's exuberance to meet new people and dogs. It's the perfect place to work on the command, "Leave it," which most dog handlers teach for good behavior.

The American River Parkway is even a movie star, of sorts. The trail was used as a backdrop in the 1997 Kurt Russell thriller *Breakdown*.

53. Folsom Lake and Mormon Island Dam

Round-trip: 13 miles
Hiking time: 6 hours or overnight
Difficulty: Easy
High point: 600 feet
Elevation gain: 400 feet
Best hiking time: Early spring; hikable year-round
Water: From the Folsom Lake
Regulations: Dogs must be leashed
Map: USGS Folsom
Contact: Folsom Lake Recreation Area, (916) 988-0205

Getting there: From U.S. Highway 50 in Sacramento, take Folsom Boulevard north for 2.8 miles. Turn right on Natoma Street and drive 3.1 miles. Turn right to stay on East Natoma Street, signed for Folsom Point. Drive another 0.7 mile and turn left to the picnic area and beach.

When the summer sun is high in the sky and everyone from Sacramento, it seems, has escaped the valley heat with their boats and personal watercraft, this is a trail best avoided by dogs and their owners. Just too much saturation.

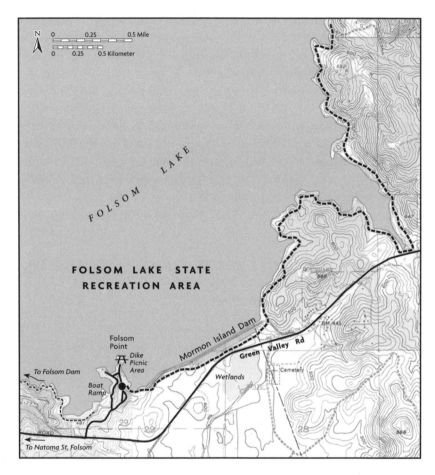

But in the months before and after the high season (May through September), this lake is ideal for a stroll with the dogs, since it offers 75 miles of shoreline. On some weekends in the early spring, late fall, and winter, you'll think you own the lake; you might not see another person for miles. Your only company, besides your trusted canine companion, will be the American kestrels, red-tailed hawks, and eagles that soar on the thermals; the honking Canada geese; and, if you're lucky, a bobcat or raccoon at sunset coming down to the lake for a drink or a meal.

Starting at the picnic area and beach, the trail winds its way past a small cove that's full of willows. You'll continue across Mormon Island Dam and the 1-mile Dike 8 Trail, where you'll get a great view of the entire 18,000-acre lake. To the southeast, you'll get a good view of the huge cottonwoods and willows clumped together in the protected Mormon Island Wetlands. Bring a good set of binoculars and a bird-watching book to spy a spectacular array of birds, from songbirds that stay in the area all year to migrating waterfowl.

You'll continue along the rocky shoreline contours, past gray pine and blue oaks, coming at 1.5 miles to a slender footpath that leads to a quaint cove. In spring, the lupine, vetch, and clover will all be in bloom.

So will the poison oak. You'll notice that this itchy plant grows as a ground cover, creeping vine, and shrub here. If your dog comes in contact with it, be sure to wash your pet off before getting back to your car, since a dog's fur can carry the itchy oils from the plant—and infect you days later (I know this from personal experience).

Folsom Lake, early spring (Marc Soares)

54. Crooked Lakes Trail to Penner Lake

Round-trip: 6 miles
Hiking time: 3 hours or overnight
Difficulty: Moderate
High point: 6900 feet
Elevation gain: 500 feet
Best hiking time: Mid-June through October
Water: From trailside lakes
Regulations: Dogs must be under control at all times, whether strict voice control or leashed; leashes recommended
Maps: USGS Graniteville, USGS English Mountain
Contact: Tahoe National Forest, Nevada City Ranger District, (530) 265-4531

Getting there: From the junction of Interstate 80 and State Route 20, take SR 20 west for 3.7 miles and turn north (right) onto Bowman Lake Road (Forest Road 18). Drive 8.4 miles on this road, and turn right at the junction signed CARR AND FEELY LAKES. Stay on this road, ignoring any smaller roads that split off on either side, and in 2.2 miles go right at the junction signed CARR LAKE. Take another right at the signed junction in 0.4 mile and follow the bumpy dirt road the last 0.4 mile to the trailhead, which is located at the Carr Lake Campground.

Weekend solitude you'll not likely find on this trail; however, if you want some of the most spectacular views of the Sierra Nevada and a string of alpine lakes where you can swim, fish, or just sit and relax for a good long while, this is the trail for you. You'll miss the crowds if you can trek midweek, but don't let a few people deter you from taking this hike. It's a drainer on the legs, no doubt, but the rewards are great.

The trail starts at the Carr Lake Campground, where you'll walk along the campground road going east until you cross a creek and turn onto the actual trail. That path hugs the shoreline of Feely Lake—favorite destination for anglers—where you'll get good views of Fall Creek Mountain

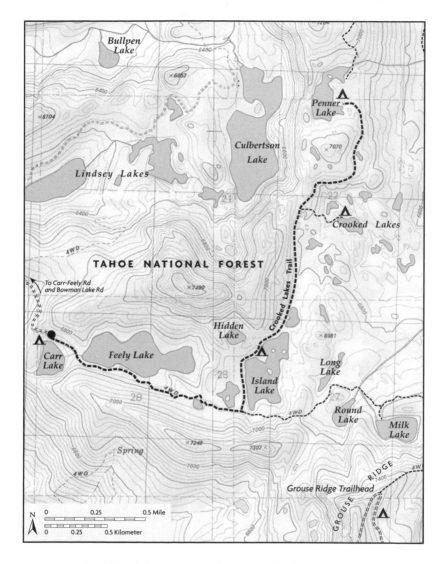

to the north. After 0.5 mile, you'll start to climb gradually, eventually leveling off at a small pond.

At just over 1 mile, you'll turn left onto the signed Crooked Lakes Trail, just after passing an unnamed lake. The path goes between this lake to the left and Island Lake to the right.

Island Lake and Penner Lake are the crown jewels of this hike. Both

Paul splashes along the edge of a shallow, grassy pond on the way to the lake.

are spectacular in terms of beauty and play opportunities. Island Lake is encased in black-flecked granite, its crystal-clear waters inviting a quick dip. It's as if someone took a dipper into the blue Sierra Nevada sky and ladled it into a rock bowl. All around, the green of the red fir and lodgepole pine forest sparkles and sets off the starkness of the serrated Sierra Nevada range.

If you can't pull yourself away, there are good campsites amid the lodgepole pines near the water's edge to the left. These are fairly popular sites, so if they're full, try one of several sites along the east shore.

After bidding Island Lake farewell at 1.5 miles, you'll enter a cool red fir forest, where you'll come upon a small waterfall coming from Island Lake's outlet. The first of the Crooked Lakes comes at 2 miles, but it's shallow, marshy, and there are better choices ahead. The path starts to lose elevation at 2.3 miles, where you'll pick up a side trail on the right of the lake that leads to another small lake. Follow this path along the creek to the best of the Crooked Lakes, a large, deep, granite-encased pool. There's one good campsite where the side trail ends.

If Penner Lake is your destination, stay on the Crooked Lakes Trail, where you'll climb steadily for 0.5 mile of rocky terrain. At 2.8 miles, you'll crest the ridge and see the expansive, rocky shores of Penner below. Hopefully, you can stay for the alpenglow sunset on this lake.

It's also the best fishing lake in this string, and a dedicated angler can almost guarantee a trout dinner. Campsites are hard to come by at Penner, but if you don't mind pitching your tent on a slab of granite, the views can't be beat.

55. Loch Leven Lakes

Round-trip: 7.4 miles
Hiking time: 4 hours or overnight
Difficulty: Moderate
High point: 6850 feet
Elevation gain: 1120 feet
Best hiking time: Year-round; busiest mid-June to late October; good winter showshoeing
Water: From Loch Leven Lakes
Regulations: Dogs must be under control at all times, whether strict voice control or leashed; leashes recommended
Map: USGS Cisco Grove
Contact: Tahoe National Forest, Nevada City Ranger District, (530) 265-4531

Getting there: The trailhead and parking area just east of the Big Bend Ranger Station on Hampshire Rocks Road off Interstate 80, about 75 miles northeast of Sacramento. Traveling east on I-80, take the Big Bend exit and turn left onto Hampshire Rocks Road. The signed trail begins across the road from the parking lot.

Winter, spring, summer, or fall, a trek to Loch Leven Lakes offers it all: Scenic overlooks. Muscle-burning uphills. Cool mountain lake swimming. Fishing. Or just plain sitting around. But you first have to get to this string of granite-basin lakes.

The first mile of this hike is steep and will leave you and the dogs panting. It's a blessing, perhaps, that this section of trail is shaded by a lodgepole pine forest. You'll reach an uncontrolled Union Pacific Railroad crossing at 1.3 miles. Be sure to keep your dogs leashed and right with you through this section to avoid a potential train accident. In this area you'll see western white pine and the occasional quaking aspen.

Once you leave the forest, at 2.2 miles, the grade evens out; then you'll reach a series of switchbacks (make sure your dogs don't cut the

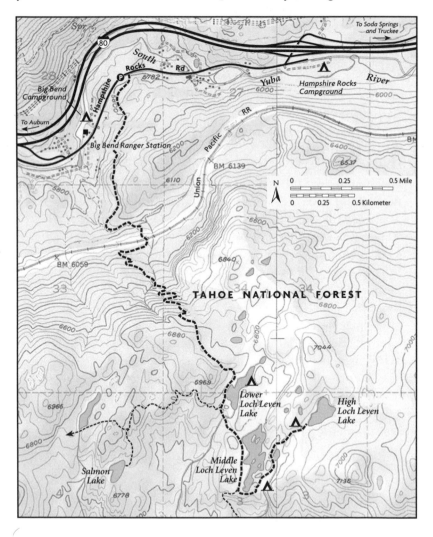

Spring brings seasonal ponds to the Loch Leven Lakes area.

switchbacks—this leads to erosion) that takes you to the top of a high ridge, where Lower Loch Leven Lake sits after 2.7 miles of hiking.

At the south end of the lake, the trail splits, with the branch to the right leading southwest to Salmon Lake. The other fork continues south, climbing and descending small ridges about 0.25 mile to Middle Loch Leven. Keep going another 0.75 mile and you'll finally hit High Loch Leven Lake.

Camping is available at all the lakes, but you'll want to spend most of your time at High Loch Leven, which doesn't get as much pressure—and the granite-island-dotted shoreline is protected by white fir, red fir, lodgepole pine, and western white pine and provides much-appreciated shade in the summer. Fishing for brook and rainbow trout is good at all the lakes.

Be sure not to abandon this hike in the winter. While strenuous, the trek on snowshoes offers a completely different perspective on the wilderness. Some cross-country skiers traverse the snow from the east on a marked trail to High Loch Leven, but most snowshoers reject the challenge. Don't be one of them. Though with no trail to follow you'll need basic route-finding skills, finding the lakes isn't that big of a problem.

One thing to be aware of in winter is crossing the Union Pacific tracks. The company uses plow trains, which in heavy snow years can pile up a mound of snow that can't easily be climbed in snowshoes. It's generally a good idea to carry a snow shovel in the backcountry, and you can use it to dig steps into the snowbanks.

56. Summit Lake Trail

Round-trip: 4 miles
Hiking time: 2 hours
Difficulty: Easy
High point: 7400 feet
Elevation gain: 200 feet
Best hiking time: June through October
Water: Bring your own
Regulations: Dogs must be under control at all times, whether strict voice control or leashed; leashes recommended
Map: USGS Norden
Contact: Tahoe National Forest, Truckee Ranger District, (530) 587-3558

A log jutting into one of the trailside lakes is hard for an adventurous dog to resist.

Getting there: From Auburn, drive 60 miles east on Interstate 80 to the Castle Peak Area/Boreal Ridge Road exit just west of Donner Summit. Take the exit, turn right, then turn immediately left onto Bunny Hill Drive. Continue 0.4 mile to the trailhead for Donner Summit and the Pacific Crest Trail.

A buddy of mine, a dog lover and travel writer, asked if I was going to include Summit Lake in this guidebook. I hadn't thought about it, since I really don't often get to this part of the state on my jaunts with the dogs.

"Oh, you have to include Summit Lake," he said. "I don't know of any dog from San Francisco or Sacramento that hasn't used this trail."

So I did a little research, and found that the trail is canine-approved by www.dogfriendly.com, a website that provides city and travel guides for people and their pets. Next thing was to take a trip out I-80 to Donner Summit and the Summit Lake Trail.

Okay, it's not much of a trail for some people, but it is a scenic trip that can be done—out-and-back—in just a couple of hours. And even in late fall, when the weather was crisp and there was the threat of snow in the air, carloads of people were streaming off I-80 to stretch their legs and let their dogs stretch too.

Dogs should be on a leash unless they behave when off leash and are under direct voice command. Normally my border collie cross Trinity is great at voice commands—until she gets into the middle of a pack of dogs. We stayed leashed the entire 4-mile round-trip.

The first mile of the hike follows the wide and inviting PCT in an easterly direction, then picks its way north for another mile, passing through a tunnel under I-80. It is best to leash your dogs and keep them close in the area surrounding the tunnel to avoid accidents. Just after emerging from the tunnel, you'll come to the junction with the Summit

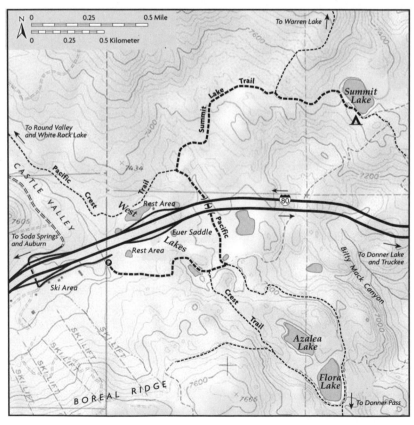

Lake Trail and take it to the right. This is where you'll leave the PCT and gain almost all of your elevation.

You'll cross two small creeks, which are separated by a low, glaciated granite ridge. The trail then bends through a meadow that's ablaze with wildflowers in the spring and early summer. The trail continues past the Warren Lake Trail intersection, where you'll want to veer right and out to the edge of a ridge. From here, it's a short walk under a canopy of pine to the southern corner of Summit Lake.

Camping is available here, but most people sit a bit and head back to the car. Don't forget to pack a light fishing rod, since the lake is full of brook and rainbow trout. If you're fishing, don't forget your California Department of Fish and Game license.

57. Martis Creek Lake and Wildlife Area

Round-trip: 5 miles or more
Hiking time: 2 hours or more
Difficulty: Easy
High point: 5906 feet
Elevation gain: 190 feet
Best hiking time: Year-round; snowshoe or cross-country ski
  in winter
Water: Bring your own
Regulations: Dogs must be under control at all times, whether strict
  voice control or leashed; leashes recommended; dogs must be
  leashed in and around developed areas such as campgrounds
Maps: USGS Truckee, USGS Martis Peak
Contact: U.S. Army Corps of Engineers, Sacramento District,
  (530) 432-6427 or (530) 587-8113

Getting there: From Interstate 80 in Truckee, take the exit for State Route 267 toward Sierraville/Lake Tahoe and head south on SR 267 for 2.8 miles, then turn left onto Martis Creek Road. In the winter, when the gate is closed, you can park in the small lot near the information kiosk. The rest of the year you can drive farther up the road and park near Alpine Meadows Campground or closer to the lake, which will make for a shorter hike.

When most people think of outdoor recreation in and around Tahoe, they envision swooping carved turns down the runs of world-class ski resorts, peak-bagging alpine ascents, or hours of strenuous trekking. The Martis Creek area just southeast of Truckee is proof that Tahoe caters to all outdoor activity levels from the extreme to the extremely relaxed.

Built in the 1970s by the U.S. Army Corps of Engineers to provide flood control for downstream communities, Martis Creek Dam opened the way for recreational opportunities in this picturesque open valley between Truckee and the Northstar California resort.

For people out to get in a good hike with their dog, Martis Creek Lake and surrounding valley is a great place to visit any time of year. Due to

The trails along the shore of Martis Creek Lake offer hours of fun exploring for you and your pup.

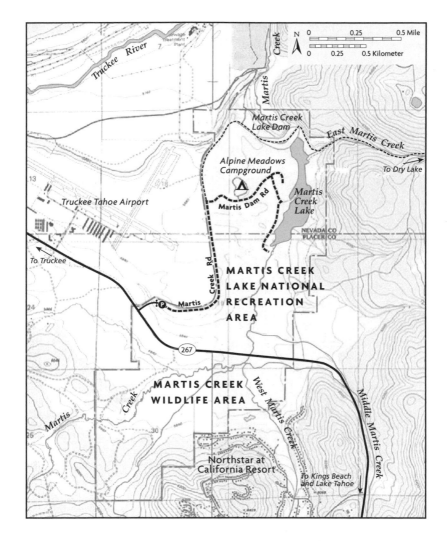

the easy, mostly flat terrain and smooth surfaces, this is also a popular destination for families and hikers with kids. Since you are likely to encounter other hikers and dogs here, be sure to keep your pooch under control and clean up after Fido to ensure continued access and a good time for everyone.

This hike embarks from Martis Creek Road, past the gate. The road climbs a slight grade for the first 0.25 mile as it contours to the north and then stays mostly flat as you walk along a plateau overlooking the lake to the southeast. Windblown scrub, punctuated with sparse stands of trees, makes a subtle foreground to the mountain vistas you'll see in every direction.

Continue to follow the road for more than 1 mile and turn right onto Martis Dam Road, following the signs for Alpine Meadows Campground and Sierra View Day Use Area. Past the campground, the road turns to dirt and sweeps down along the lakeshore. Here you'll have more opportunities to see wildlife in and around the lake as well as the subtle colors in the valley and surrounding hills.

You can explore along the road as much or little as you and your pup have energy for. The road terminates near the south end of the lake at approximately 2.5 miles. You can then, or at any point in between, turn around and retrace your steps back to your car.

Other hiking options abound in this area. Those seeking more adventure can take side trails across Martis Dam to Dry Lake. Also popular are the dirt trails that loop around the Martis Creek Wildlife Area on the south side of SR 267. To reach these, walk or drive slightly farther south on SR 267 and follow the signs to the parking lot for the area, which skirts the north boundary of Northstar California resort.

58. Alpine Meadows to Five Lakes

Round-trip: 4 miles
Hiking time: 2.5–3 hours or overnight
Difficulty: Moderate to strenuous
High point: 7571
Elevation gain: 1147
Best hiking time: Mid-July through October
Water: Bring your own
Regulations: Dogs must be under control at all times, whether strict voice control or leashed
Maps: USGS Tahoe City, USGS Granite Chief
Contact: Tahoe National Forest, Nevada City Ranger District, (530) 265-4531

Granite rock formations and boulders are cast in the first hint of alpenglow as the sun begins to set.

Getting there: From Truckee, take State Route 89 south toward Tahoe City for 10 miles. Turn right onto Alpine Meadows Road and drive 2.1 miles to the trailhead, which is on the right just past the intersection with Deer Park Drive.

From Tahoe City, go north on SR 89 for 3.8 miles, turn left onto Alpine Meadows Road, and follow the same route to the trailhead.

If giant slabs of granite, alpenglow sunsets, and shimmering alpine lakes sound good to you, then the trek to Five Lakes from Alpine Meadows in Tahoe is a must-visit. In addition, you and your dog will get a fantastic workout as you climb along this beautiful trail and into the pristine Granite Chief Wilderness, which surrounds the lakes.

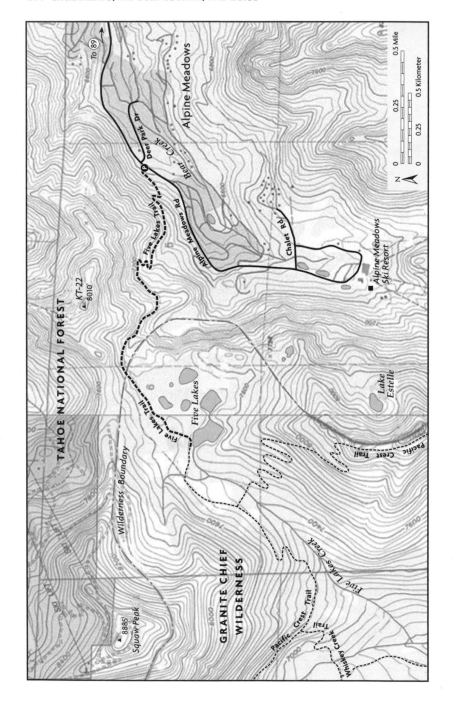

If you can schedule your hike to coincide with sunset, without leaving yourself a dangerous descent back to the car in the dark, do it. The best way to witness the wonder of this area is with the rays of sunlight filtering through the atmosphere, casting everything in that magical pink glow.

The hike starts on private property, so be sure to respect the owner's wishes by staying on the trail and being courteous to others you may encounter.

From the trailhead, this hike gains elevation in a hurry as you navigate each successive switchback and traverse. The first section seems relentless, and there isn't much to see except for the forest of scrub that immediately surrounds you, but as you approach the 0.5-mile mark the views really open up and draw you ever farther up the trail to see the next brilliant vista.

As you work your way up the ridge to the north, near the 1-mile mark you'll pass under an old line of chairlift towers; these may have been used in the past to access the ridge to the north.

The views improve even more as you begin a series of mostly gentle climbing pitches and a few more switchbacks. In the late afternoon the rocks and stacks of giant boulders on your right take on lovely pastel hues in contrast to the lighter tints of the granite across the valley to your left.

Toward the top, the trail switches back a few more times and navigates a couple of sections where steps have been cut and worn into the granite. The top of the climb is near 2 miles, and you'll pass a sign letting you know you've entered the Granite Chief Wilderness. The lakes are only a little farther down the trail.

Several unsigned trails split off to the left from the main trail to explore the various lakes. If you follow the main trail, you'll pass a sign pointing left for Five Lakes and the Pacific Crest Trail. This trail will bring you right to the shore of the largest of the lakes in the basin at the 2-mile mark.

After you've explored the lakes to your heart's content—they are great for swimming and fishing—it is time to return to civilization via the same trail you took to get here. Be sure you watch your step on the way down, especially if you have come up late in the day and are descending as daylight fades.

59. Caples Lake to Emigrant Lake

Round-trip: 9 miles
Hiking time: 5 hours or overnight
Difficulty: Moderate
High point: 8600 feet
Elevation gain: 950 feet
Best hiking time: Mid-July through late October; snowshoe in winter
Water: From the lakes
Regulations: Dogs must be under control at all times, whether strict voice control or leashed; it is recommended that dogs be leashed; obey all trail signs
Map: USGS Caples Lake
Contact: Eldorado National Forest, Amador Ranger District, (209) 295-4251

Getting there: From the community of Meyers, at the junction of U.S. Highway 50 and State Route 89, drive south on SR 89 for 11 miles to SR 88. Turn west on SR 88 and drive 13.6 miles to the west side of Caples Lake and the trailhead parking area, which is just under 5 miles west of Carson Pass. The trailhead begins near the restrooms. You'll need a wilderness permit to camp near Emigrant Lake, available from the Amador Ranger District.

This is a popular hike, since you'll get two great lakes—the first right outside your car door and the second after a surprisingly easy trek into the rugged, 105,165-acre Mokelumne Wilderness Area. This wilderness area, designated by Congress in 1964, straddles the crest of the central Sierra Nevada within the Stanislaus, Eldorado, and Toiyabe national forests.

Because of increased outdoor activity near Carson Summit, officials with the Eldorado National Forest have had to create an area known as the Carson Pass Restricted Area, which encompasses your destination, Emigrant Lake. As of this writing, people cannot camp within 300 feet of the lake so that the shoreline can heal. Also, campfires are not permitted. These rules apply year-round. However, dogs are still allowed, and this

There are many places to explore on the shoreline of Caples Lake.

is too scenic a trip to miss. Consider making this a day hike, instead of an overnighter.

Come in late summer, and you'll have the opportunity to sample several great swimming spots. It is also possible to do this hike past the late-October date suggested; indeed, many people are finding that

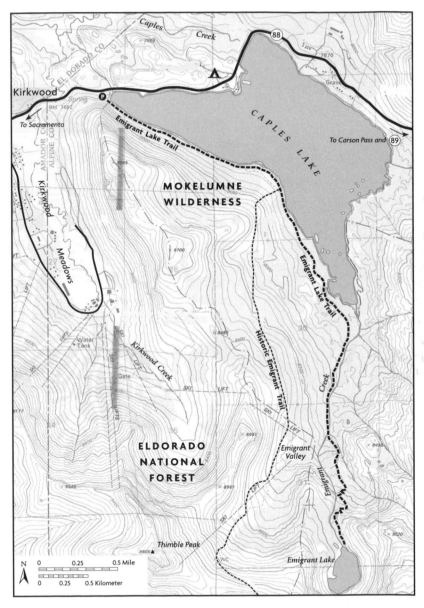

snowshoeing here—as well as snow camping—is a great way to visit the area minus the crowds. The Carson Pass Restricted Area plan states that you cannot snow-camp unless there's at least a foot of snow on the ground, which usually is the case by Christmas. If you do opt for a snowshoe or cross-country adventure, make sure you have good map and compass skills, as well as having the foresight to pack winter survival gear that will get you to your destination and back.

The trail starts off among aspen and a mixed conifer forest of red fir and lodgepole pine. At 1.2 miles, you'll reach a junction which heads uphill to the right signed HISTORIC EMIGRANT TRAIL. This trail brought thousands of emigrants to California. Go past this trail and continue straight ahead, following the signs for the Emigrant Lake Trail. From here, the trail crosses four seasonal creeks over the next 1.2 miles, each bordered by lush streamside plants like willow and alder. The path then winds along Emigrant Creek as you finally bid farewell to Caples Lake.

You'll start to climb, gently, through a meadow where granite boulders abound. Here, mountain hemlock comes into view, as the trail hugs the creek thick with willows, and you'll come to a trail fork at 3.4 miles.

At 4 miles, you'll get the chance to boulder-hop across Emigrant Lake's outlet stream, where you'll catch the first look at the Sisters' rocky spires to the east. At 4.3 miles, the trail levels out and parallels a small meadow. At 4.5 miles from the trailhead, you'll reach Emigrant Lake, set in a deep granite basin. Notice how the power of the glacier can literally move mountains. From the lake's south shore, a talus-tumbled cliff rises nearly vertical from the water's edge.

60. Lake Margaret

Round-trip: 5 miles
Hiking time: 3 hours or overnight
Difficulty: Easy to moderate
High point: 7741 feet
Elevation gain: 550 feet
Best hiking time: Early July through late October
Water: From streams and Lake Margaret
Regulations: Dogs must be under control at all times, whether strict voice control or leashed; it is recommended that dogs be leashed; obey all trail signs
Map: USGS Caples Lake
Contact: Eldorado National Forest, Amador Ranger District, (209) 295-4251

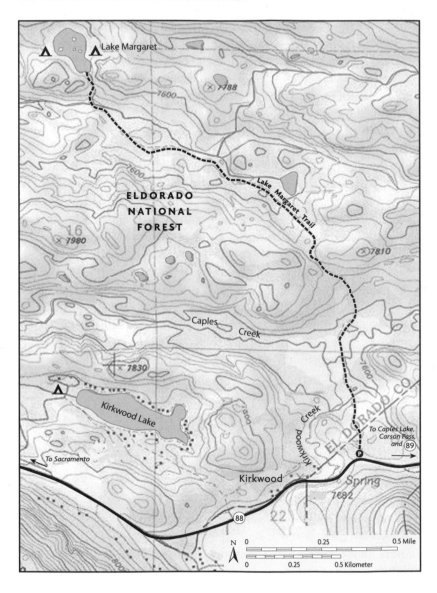

Getting there: From the community of Meyers at the junction of U.S. Highway 50 and SR 89, drive south on SR 89 for 11 miles to SR 88. Turn west on SR 88 and drive 13.8 miles to the brown Forest Service sign for Lake Margaret trailhead on the north side of the road. The parking area is 5 miles west of Carson Summit and 5.2 miles east of Silver Lake. You'll

Lake Margaret is a swimmer's (or dogpaddler's) paradise.

need to get a campfire permit from the Eldorado National Forest (available at Amador Ranger District) if you plan to have a fire or use a stove.

For little effort, this hike offers a lot of nature: a cool, inviting granite-basined alpine lake, a great burbling stream, and killer views. This is a trail built for children, families, and those households with a new puppy. Here, you'll get the chance to teach some leash lessons and get your new arrival used to hiking the trails of California and beyond.

The trail starts with a downhill trek through lodgepole pine and dense white fir toward a seasonal creek at just 0.2 mile. Here, the trail bends east; make sure to look straight ahead at the high mountain ridge just north of Caples Lake. The path parallels, then crosses, another seasonal stream, and at 0.5 mile you'll reach Caples Creek, where a grassy meadow makes the perfect stop for a snack (and a quick dip in the clear creek waters).

You'll next climb a short grade (maybe 150 feet) bordered by granite hillsides. The trail levels out again and skirts a stagnant, lodgepole-and-willow-choked pond on the left at 1.2 miles and immediately crosses more granite. A larger pond awaits at 1.6 miles. You'll soon cross a stream and pass through a dense mountain alder thicket. At 2.2 miles, aspen become your guardians along the path for nearly 300 yards, where you'll come to a stream that must be traversed across a log.

After getting past the log bridge, you'll hit your last ascent to the final destination. Follow cairns, or ducks—a pile of rocks that have been left by hikers to mark the trail—up the gently sloping granite hillside. After this short climb, you'll reach the cool, deep waters of Lake Margaret. This is a swimmer's paradise, as huge slabs of granite lie just below the water's surface, making it a great place to sit and soak up the abundant sunshine.

Campers will find two nice campsites on the lake's eastern shore, as well as two along the western shore. If you're lucky, you might even catch a few trout for cooking over a small warming fire.

SHASTA- CASCADE

61. PCT to Seven Lakes Basin

Round-trip: 6 miles
Hiking time: 5 hours or overnight
Difficulty: Approach hike is easy, but the trek down into the basin and back is moderate
High point: 6900 feet
Elevation gain: 1250 feet
Best hiking time: Early June through late October
Water: Only from Seven Lakes Basin lakes; bring your own for the approach hike
Regulations: It is recommended that dogs be leashed
Maps: USGS Mumbo Basin, USGS Seven Lakes Basin
Contact: Shasta-Trinity National Forest, Mount Shasta Ranger District, (530) 926-4511

Getting there: From Interstate 5, take the Central Mount Shasta exit and turn west onto West Lake Street, which soon becomes Hatchery Lane. Turn left onto South Old Stage Road and stay right where the road forks onto W. A. Barr Road. Staying on W. A. Barr Road, cross Box Canyon Dam and follow the road as it arcs around Lake Siskiyou. Follow the paved, scenic road (which soon becomes Forest Road 26) 13.4 miles past Lake Siskiyou Camp-Resort to Gumboot Saddle and park in the signed area on the right, which is 2.2 miles past the turnoff to Gumboot Lake and its free campground.

Paul perches on a ridgeline just off the PCT with Mount Shasta in the background.

The drive in to this trailhead alone is enough to lower your heart rate, as well as your stress level. Get on the trail, and you'll soon realize that this trek requires little effort and the rewards are fantastic.

While trekking along the wide Pacific Crest Trail, you can't help but stop often to take in the 360 degrees of panoramic pleasure. From various points, you'll glimpse 14,162-foot Mount Shasta, the granitic splendor of Castle Crags, the volcanic magnificence of Gray Rocks, the Trinity Divide, the Trinity Alps, and the best of the Klamath Mountains. Add to that a couple of dandy lakes where swimming and fishing are king, and you've got the makings of the quintessential weekend getaway.

The trail into the basin begins at the crest of Gumboot summit, just before the parking area. After you park, walk back up the road a short ways and look for the PCT marker to the left and right. Take the PCT to the right (south) and after several minutes of forested walking, you'll burst forth into an opening, where several rocky clearings give an unimpeded view of the mountains and forests of this heavily glaciated and volcanic area. In spring, the path will be flecked with wildflowers, notably yellow sulfur flowers, sweet pea, and blue lupine.

You'll reach a PCT thru-hiker campsite off to the left of the trail in just 0.3 mile. It's here that you'll get your first look at a towering Mount Shasta, and depending on the time of year, it'll be cloaked in white or wearing the browns and grays of summer. Soon, Mount Eddy, the head-waters of the Sacramento River, and Gumboot Lake come into view. Look west for great views of Mumbo Lake (great for trout) and the forested Mumbo Basin.

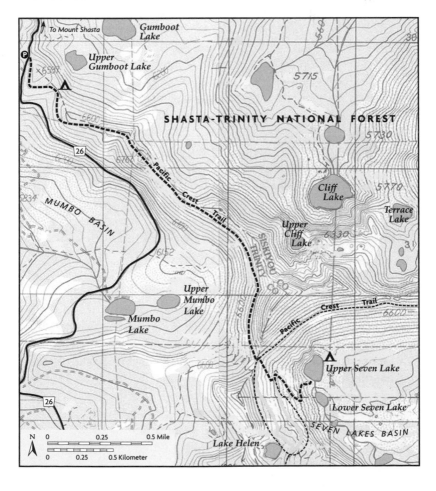

The trail comes to its first junction at the saddle at 2.5 miles. From this vantage point, you'll be able to spot Boulder Mountain rising above the basin's largest lake, Echo (it's privately owned, the owner is notoriously cranky, and it's best left unexplored). You'll also get views of Lassen Peak, Magee Peak, and Burney Mountain to the southeast.

To quickly make the descent into Seven Lakes Basin, go left at the junction on the PCT and within another 30 feet take the faint, unmarked trail that dips down to the right. It will soon intersect an old four-wheel-drive path. Turn left onto the path and follow it to Upper Seven Lake, about a 0.5-mile distance. Upper Seven Lake is ringed with rocks and vegetation, but its north shore has a dandy beach that just begs you to take a dip. The lake has a healthy population of brook and rainbow trout, which will rise to a fly or copper-colored lure (I never leave home without a 0.25-ounce copper Kastmaster).

The best campsites are the farthest east of two spots that are too close to the water's edge; Lower Seven Lake is 100 yards to the south. It's shallow, muddy, and has no campsites. Most of the lakes in the basin are privately owned, so be respectful, don't build campfires, and be sure to follow Leave No Trace ethics.

Trails snake their way throughout the basin, which allows for some great exploration of this area. This hike is a good primer for families who want to get into the backpacking lifestyle.

62. Castle and Heart Lakes

Round-trip: 3.4 miles
Hiking time: 3 hours or overnight
Difficulty: Moderate to strenuous
High point: 6035 feet
Elevation gain: 700 feet
Best hiking time: Mid-May through late October; snowshoe the rest
of the year
Water: From Castle Lake
Regulations: It is recommended that dogs be leashed
Maps: USGS Seven Lakes Basin, USGS Dunsmuir
Contact: Shasta-Trinity National Forest, Mount Shasta Ranger
District, (530) 926-4511

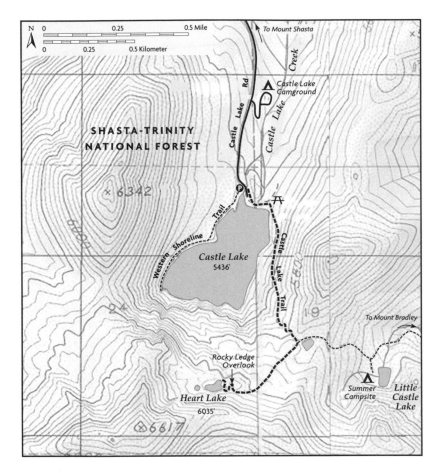

Getting there: From Interstate 5, take the Central Mount Shasta exit and turn west onto West Lake Street, which soon becomes Hatchery Lane. Turn left onto South Old Stage Road and stay right where the road forks onto W. A. Barr Road. Stay on W. A. Barr Road for 2.2 miles, crossing Box Canyon Dam, and turn left at the signed Castle Lake Road. Follow it 7.1 miles to the paved parking lot. The road is plowed throughout the winter, though at times not all the way up to the lake.

Since 1968, students from the University of California at Davis have been studying Castle Lake in the area of limnology, from the Greek word *limne*, which means "marsh" or "lake."

The science helps researchers understand some things about the

Trinity gazes down at Castle Lake.

world's fresh water: how healthy it is, what's happening to it, and how water quality can improve with time—and interference by people. What the budding researchers have found is that despite heavy year-round use, Castle Lake continues to be one of the most unspoiled subalpine lakes in the world. Start at Castle Lake and take this trip up to tiny Heart Lake, and you'll have a great appreciation of these north-state gems.

This trek in fall offers up many fewer people, and you'll be able to see the gradual color change, from greens to golds and browns. In the winter months, you'll still be able to pick your way through the forest and up the ridge, but if the snow is too deep, you can satisfy your exploration needs by following the western shoreline of Castle Lake.

At its start, the trail crosses Castle Lake's outlet stream and heads east around the lakeshore. From there it ascends in earnest toward Mount

Bradley Ridge and tiny Heart Lake just below. This steep and rocky path soon bursts from the canopy of alder, oak, and pine and affords the first overall glimpses of the glaciated Castle Lake basin.

Reach a saddle in little more than 0.5 mile and keep looking for the turnoff to Heart Lake, which is an unmarked trail to the right that leads to a seasonal marsh. The way can get convoluted in this area as many small paths shoot off from the main trail. Thankfully, most of the offshoots lead to the same place and the main trail is fairly well worn. When in doubt, continue to work your way uphill to the southwest and toward the ridge. Follow this path through the upper meadows (erupting with wildflowers in the spring) another 0.5 mile to Heart Lake.

Let the dogs take a dip, soak your own dogs, and don't forget to hike over to a rocky ledge for a breathtaking view of Castle Lake and Mount Shasta to the north. Side trips include a trek up to the ridge above or a short downhill hike to Little Castle Lake, where there's an inviting summer campsite.

To extend your stay in this outdoor playground, visit the Forest Service's Castle Lake Campground, about 0.5 mile north of the Castle Lake parking lot. This free campsite has portable toilets (there also are toilets at the parking lot), but no drinking water. With such close proximity to one of the world's most unspoiled lakes, you can drink up (purify first) the cool, clean waters of Castle Lake above.

63. Squaw Valley Creek Trail

Round-trip: 5–8 miles
Hiking time: 3–6 hours or overnight
Difficulty: Easy
High point: 2800 feet
Elevation gain: 200 feet
Best hiking time: March through November
Water: From Squaw Valley Creek
Regulations: It is recommended that dogs be leashed
Maps: Free from the Shasta-Trinity National Forest; USGS Girard Ridge
Contact: Shasta-Trinity National Forest, McCloud Ranger District, (530) 964-2184

Getting there: Turn right at the McCloud central business district and follow the signs for Squaw Valley Creek Road and the McCloud Reservoir. Continue on this road for 6.1 miles. Just past an RV and camp park named Friday's Retreat, turn right onto Squaw Valley Creek Road. The sign says rough road, but this dirt path can be handled easily in the family sedan. Continue on this road for 3.1 miles, where you'll cross over a concrete bridge. The parking area, trailhead, and restroom will be on your immediate left once you cross the bridge.

Simplicity is the basis of greatness, and people who take the time to discover this hike will find something new to cherish each and every time out.

Over time, Squaw Valley Creek has sliced the surrounding dark basalt rock into a cascade of cool pools under a canopy of mature, mixed conifer forest that includes Pacific yew, incense cedar, and Douglas fir. The undercanopy includes black oak, willow, dogwood, alder, and vine maple, with wild ginger, iris, and wild rose clinging to the mossy ground. Indian rhubarb grows thick at the water's rocky edge, hiding delightful spots where man and beast can soak on hot summer days.

Given the elevation, poison oak also does very well here. Be sure to wash your dogs before loading them back in your car, and give them a good bath when you get home. The volatile oil that causes your skin to itch—urushiol—sticks to dog fur and can cause a breakout days later.

Every season brings a new reason to visit this trail, which offers a lot of level ground and a few gentle climbs. Spring, when the dogwoods are in bloom, brings anglers to the creek, where native rainbow trout will rise to suck down a meal of hatching aquatic bugs. Summer is the time for birders, swimmers, and wildlife watchers. Pack the binoculars for the chance to view mountain quail, common nighthawk, hairy woodpecker, Pacific-slope flycatchers, Swainson's thrush, cedar waxwing, evening grosbeak, and a host of other species. If you're quiet, there's always a chance to glimpse a black-tailed deer munching on vegetation or a black bear sipping from the creek. Fall brings on a burst of color from the undercanopy. The creek, which rarely dips from view along the trail, flows through a blaze of orange, crimson, and yellow.

A sturdy wooden bridge takes hikers across Cabin Creek, then the trail hugs the west side of Squaw Valley Creek for the duration of the trek. While the Forest Service has completed 5 miles of trail, most hikers turn

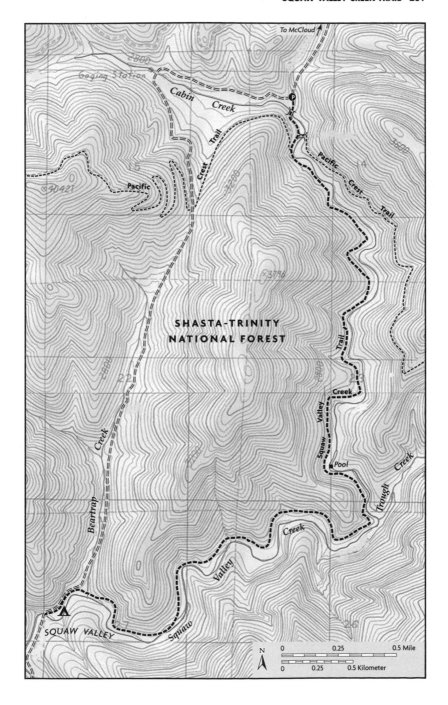

A wooden bridge crosses Squaw Valley Creek, connecting the Squaw Valley Creek Trail with the Pacific Crest Trail.

around at or near the 2.5-mile mark due to the increasing abundance of poison oak beyond that point. Be sure to leave yourselves plenty of time to play in the chilly water, and bring a water filter so you can drink from this spring-fed creek.

At Cabin Creek, the 2650-mile Pacific Crest Trail crosses the Squaw Valley Creek Trail. During the summer months, there's always the possibility of talking with thru-hikers about their adventures.

While the chance to take a dip along this stream is constant, a not-to-be-missed pool is located near the 2.5-mile turnaround point. A wide, smooth section of basalt makes for a great place to catch some sun and have a picnic. Soft sand coats the bottom of this pool, big enough and deep enough for several people—and their dogs.

If you choose to go past the normal turnaround, the dense under-canopy will slowly begin to swallow the trail at about 4 miles. Along a rocky wall, the trail finally gives over to a thicket of alder, and it's time to turn back.

For the adventurous, this hike can be turned into an overnight trip, with good campsites near the south terminus of the trail. Camp at least 200 feet from the creek and be sure to follow Leave No Trace ethics.

64. McCloud Waterfalls

Round-trip: 3.2 miles
Hiking time: 2 hours or overnight
Difficulty: Easy
High point: 3600 feet
Elevation gain: 200 feet
Best hiking time: Year-round; snowshoe in winter, falls more
   powerful in spring
Water: From Fowlers Campground; or from the river
Regulations: Dogs must be leashed
Map: USGS Lake McCloud
Contact: Shasta-Trinity National Forest, McCloud Ranger District,
   (530) 926-2184

Middle McCloud falls in mid-spring (Marc Soares)

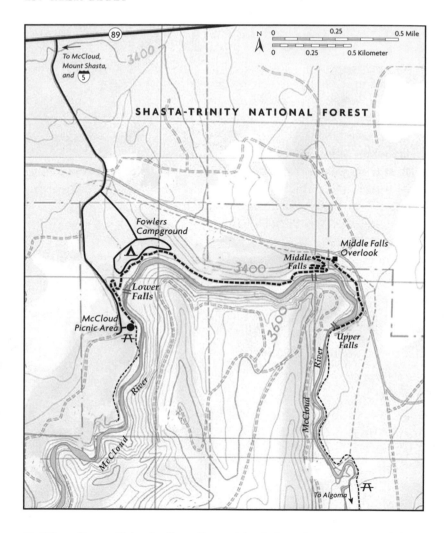

Getting there: Take the State Route 89 exit from Interstate 5 and drive 10 miles to the town of McCloud. Continue on SR 89 5.2 miles past McCloud and turn right at the sign for Fowlers Campground. Go about 0.5 mile, stay straight where the road forks, and bear right again in another 50 yards. Then continue another 0.5 mile to the trailhead and the Lower Falls of the McCloud Picnic Area.

To tune in to a wild river boasting a trio of fantastic waterfalls on a hike that's a piece of cake seems too good to be true, but that's what you get with this trek. These three exhilarating falls are all granite-ringed, but that's where the similarities end. The Lower Falls are by far the tamest. The Middle Falls radiate a spiritual feel; a soul can easily find deep peace on one of the big rocks at the scene. The Upper Falls aren't as photogenic as the Middle Falls, but are perhaps the most unique looking, and certainly carry the most water force.

You get a lot for a little energy expense, unless you make it a much longer hike or even a backpack trip by continuing on a new trail section (built in the late 1990s) along the banks of the fast-flowing McCloud River. After 14 miles, you come out of a very remote river region into the tiny community of Algoma. There are no fees for the hike and no permit required unless you intend to stay the night along the river.

Start your journey at the Lower Falls. Up to 40 feet wide in late spring, these falls spill 15 vertical feet into a foamy avalanche of white froth, then into a 25-yard-long pool. Picnickers and anglers relax along the granite slab field overlooking the inspirational scene.

Continue along the river; Fowlers Campground borders this narrow channel of clear and cold water starting at 0.2 mile. Soon after, note an eroded and steep cliff face on the other shore at 0.8 mile; look for the 20-foot-tall, rare Pacific yew (redwood-like needles) at trailside. Shortly, you'll see but not hear a fast-moving sheet of white just beyond a big rock outcrop so imposing it causes the course of the river to veer.

Set in a steep and rocky canyon dotted with majestic Douglas firs, rectangular-shaped Middle Falls are some 30 yards wide with a spectacu-lar drop-off half that number. The trail then snakes up and away from the river, reaches a prime vista down on the Middle Falls, ascends some long, wooden steps, and culminates on a rocky rim. From a nearby rocky perch beneath a cluster of ponderosa pines, check out a clear view of the falls setting.

The surging white water in the canyon resembles a wild scene from the Colorado River. Look forward to pleasing views of Mount Shasta and mountains of the Trinity Divide along this stretch of the return route. At 1.4 miles you reach a shady section featuring a staggeringly steep wall of lichen-coated gray rock on the left side of the trail. The first sighting of the Upper Falls promptly ensues just past this 20-foot-high corridor.

Hemmed in on both sides by steep granite cliffs, these falls are an extremely powerful chute of pure white water. Looking down on the rushing water, it's easy to imagine a bursting dam. Make your way down the spur trail to the edge of a large and round swirling pool (ideal for trout fishing). From here you can just retrace your steps to return to your car.

65. Mount Eddy and Deadfall Lakes

Round-trip: 9 miles
Hiking time: 6 hours or overnight
Difficulty: Approach hike is easy, but the trek to the summit of Mount Eddy and back is strenuous
High point: 9025 feet
Elevation gain: 2850 feet
Best hiking time: Early July through mid-October
Water: From lakes and streams; none past Upper Deadfall Lake
Regulations: It is recommended that dogs be leashed
Maps: USGS Mount Eddy, USGS South China Mountain
Contact: Shasta-Trinity National Forest, Mount Shasta Ranger District, (530) 926-4511

Getting there: Driving north on Interstate 5, go 2.5 miles past the North Weed Boulevard exit and take the Edgewood/Gazelle exit. Go under the freeway, turn right at the stop sign, and take a signed left at Stewart Springs Road in 0.3 mile. In 4 miles, turn right onto Forest Road 17, known also as the Parks Creek Road. Follow this winding, often one-lane paved road 9.1 miles to Parks Creek Summit and the Deadfall Lakes parking area on the right.

Most Northern Californians give snowmelt from the flanks of Mount Eddy the nod as the headwaters of the Sacramento River, at 384 miles the longest river in California. One look from the windswept, flattened top of this peak, and who's to argue?

There's no argument when it comes to shouldering a pack into the Deadfall Lakes Basin, where man and beast can find cool, clear waters to swim, and humans can chase rainbow and brook trout in Lower and Middle Deadfall Lakes. This is a great destination for families with younger children, since the trail gains little elevation to and from the

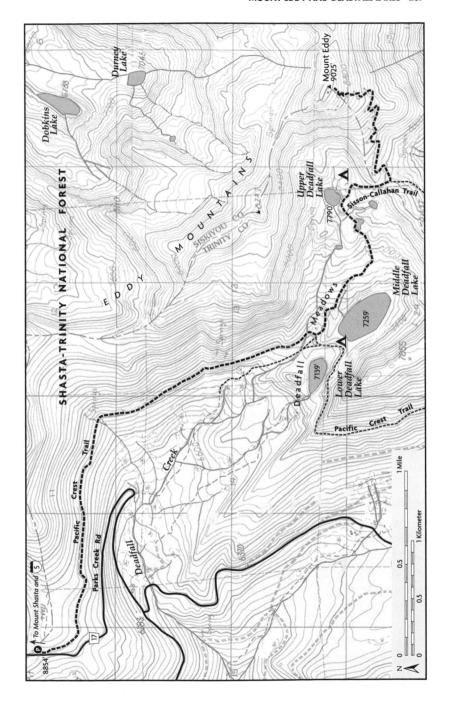

The clear waters of Middle Deadfall Lake are irresistible after the hike into the basin.

basin. It's the hike to the peak that will have adventurers wheezing.

The trail begins to the west of the parking area (just past the information kiosk). You'll be following the Pacific Crest Trail into the basin, which stays wide and level through a forest of red and white fir, ponderosa, and Jeffery pine and shady patches of yarrow and dwarf larkspur.

In less than a mile, the trail intersects a dirt road and continues directly across it. As you near 1.5 miles, you'll cross a seasonal creek, and then pass another gurgling spring before reaching the stunning Deadfall Meadows at 2.5 miles. The wildflower display lasts well into summer, with sage, yellow lupine, white-flowered angelica, corn lily, and red columbine. Western white fir dominates the landscape until the path crosses burbling Deadfall Creek and reaches a signed junction a few steps later. Go right and you'll soon reach the swimmable waters of Lower Deadfall Lake, where a few campsites beckon. Turn left and you'll be following the historic Sisson-Callahan Trail, along which Middle Deadfall Lake awaits to the right.

The emerald-green waters of Middle Deadfall Lake at 3 miles make for a wonderful base camp to attack the summit of Mount Eddy. Fantastic campsites lie on the lake's west and northern shores (fishing for rainbow and brook trout also is at its best here).

At 3.1 miles, you'll reach the first of three ponds where you can purify water for the last push up to the summit. At 3.3 miles, you'll reach Upper Deadfall Lake and get the awesome view of this trek's prize—the red-stained rocks of Mount Eddy. Continue climbing to Mount Eddy Pass for a commanding view of the Deadfall Basin, the whole of the Trinity Alps, and Lake Siskiyou.

Go left at the signed trail fork to leave the Sisson-Callahan Trail, and climb relentlessly on switchbacks for another 0.7 mile. Just when you think you've run out of breath, you'll gain sight of a jumbled pile of wood—the remnants of an old fire lookout—and the summit of Mount Eddy.

Here's where, surprisingly, you'll get your first glimpse of Mount Shasta since leaving the trailhead. Officially, the high point of the peak is a windswept corner on the western edge. Hikers have built a rock circle around the high point.

66. Bailey Cove Loop

Round-trip: 2.5-mile loop
Hiking time: 2 hours
Difficulty: Easy
High point: 1126 feet
Elevation gain: 349 feet
Best hiking time: Year-round
Water: At the trailhead and from Lake Shasta
Regulations: It is recommended that dogs be leashed
Map: USGS O'Brien
Contact: Shasta-Trinity National Forest, Shasta Lake Ranger
District, (530) 275-1589

Getting there: Take the Shasta Caverns Road exit off Interstate 5, about 15 miles north of Redding. Drive east 0.4 mile on Shasta Caverns Road and turn right onto Bailey Cove Road. Continue another 0.7 mile to where the road ends at the parking lot.

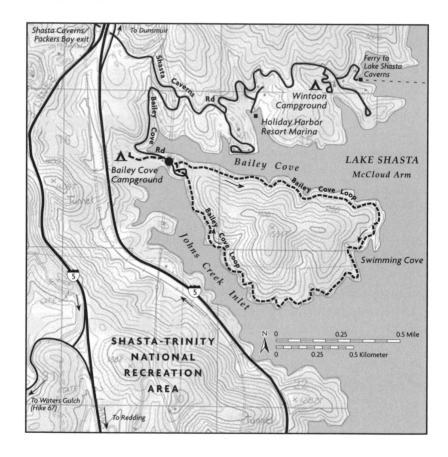

Mix equal parts of rambunctious dog, fishing rod, brilliant fall afternoon, and a family, and you've got a tonic called the Bailey Cove Loop. This hike takes in a few lovely miles of shoreline on California's largest man-made lake.

Lake Shasta was created when Shasta Dam was built in 1945, harnessing the waters of the Sacramento, McCloud, and Pit rivers. The lake has 365 miles of shoreline, one for every day of the year.

Here, you'll get to explore a prominent peninsula that once was a mountain. This well-maintained trail attracts anglers who sling lines into the numerous coves, as well as mountain bikers and families out for a stroll. You'll get a glimpse of Holiday Harbor, one of the many marinas that cater to the myriad of houseboaters who make annual pilgrimages to the lake.

Poison oak climbs on nearly every tree in the first section of the Bailey Cove Trail.

Commanding the view is 3114-foot-high North Gray Rocks. This limestone formation houses the splendor of the renowned Lake Shasta Caverns (www.lakeshastacaverns.com), where people can take a boat ride across the lake and get a peek at the water-created formations in the cave. Limestone, it should be noted, is the compressed skeletal remains of marine life that lived more than 200 million years ago. This soft rock is transformed into elegant calcite crystal formations.

The trail starts in a clockwise direction from a large canyon live oak and some smallish ponderosa pine. While mostly flat, the trail is tantalizingly close to the water's edge, and you'll have a hard time getting the dogs to stay on the trail—mine love to swim along—as the footpath swings south out of the cove through gnarled whiteleaf manzanita. In the few sunny spots, poison oak grows tall and lush, so beware and make sure to wash your dog off before she climbs back into your car.

At 1.3 miles, the trail meanders under a grove of knobcone pine and reaches a gulch with easy access to a small cove. Move past a collection of common mullein plants (marked by large, gray fans for leaves) to a flat space to swim and have a snack. You'll find plenty of secluded lakeside perches on this trail. The final mile loops above the cove formed by the Johns Creek Inlet and affords the sunniest locations on this trek. You'll find the canyon live oaks here grow like shrubs.

67. Waters Gulch Creek to Packers Bay

Round-trip: 5-mile loop
Hiking time: 4 hours
Difficulty: Moderate
High point: 1535 feet
Elevation gain: 1049 feet
Best hiking time: Year-round
Water: From Lake Shasta
Regulations: It is recommended that dogs be leashed
Map: USGS O'Brien
Contact: Shasta-Trinity National Forest, Shasta Lake Ranger District, (530) 275-1589

Getting there: From Interstate 5 north, about 15 miles north of Redding, take the Shasta Caverns/Packers Bay exit. Drive under the freeway and get back on I-5 going south. Drive 1 mile and take the Packers Bay exit. Turn right, drive 1 mile, and park in the small paved lot on the right.

A buddy of mine begged me not to include this hike in this guide. "Awwww, let's just keep it for ourselves," he said. "And the dogs."

Sorry, but this is one great hike, a chance to see the Sacramento Arm of Lake Shasta up close and personal, all the while giving the hounds a chance to run off all that pent-up energy. There's even the potential to explore Waters Gulch Creek, a slim waterway that loses its intensity during the summer but comes crashing back in the winter.

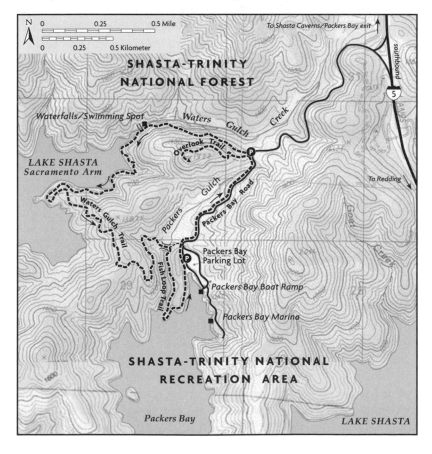

This swimming spot is a great place to cool your heels (and paws) on a hot day.

Here is where the lake takes a slight departure from the surrounding forest. The hike goes through a stand of black oak, California's most colorful oak. In spring and early summer, its leaves are as green as the waters of Lake Shasta; in the fall, whole hillsides turn a mix of orange and yellow. And thanks to my guide-writing friend, Marc Soares, I now know to look for the recently discovered Shasta snow wreath, which is a shrub in the rose family.

Begin your hike with a good workout and hike to the top of the Overlook Trail, so named because it offers a secluded look at the crown jewel of the Central Valley Water Project: Lake Shasta.

From this point, descend the mostly shaded 0.5-mile trail and head for the signed Waters Gulch Trail, which promptly leads to its namesake creek. The north slope is festooned with Douglas fir, no doubt drinking heartily on the moisture afforded the slope. Here, you'll find a slender spur trail that will lead you to a small but powerful waterfall. The falls are protected by a fragrant grove of bay laurel trees, which will add to your enjoyment of the rushing waters.

To find a clear pool at the end of the falls, walk another 100 yards down the main trail. Be careful when climbing down a small side trail, where a tiny seasonal creek on the opposite shore topples into Waters Gulch Creek and into the lake. If the lake is full, you can swim some 20 yards and soak in the tiny whirlpools created by the falls. As an added bonus, there are plenty of flat boulders on which to sun yourself.

Get back on the trail and you'll find yourself in a sea of dogwoods, bigleaf maple, and alder. The scene shifts from crashing waters to a more serene setting where the trail follows the wooded shoreline and several wooden bridges cross the babbling streams that lead to driftwood-strewn coves. Everything is cool and green, which allows the mind to wander and the soul to be freed.

At 2.5 miles, the trail begins to climb inland under black oak—through an area scorched by a prescribed burn in the early 2010s—to a wooden bench at 3 miles. Here your lake views disappear, replaced by steep west and southern slopes packed with chaparral plants, mostly gray pine and scruffy canyon live oaks

As you descend, just before the 4-mile mark cross a bridge over a small stream and take the signed Fish Loop Trail to the right. After rounding another point you'll come out near the lakeshore at the south end of Packers Bay parking lot. From here, walk up Packers Bay Road another 0.5 mile to return to the trailhead and your vehicle.

If you and your dog are tired, you can shave 0.5 mile off your trek by skipping the Fish Loop Trail altogether. To do this, stay straight at the junction and within about 100 yards you'll find yourself at the north end of Packers Bay parking lot where you can make the same walk up the road to your car.

68. Clikapudi Trail

Round-trip: 8.2-mile loop; 4.2 miles out-and-back to Clikapudi Bay
Hiking time: 3–6 hours
Difficulty: Moderate
High point: 1423 feet
Elevation gain: 900 feet
Best hiking time: Year-round
Water: From Lake Shasta, or Jones Valley Boat Ramp
Regulations: It is recommended that dogs be leashed
Map: USGS Bella Vista
Contact: Shasta-Trinity National Forest, Shasta Lake Ranger
    District, (530) 275-1589

Getting there: Take State Route 299 east from Redding and drive 6 miles to the community of Bella Vista. Turn north on Dry Creek Road and drive 5.5 miles to the junction with Bear Mountain Road. Continue straight at this junction (you are now on Bear Mountain Road) another 1.1 miles to Jones Valley Road. Go right on Jones Valley Road and drive 1 mile to a small gravel parking lot on the left, just past the 25-mile-per-hour sign. The trail starts across the road next to the sign.

Two massive fires scorched the Clikapudi Trail area in a five-year period from 1999 to 2004. First the Jones Fire and then, five years later, the Bear Fire damaged many local communities and drastically changed the landscape as well as this multiuse trail.

Fortunately, the Forest Service has been diligent, and this well-constructed trail again attracts everyone from families and their dogs to fishermen and mountain bikers. Yes, this is a popular destination, but in the off-season (October through May) you and your dog can find the kind of seclusion many millionaires pay top price to achieve.

During the summer months, it's best to have the dogs on leashes to avoid entanglements with surprised anglers and mountain bikers completing the twisted path, which is rated as a Top 10 single-track

The extra distance of the Advanced Loop pays off in views.

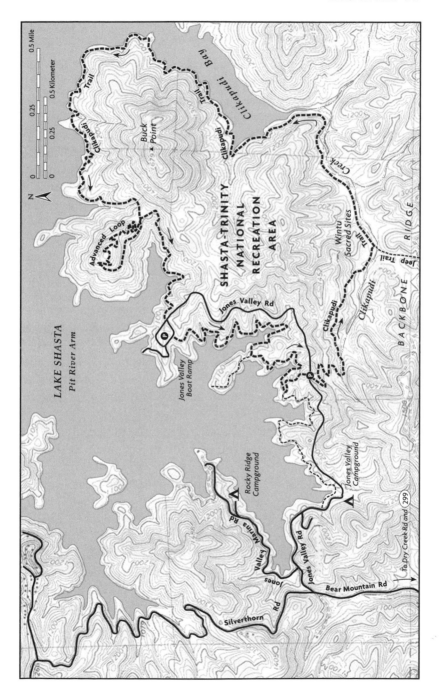

destination in California ("single-track" because the path is just wide enough to accommodate one rider).

From the get-go, this yard-wide path climbs nearly 0.5 mile through steep hillside covered with scrub. From the top it then heads down into a narrow slot that stays close to a seasonal stream.

As you descend the next section of trail, you'll unknowingly pass two unsigned protected Wintu sites and cross Clikapudi Creek. Before 1.5 miles you'll pass a wooden post on the right side of the trail and see the faint remnants of an unsigned Jeep trail that climbs the ridge to the south. Notice how Clikapudi Creek now gets deeper, faster, and stronger as it enters Clikapudi Bay. Just past the inlet, there's a grove of willows that makes for a great spot to take a dip, sling a line, and generally relax—a reward for making it this far.

Continue on and you'll get to a wooden bridge that crosses a drift-wood-strewn, quiet inlet cove at just over 2 miles. The area is full of wild California grapevines.

Pass through some scrubby canyon live oak and whiteleaf manzanita to a vista point that overlooks twin peninsulas and a curvaceous spot along the lake's Pit River Arm at nearly 3.5 miles. The trail now swings around another inlet stream and picks up the mixed knobcone, ponderosa, and Douglas fir forest. The trail will hug the shore, allowing for numerous dunks in the lake for the dogs. You'll find plenty of driftwood to toss out for hounds that like to fetch.

Soon, the trail turns slightly inland, hugging the hilly contours of a deep inlet. This short, steep climb takes you to a small saddle area on the western flank of Buck Point. A new trail loop, the Advanced Loop, which opened in 2007, takes off to the right at just beyond the 4.5-mile mark. If you'd like to add another mile to your trek and see what are perhaps some of the best views of the whole hike, take this trail. This loop is loose and rocky as well as being very popular with mountain bikers, so keep an eye out and watch your step.

Once you complete the Advanced Loop, head down the trail to the Jones Valley Boat Ramp parking lot, where there's water and public restrooms. Pick up the trail again at the southwest corner of the parking lot. In the next 1.5 miles you'll work your way along the lakeshore past a few more of Lake Shasta's coves.

At 8 miles, watch out for a sharp switchback trail junction on your left. Take this trail to the left and make the short climb back to your car.

69. Boulder Creek Falls

Round-trip: 5.5 miles
Hiking time: 3 hours or overnight
Difficulty: Moderate
High point: 2241 feet
Elevation gain: 1279 feet
Best hiking time: Year-round; streams might not be passable in
early spring
Water: From Boulder Creek
Regulations: Dogs must be leashed
Maps: USGS Whiskeytown, USGS French Gulch
Contact: Whiskeytown National Recreation Area, Whiskeytown
Unit, (530) 246-1225 or (530) 242-3400

Getting there: Take State Route 299 west from Redding 12 miles (1.5
miles past the Oak Bottom Campground turnoff) and turn left onto Judge
Francis Carr Powerhouse Road. After 0.3 mile past the power plant, the

Otis and Bella are ready to hike again after getting a cool drink from a stream.

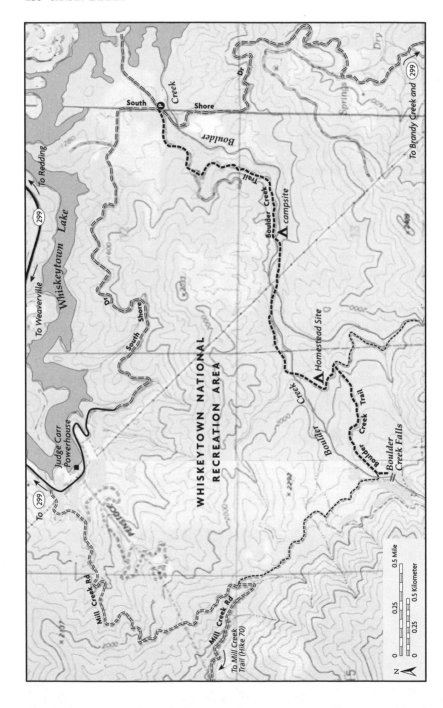

road becomes the dirt South Shore Drive. You'll reach a crossroads at 2.4 miles, where there's room to park along the shoulder of the road. The trail is beyond the gate to the west.

This hike leads, arguably, to the prettiest waterfall in Whiskeytown National Recreation Area: a spectacular 120-foot drop that changes its attitude with the changing seasons. Better still, the best vantage point of the falls is on a mossy granite slab across the ridge from where Boulder Creek begins its tumble to Whiskeytown Lake.

By late winter and early spring, the falls are at their most frothy white; be prepared to get a little wet on the three stream crossings on the way to the falls. But in summer, when the temperatures are hovering around 100 degrees, cool, inviting Boulder Creek is a hiker's delight, with many pools that teem with tiny rainbow trout and native sculpin, a small bottom-dwelling fish.

If you've never had a backcountry experience with your pet, here's the place to change that, all while being little more than 10 miles from the heart of Redding. Along the way to the falls are two seldom-used backcountry campsites, shaded in oak and pine forest, within the harmonious sounds of the creek rushing over granite boulders.

The trail starts off along an old fire road, where you should keep a sharp eye out for the numerous fence lizards and the occasional alligator lizard. A treat to see, if they are out sunning themselves, are the beautiful (and nonvenomous) California mountain king snakes. This red/black/white-striped reptile is a natural enemy of the rattlesnake and sometimes is confused with the deadly poisonous coral snake (which has red/yellow/black bands). This trail is the only one in Whiskeytown where I've ever seen king snakes. Please don't let your dogs get too curious, as the king snake will still snap at a curious, wet nose.

The trail climbs steadily for nearly a mile, and then descends to the first crossing of Boulder Creek at 1 mile. Soon, you'll pass the first trailside campsite. Traveling on, you'll come up on two gigantic sugar pines, by far the largest species of pine on this hike, and the second stream crossing. The trail will veer from the creek after the third crossing, where you'll reach the second campsite and the site of an old homestead. This is a great place to stop for lunch and walk around and imagine what it would have been like to live—and work—in such beautiful surroundings.

Go right near the 2-mile mark at the trail junction signed BOULDER CREEK FALLS 0.75 MILE. Shasta Bally, at 6209 feet in elevation, looms close (its snowmelt feeds Boulder Creek) just before the trail descends toward the creek. Look for a trail to the left that begins a short ascent alongside the creek. Climb the twisting stairs until you reach a large granite boulder, big enough for two people and two dogs, and take a moment to listen to the rushing sounds of the falls.

The falls are adorned by bigleaf maples. Actually, Boulder Creek Falls is a series of three drops. The highest falls cascade into the middle falls, which plummet into a pool surrounded by slick, mossy rocks. Water then spills over and drops 75 feet into a deep, clear, sandy-bottomed pool.

Retrace your steps back to your car, or you have the option of continuing along the fire road (at the base of the trail to the falls) and hiking west toward Mill Creek Road, where it is possible to link up with the Mill Creek Trail (Hike 70).

70. Mill Creek Trail

Round-trip: 5 miles or more
Hiking time: 2.5–3 hours
Difficulty: Moderate
High point: 1986 feet
Elevation gain: 1023 feet
Best hiking time: Year-round, but stream might not be passable in early spring
Water: From Mill Creek
Regulations: Dogs must be leashed
Map: USGS French Gulch
Contact: Whiskeytown National Recreation Area, Whiskeytown Unit, (530) 246-1225 or (530) 242-3400

Getting there: Take State Route 299 west from Redding 13 miles (2.5 miles past the Oak Bottom Campground turnoff) to a signed parking area for the Tower House Historic District on the south side of the highway. The parking area is just east of the bridge over Clear Creek, which is 0.1 mile east of Trinity Mountain Road.

Splashy creek crossings and a dandy swimming hole are just a couple of the many great reasons to come to the west side of Whiskeytown and hike the Mill Creek Trail. Another great reason is the fact that even though this hike can leave your chest heaving from exertion, Mill Creek's deep, shady canyon offers temperatures considerably cooler than surrounding areas during the brutally hot summer days that Mother Nature can sometimes dish out.

Bella scans the trail ahead.

Truly a delight for water-loving dogs, as well as hikers who don't mind getting their feet wet every once in a while, this trail crosses boulder-strewn Mill Creek eighteen times in 1.2 miles, and the creek holds several pools where you can both rest. You'll also get a good look at how nature remakes itself, seeing how the land has reclaimed an old mining operation.

A note about poison oak: there's a ton of it on this hike. Make sure you have a supply of over-the-counter soap such as Dawn or Simple Green in the car to wash yourself off, and be sure to dip the dogs in the waters of Clear Creek before driving home. I couldn't figure out how I kept breaking out in an itchy red rash a week after coming back from this hike. The oils from the plant had been transferred to the dogs' fur, which kept getting transferred to me. It took two shots of steroids to get rid of the reaction.

After parking, go west toward the information kiosk and cross Clear Creek on an elegant footbridge. A sandy path then leads you south past the Camden House, over another bridge, and continues past a private residence before you reach the historic El Dorado Mine, a gold-mining operation that was active until 1967. Beyond the mine the wide trail narrows and civilization starts drifting away. Stay straight, following the signs for the Mill Creek Trail at the junction with the Clear Creek Vista Trail just past the 0.5-mile mark.

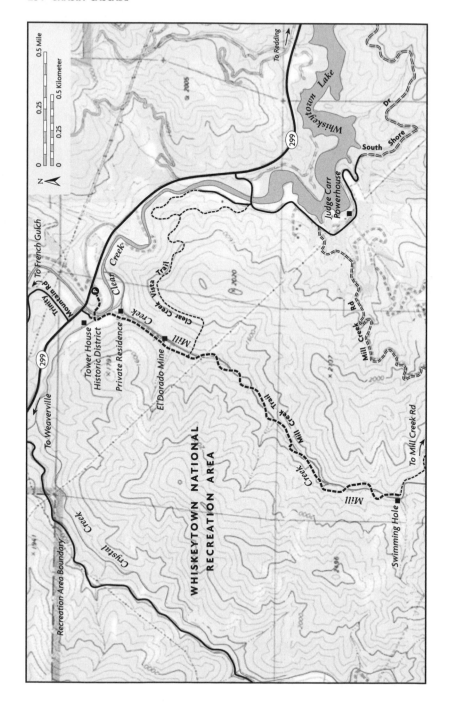

After entering the shaded forest, you'll see your first chance at a swimming hole. If you can hold off, the swimming areas get better—a lot better. After just 2.5 miles of winding trail, you'll come upon one of the best secluded swimming holes in California—a 15-foot-diameter, 5-foot-deep sandy-bottomed soaking pool fed by a 5-foot, cascading waterfall. It's a place to rest, strip down, and take a dip—if only briefly. The water is sooooo clear and cold that it takes your breath away.

After a rest, it's time to retrace your steps to the car. This hike can be extended another 1.5 miles to where the Mill Creek Trail becomes a dirt road. From there you can head east to meet up with the west end of the Boulder Creek Falls Trail (Hike 69) or continue west on Mill Creek Trail to eventually meet up with the James K. Carr Trail to Whiskeytown Falls (Hike 71).

71. Whiskeytown Falls

Round-trip: 3 miles
Hiking time: 2 hours or overnight
Difficulty: Moderate
High point: 2946 feet
Elevation gain: 1324 feet
Best hiking time: Year-round
Water: From the creek
Regulations: Dogs must be leashed
Map: USGS French Gulch
Contact: Whiskeytown National Recreation Area, Whiskeytown Unit, (530) 246-1225 or (530) 242-3400

Getting there: Take State Route 299 west from Redding nearly 14 miles (0.8 mile past the signed parking area for the Tower House Historic District on the south side of the highway) and turn left onto Crystal Creek Road. Drive 3.7 miles up Crystal Creek Road, past the parking area for Crystal Creek Falls, to the signed Whiskeytown Falls Trailhead on the left side of the road. There are ample parking spaces, an information kiosk, and a pit toilet at the trailhead. The trail leaves from the east end of the lot past the toilet.

It would be a serious lapse in judgment to write a hiking guide with trails in Whiskeytown National Recreation Area and leave out this little hike up to the park's namesake waterfall, Whiskeytown Falls.

Before 2005 there was no trail to these falls. In fact, they remained officially undiscovered until then, and very few people knew about or had visited them. This situation was remedied with the construction of the James K. Carr Trail, commonly referred to as the Whiskeytown Falls Trail. Make the trek to the falls with your pooch, and you'll see why this has become one of the favorite and most visited areas of the park.

The trail leaves the lot just beyond the toilet and descends to cross Crystal Creek over a small wooden bridge. The trail then climbs steeply up and around the other side of the canyon before leveling off slightly.

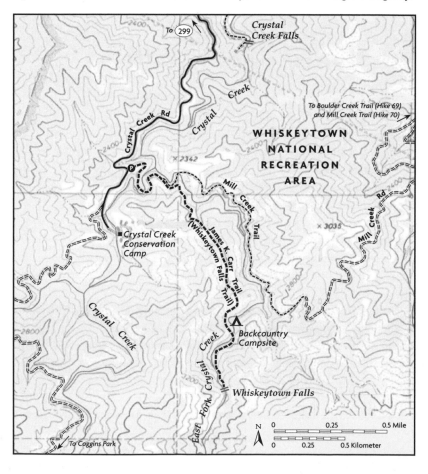

Whiskeytown Falls rushes over the rocks to a deep pool at the bottom.

Very soon you'll go right at the junction on the trail signed WHISKEY-
TOWN FALLS. To the left is an option for a longer trek and the possibility
of linking up with the Mill Creek Trail (Hike 70) or Boulder Creek Trail
(Hike 69).

Past this first and only junction, the trail gets steep but always seems to level off just in time for a breather. Benches placed at regular intervals along the way are a blessing if you get winded and need a place to sit and rest.

This hike is just challenging enough to make you feel like you have really accomplished something, but it is also easy enough so that just about anyone with some grit and determination can make it.

This middle section of the hike takes a route away from the creek, but as you near 1 mile a slight downhill section takes the trail across a hillside directly overlooking the creek below. This stretch is a very nice change from the almost relentless climbing, and you can almost sense that you are drawing near the falls.

Round a corner and pass by a nice campsite, and at 1 mile you'll cross the creek on a wooden bridge, the rushing water below cascading over a granite slab dark green and black with rich aquatic moss.

In another 100 yards, as you pick your way along the left side of the creek, you'll reach the base of the falls and look up in wonder at the multi-tiered torrent that cascades over the slick rocks from the cliffs above.

A bench at the base of the falls provides a great place to sit and take it all in, but there is also a huge fallen log near the pool where you can sit closer to the rushing water and get some good photos.

From here you have the option to take the steps up to two different overlooks for more views of the cascading water. You may want to forgo this part with Fido unless he or she is very sure-footed—the rocks get very wet and slippery here from the falls' misty spray. There is a very sturdy metal handrail, which inspires confidence as you ascend and descend.

Once you are done basking in the cool spray, it is time to head back down the trail, retracing your steps back to the car.

72. Meiners Loop to Mule Mountain Pass

Round-trip: 5.7 miles
Hiking time: 2.5 hours
Difficulty: Moderate
High point: 1745 feet
Elevation gain: 982 feet

Best hiking time: Year-round

Water: Bring your own, for you and your dog

Regulations: Dogs allowed off leash under strict voice control

Maps: USGS Redding, USGS Igo; Swasey Recreation Area map available at Wintu Trailhead

Contact: Bureau of Land Management Redding Field Office, (530) 224-2100

Getting there: From Redding, take State Route 299 west 0.6 mile past the Redding city limits. Turn left on Lower Springs Road, continue 1.8 miles, and turn left on Swasey Drive. In just under 1 mile turn right into the signed Swasey Recreation Area. Head west up the access road and stop at the Wintu Trailhead kiosk on the right for a map. Continue up the access road another 0.5 mile and park at the Meiners Trailhead.

The Swasey Recreation Area is a real gem, offering sweeping mountain vistas, babbling Olney Creek, all kinds of plant and animal life, and many dog-friendly trails. Swasey's views, sights, and sounds will help you forget your worldly cares as you enjoy your time in nature. All of this is just a ten- to fifteen-minute drive from downtown Redding.

A great view of Shasta Bally presents itself near the top of the Escalator Trail.

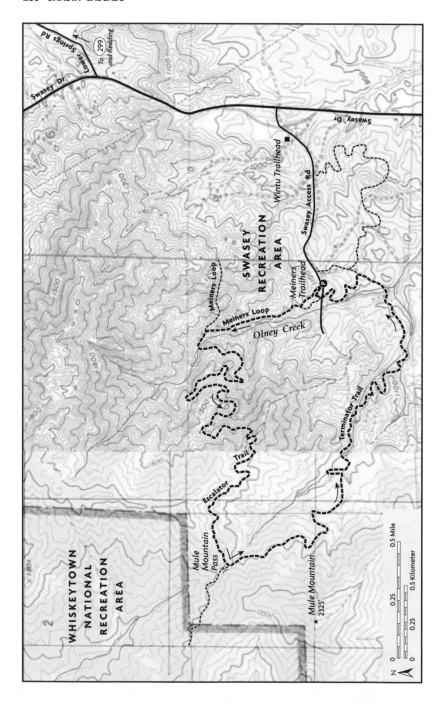

This loop offers plenty of varied terrain, swooping single-track, gentle climbs, steep technical, rocky descents, and outstanding views of Shasta Bally to the west and Lassen Peak across the valley floor to the east.

Enter the trail across the dirt access road at the north end of the Meiners Loop trailhead. This first section sweeps gently through the oaks, manzanita, and small meadows as it winds its way north along the rolling hillsides above Olney Creek. The creek provides an opening soundtrack for your hike, and small sections of embedded rocks give way to mostly even, well-graded trail—easy on both your feet and your dog's paws.

Continue straight at just under 0.5 mile as a lower section of the Meiners Loop joins from the left. At the next junction, depart the Meiners Loop and head straight onto the signed Escalator Trail.

Just beyond this junction is a perfect area for a short pit stop, when the creek is running. Take a moment's rest and let your dog cool his or her feet and get a drink, because water will be scarce for the next several miles.

From here, begin your climb toward Mule Mountain Pass. A series of switchbacks greet you in the first half of the climb. Just past the 2-mile mark, you'll find a small clearing with picnic benches that is a great place to sit down, rest, and have a snack or picnic lunch.

Next, tackle the final 0.5 mile of the climb. At 2.5 miles, as you traverse south and reach a ridgeline, a small landing presents itself. This spot provides one of the finest views of the whole hike. Here you'll get your first glimpse of Shasta Bally to the west through Mule Mountain Pass. From here the trail levels slightly and winds farther up the ridge and finally reaches the high point of the hike.

After a short descent, at just over 3 miles you'll reach Mule Mountain Pass. To the west a trail drops into Whiskeytown National Recreation Area. Take the steep and rocky Terminator Trail to the southeast. As you descend, be aware that the trail is also popular with mountain bikers, so keep your ears and eyes peeled as you go.

As you reach the 4-mile mark of your journey, several small creek crossings offer your pooch more water-playing and drinking opportunities. Cross Olney Creek at just over 5 miles and shortly thereafter take a left at the four-way trail junction to reenter the Meiners Loop.

At 5.5 miles the Meiners Loop continues up and to the right. Cross the access road and follow the signs back to the trailhead and your car.

73. Sacramento River Trail

Round-trip: 6–9 miles (or more)
Hiking time: 3 hours
Difficulty: Easy
High point: 560 feet
Elevation gain: 250 feet
Best hiking time: Year-round
Water: At the trailhead
Regulations: Dogs must remain leashed
Maps: USGS Redding; printable maps also available online at
www.healthyshasta.org
Contact: City of Redding Trails and Parks Department, (530) 224-
6100 or Community Services Division, (530) 225-4009

Getting there: From Interstate 5 in Redding, take the State Route 299/44 exit and head west over the Sacramento River. Take the Auditorium Drive exit, turn right, and follow the signs for Turtle Bay and the Sundial Bridge. The parking area is on the left across from the access road to the bridge.

If your impression of Redding is the choking gas fumes and fast-food neon along the busy Cypress Avenue exit off I-5, then you're missing an oasis just a few miles from the bustle of the freeway.

Thank the city of Redding for having the foresight to incorporate the city's signature river—it cuts the city in half—into a recreation trail that is used by walkers, cyclists, roller-skaters, kayakers, canoeists, and anglers. The Sacramento River Trail, extended by the 2004 completion of the Santiago Calatrava–designed Sundial Bridge, won the American Trails Association's 2002 Best Trail Award.

More recent extensions and additions have made this great trail even better and added more options, mileage, and variety for its users. The Sacramento River Trail remains one of the last places along the Sacramento—at 377 miles, California's longest river—where you can see the riparian forest as it was when the first settlers rode wagon trains to the water's edge.

From the parking area, the trail crosses the spectacular Sundial Bridge and follows the north side of the river to the unique concrete Ribbon

Bridge that spans the river near Keswick Dam, then returns along the south side of the river to the historic Diestelhorst Bridge (built in 1918) and back to the parking area, a round-trip of about 9 miles. While this might be too long for some, smaller chunks of the trail can be taken to shorten the trip. Several side loops are also available, such as the Arboretum Perimeter Trail, the new Forest Camp Loop, and Dana Drive extension. These can be added for a longer excursion or done alone if you are short on time.

To begin your hike, cross the Sundial Bridge and follow the trail to the left, up the river. The trail is wide and inviting, with a thicket of alders, willows, oaks, Himalayan blackberry, live oak, and wildflowers growing right up to the asphalt. You're likely to hear "Passing on your left" as cyclists come up to pass. Be courteous and take up the slack on the leash.

There are many good spots, with benches to rest, where the dogs can play in the waters of the Sacramento. Since it flows from the bottom of mighty Shasta Dam, the river stays at a chilly 52 degrees nearly year-round—refreshing for pets and nearly hypothermic for humans.

Near the 1-mile mark, pass under the North Market Street Bridge and continue on the trail as it follows the river's edge through Caldwell and

There are a lot of places along the River Trail to get down to river level and explore.

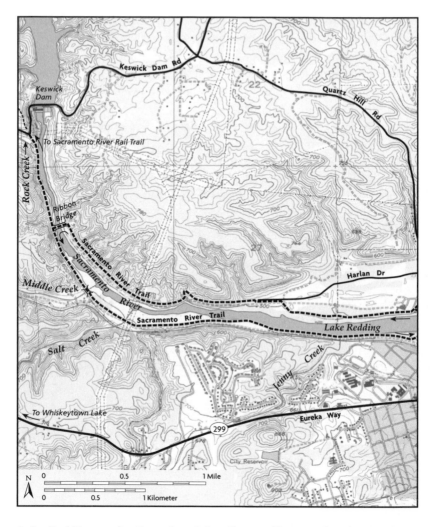

Lake Redding parks. Just after 1.5 miles you'll go under the Southern Pacific Railroad, Benton Drive, and Diestelhorst bridges.

Continue along the north side of the river, then cross the river via the Ribbon Bridge at 4 miles. Built in 1990, the 13-foot-wide, 420-foot-long concrete stress-ribbon bridge is unique to this continent (this bridge type has been used in the Czech Republic, Switzerland, and Germany). The bridge hangs suspended from the banks of the river—there are no supports sunk into the water—nearly 30 feet above the emerald-green waters of the "Sac."

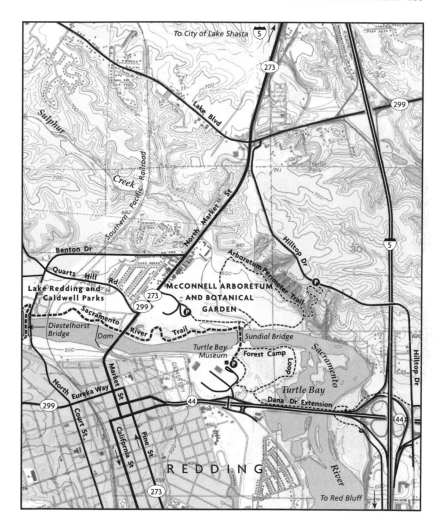

Once across, go left to begin your return trek along the south side of the river. The southern Sacramento River Trail is more flat and straight but just as lovely, so be sure to stop every so often to watch for river otters, osprey, bald eagles, snowy egrets, and other wildlife, while the dogs cool off in the river.

Work your way back downstream toward the Sundial and at 7 miles cross back over the river via Diestelhorst Bridge. From here, retrace your earlier path back to the Sundial Bridge and over the river to where you parked.

74. Magee Peak

Round-trip: 12.6 miles
Hiking time: 2 days
Difficulty: Strenuous
High point: 8549 feet
Elevation gain: 3200 feet
Best hiking time: Mid-June through October; mosquitoes trouble-some from spring through July
Water: Only from Everett and Magee lakes, or bring your own
Regulations: Dogs must be leashed in developed areas; elsewhere dogs must be under their owner's control at all times, whether on a leash or under strict voice control
Map: USGS Thousand Lakes Valley
Contact: Lassen National Forest, Hat Creek Ranger District, (530) 336-5521

Getting there: From the town of Old Station east of Lassen Volcanic National Park, take State Route 89/44 east. Stay north on SR 89 at the junction where SR 44 splits off to the east. Go 11 miles north on the highway and turn west onto the signed Forest Road 26, Thousand Lakes Wilderness. The turn is 0.4 mile north of the Hat Creek Work Center. Don't be tempted by all the lesser logging and fire roads; stay on the signed road for FR 26, Thousand Lakes Wilderness, and Cypress Camp. Go right at the first junction at 3.6 miles. Stay left in another 1.5 miles where the road forks. In less than 1 mile, stay right when the road forks again. In another 2 miles turn left to depart FR 26 at the junction signed National Forest Wilderness. Continue 2.3 more miles, again ignoring lesser roads, and turn left at the junction signed for Cypress Trailhead. Follow this road 0.3 mile to the trailhead.

My dogs and I absolutely love cirque-surrounded, subalpine lakes. On this hike, you'll pass two beautiful examples that are much less visited than lakes in nearby Lassen Volcanic National Park—and you'll top out on one of Shasta County's Top 10 highest points.

The trail starts at the south end of the parking lot just past the pit toilets. Within the first 100 yards of hiking, cross boulder-strewn Eiler

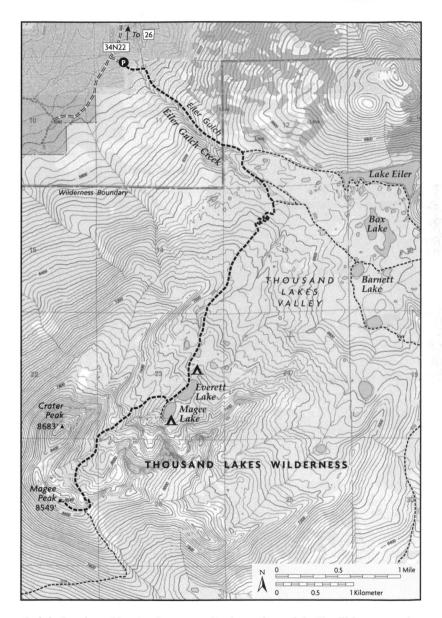

Gulch Creek and begin the steep climb up the gulch. You'll know you're on the right path—it's well-worn, as this is a popular weekend backpacking destination—as you climb southeast at a good clip, through a canopy of Jeffrey pine, white fir, and the occasional western juniper.

Lake Eiler's northeast shore (Marc Soares)

As you huff and puff up the climb, look for a sign for Thousand Lakes Wilderness that officially welcomes you to the area. Beyond the sign, at 1 mile, go right at the trail junction signed simply MAGEE. Soon you'll come upon the next trail junction and take a right again signed for Everett Lake, Magee Lake, and Magee Peak.

Through this section of trail you'll pass an amazing display of flora, from brilliant green lichens clinging to the trunks of trees, to tobacco brush, numerous wildflowers, lodgepole pine, red and white fir, and stubby pinemat manzanita.

Pine-encrusted Everett and Magee lakes are about 2 miles farther from the last trail junction. Both lakes sit at 7200 feet in elevation. Both also offer good swimming and fishing opportunities—the lakes are stocked with fish every spring by airplane—and good camping spots. I prefer to stay at Magee Lake, since there's more room to spread out, as well as more campsites. Make sure if you're close to other campers that you have control of your dogs, and let people around you know you're hiking with animals. This just cuts down on any problems.

From the lakes, it's nearly another 2-mile push to the summit. To get there, pass by Magee Lake and bear right at the trail fork. As you climb, the canopy of pine opens, allowing fantastic views of the surrounding countryside. This is volcano country, meaning the surrounding rock is sharp and porous, so it's a good idea to pack your dog's booties.

At about 1.5 miles from the lake, you'll crest the ridge and then follow the trail another 0.3 mile to the summit, at 8549 feet elevation. Notice that you and your dog (or dogs) are standing on the rim of an ancient volcano that encompassed Peak 8446 (0.3 mile to the southeast), 8683-foot Crater Peak (0.5 mile north), and others. Though glaciers finished the contours of the Hat Creek area, it was volcanoes that first carved up the landscape.

75. Baker Lake to Hat Creek Rim

Round-trip: Up to 7 miles
Hiking time: 1–5 hours
Difficulty: Easy
High point: 5300 feet
Elevation gain: 500 feet
Best hiking time: Year-round; hot in the summer, a great snowshoe route in winter
Water: Bring your own
Regulations: Dogs must be leashed in developed areas; elsewhere dogs must be under their owner's control at all times, whether on a leash or under strict voice control
Map: USGS Old Station
Contact: Lassen National Forest, Hat Creek Ranger District, (530) 336-5521

Getting there: From Redding, travel east on State Route 44. Park for free in the turnout near Forest Road 33N20, which is a few miles above the junction of SR 89/44, northeast of the town of Old Station and 2.2 miles south of the Hat Creek Rim Overlook sign.

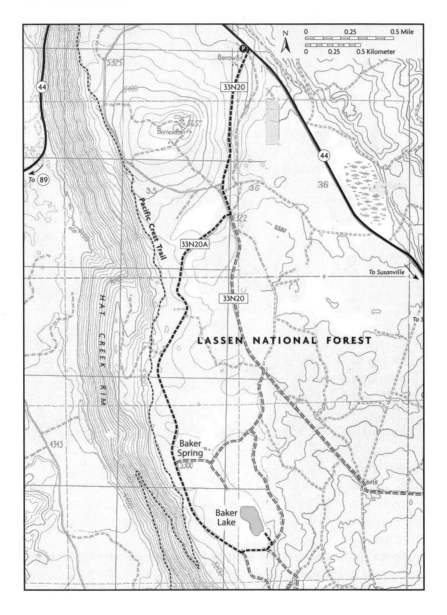

The Hat Creek Rim is a 1000-foot ridge that invites all sorts of outdoor enthusiasts to play—from dog walkers and hikers, to mountain bikers and even hang-gliding enthusiasts. It's not unusual to see multicolored gliders floating on the thermals created when wind sweeps up the valley all

At nearly any time of year, startling beauty can be found along the hike to Baker Lake.

summer. Indeed, the rim hosts a large hang-gliding event every Labor Day.

While this hike is a blast in the spring, summer, and fall, winter is the time dogs will love this jaunt the most. And so will you. If you've never tried snowshoeing, this is just the trip to learn. You'll travel through a volcanic world that is softened by snow, and the terrain is flat and the path is wide. If you go when there isn't snow on the ground, consider packing your dogs' protective booties to guard their paws from the sharp volcanic rock that dominates this area.

The tone of this hike is ease. It starts on cinder-covered FR 33N20. Ignore the branch roads until you get to an obvious branch at 1.2 miles, where you'll start climbing up signed FR 33N20A. This is the route you'll stay on all the way to Baker Lake, probably snow covered in winter, since this is a shallow wisp of a waterway.

Because of a devastating forest fire many years ago, you'll march through a forest of Jeffrey pine that's uniform in size. The forest was planted after the fire; you can see the blaze's full power on display from Hat Creek Rim.

After a slight downhill at 1.6 miles, look for open views of Prospect Peak to the south. Then, when you come to an outlook at the rim at about 3 miles, hike some 75 yards to one of the most spectacular vistas of Lassen Peak, especially striking when decked out in its winter cloak. This is a postcard-worthy picture; make sure you bring your camera.

I usually get to Baker Lake, at 3.5 miles in, have a snack, cook up some hot chocolate, and let the girls gnaw on a rawhide chewy before backtracking to the truck. You can turn around any time you like.

76. Crystal and Baum Lakes

Round-trip: 5 miles (to Baum Lake Dam and the loop around Crystal Lake)
Hiking time: 3 hours
Difficulty: Easy
High point: 3000 feet
Elevation gain: 100 feet
Best hiking time: Year-round; snow possible in winter
Water: From Baum and Crystal lakes
Map: USGS Cassel
Regulations: Dogs must be under their owner's control at all times, whether on a leash or under strict voice control
Contact: Lassen National Forest, Hat Creek Ranger District, (530) 336-5521; Pacific Gas and Electric Co., (800) 743-5000 or www.pge.com/about/environment/pge/recreation/

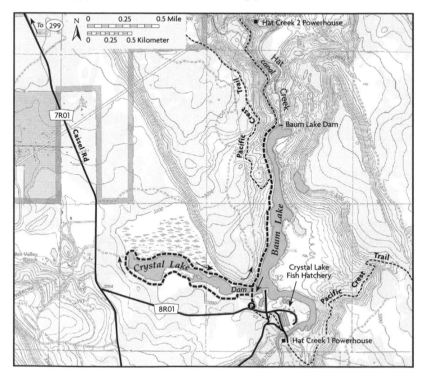

Getting there: From Redding, take State Route 299 east to the intersection of SR 299/89, about 54 miles from Interstate 5. From the intersection, drive another 2 miles on SR 299 and turn south onto the paved Cassel Road. Go 2 more miles and turn left at the sign for the state-run Crystal Lake Fish Hatchery. Drive another mile and turn left into the paved parking lot of Baum Lake.

On a good day, my dogs will let me fish after hiking for a good hour, but those days are few and far between. While Scully will plop down and watch the world go by, Trinity is often unwilling to afford me that luxury. She's constantly getting in the water, swimming, jumping, and making sure I see her. Crystal and

Crystal and Baum lakes offer great fishing and solitude.

Baum lakes are full of fish—German brown, brook, and rainbow trout. Big ones, up to 20 pounds, along with planted fish that are just right for the grill, at a half pound each.

And while I do get to fish once and again, I always enjoy going back to these lakes for the hike it affords the dogs and me. I manage to see something different each time out. The lakes offer a peace that is hard to find these days. Osprey and hawks circle overhead (there's always a chance to watch the osprey hunt, grabbing a fish from the lake and turning it so it faces forward to be more aerodynamic), while all manner of shorebirds and waterfowl squawk, chirp, whistle, and honk.

The trail network traces the shoreline of both lakes and is used by anglers and hikers alike. Start from the parking lot and take the path that leads to a dam that separates the two lakes. At a grove of ponderosa pine, look north for a great view of Mount Shasta. Turn left before the dam then follow Crystal Lake's southern shoreline. It's an easy hike around the lake, where you're likely to see white pelicans bobbing on the water during their migration inland. You'll pass grasslands and low brush, like squawbrush, sage, and western juniper once you've looped around to the north side of the dam.

Turn left here onto the 1.5-mile path along Baum Lake's western shoreline, where you'll link up with the Pacific Crest Trail. Follow the trail north—it's obvious—where you'll soon get to a split in the trail. The upper fork goes up a slope, crosses a fence, and reaches another fork. The PCT heads left and uphill from the midslope trail, but you can stay right and you'll reach the lower trail, which never leaves the shore.

From the Baum Lake Dam you can continue on to the Hat Creek 2 Powerhouse, or just retrace your steps to the dam separating Baum and Crystal lakes, where you might snatch a few minutes to cast a line for dinner.

77. Hat Creek Trail

Round-trip: 8.6 miles
Hiking time: 5 hours or overnight
Difficulty: Easy
High point: 4300 feet
Elevation gain: 400 feet
Best hiking time: Year-round
Water: From Hat Creek
Regulations: Dogs must be leashed in developed areas; elsewhere
   dogs must be under their owner's control at all times, whether
   on a leash or under strict voice control
Map: USGS Old Station
Contact: Lassen National Forest, Hat Creek Ranger District,
   (530) 336-5521

Getting there: Go north on State Route 89/44 through the town of Old Station. Stay on SR 89 at the junction where SR 44 turns to the east. Drive 0.3 mile and turn left into Cave Campground. Park in the small lot to the left near the entrance.

From late April through mid-November, this trail is teeming with anglers, sniffing out the best places to chase the thousands of rainbow and brook trout the California Department of Fish and Game plants each general trout fishing season.

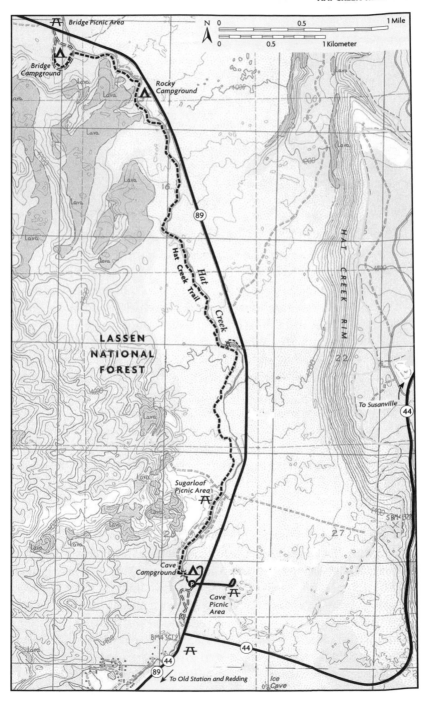

Hat Creek presents a picturesque riffle around every corner.

Oh, you'll see others on the trail, retired folks walking hand-in-hand as they take a break from their recreational vehicle wanderings, teens heading to secret swimming holes, and certainly, dog walkers—and happy dogs who rush from the trail to Hat Creek for a dip or drink. The rushing waters of spring-fed Hat Creek and the canopy of riparian forest bring trekkers here all year, from the crunch of fall leaves, through the crunch of snow in winter and the renewed energy of spring, all the way through the heat of another Northern California summer.

From the parking area, cross the wooden bridge over Hat Creek and pick up the trail on the right. At just about 1.5 miles from the bridge, you'll reach another concrete bridge and gorge that shows off the power of this little stream. A narrow slot has been cut through the porous lava rock, where mini-waterfalls crash through the channel, until the stream slowly widens. The wide, sandy trail never leaves Hat Creek for more than a few yards, since, after all, it's a fishing access trail.

Soon you'll come across a grove of white-trunked aspens, which are rich green in summer and golden in fall. You'll also notice the mix of huge ponderosa pine and incense cedar, species that aren't so water-friendly, mixing with water-loving species like alder and willow. There's even live oak and, off the trail, a maze of chaparral shrubs like bitterbrush, mountain mahogany, greenleaf manzanita, western juniper, California sage, and rabbit goldenweed mixed in for good measure.

In the spring and summer, you'll find black-tailed deer here, also songbirds, Steller's jays loudly begging for a dropped crumb, osprey, and the occasional eagle. I've heard of people spotting bobcat, but I have never seen one of these elusive cats here.

While the trail is mostly shrouded by the riparian forest, there are views of the surrounding volcano-enhanced landscape. Lassen Peak, ghostly white in winter, is prominent on the return trip to your car. But also look for Sugarloaf Peak, Hat Creek Rim (in summer, hang gliders use the rim as a take-off point), Freaner Peak, and Burney Mountain.

At 1.8 miles, you'll reach another stand of aspen, then another waterfall a short time later. At 2.2 miles, you're treated to a second waterfall, while entering a strip of conifer forest of white fir and sugar pine. Walk another 0.25 mile and you'll come across a third waterfall. The scene is repeated at 2.7 miles.

At 3 miles, you'll be treated to views of Magee and Crater peaks toward the west, from another stand of aspen. The trail leads to another wooden bridge, announcing Rocky Campground at 3.8 miles. Traverse the basalt talus here, where you actually look down on Hat Creek, then continue on to Bridge Campground at 4.3 miles and the terminus of the trail. You could opt to use a car shuttle for a one-way option, or turn around and go back the way you came.

78. Caribou Wilderness Area

Round-trip: 6.8 miles
Hiking time: 5 hours or overnight
Difficulty: Moderate
High point: 7100 feet
Elevation gain: 600 feet
Best hiking time: Fall; hikable year-round, be prepared for swarms of mosquitoes in spring
Water: From lakes
Regulations: Dogs must be leashed in developed areas; elsewhere dogs must be under their owner's control at all times, whether on a leash or under strict voice control
Map: USGS Bogard Buttes
Contact: Lassen National Forest, Almanor Ranger District, (530) 258-2141

Getting there: From Susanville, drive north on State Route 44 for approximately 35 miles and turn left (west) on Forest Road 10 just before the Bogard Work Center. Follow FR 10 for 6 miles and turn right on Forest Road 32N09, following it 2.6 more miles to the Cone Lake parking lot and trailhead.

Note that if you would like to try an alternate hike, you can also approach the southern Caribou Lakes from the south. From Chester, go east on State Route 36 for 5 miles, then turn left on FR 10. Follow the road 9.5 miles and turn left on Forest Road 30N25. Continue a short distance to the Indian Meadow parking area.

Fall is the best time of year for hardy souls to make those final backpacking trips before the blanket of winter tucks everything up in white—and the Caribou Wilderness Area on the back side of Lassen Volcanic National Park is probably my favorite camping destination with the girls.

Backpackers might need to get out their silk sleeping-bag liners for a bit of extra warmth, but the prospect of a few last weekends in the woods is alive and well. No matter that you can see your breath as you light the stove for that must-have cup of coffee after slipping from your cocoon of bag and tent.

The relative flatness of the Caribou Wilderness makes it a good choice for families with children.

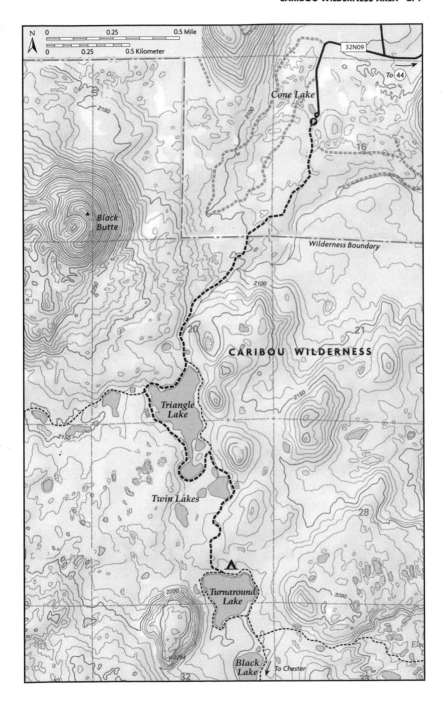

N

0   0.25   0.5 Mile

0   0.25   0.5 Kilometer

32N09

To 44

Cone Lake

P

16

2150

2100

Black
Butte

Wilderness Boundary

2100

20

21

CARIBOU WILDERNESS

2150

Triangle
Lake

Twin Lakes

28

2150

Turnaround
Lake

2200

2200

Black
Lake

To Chester

32

In the fall, you just might be the only overnight guest in the 20,500-acre wilderness that's all of 9 miles long and 5 miles wide. The entire wilderness sits at about 6900 feet along a rolling volcanic plateau, so the hiking is easy. In fact, the highest point is the 8374-foot Red Cinder, a peak that straddles the wilderness and Lassen Volcanic National Park.

Sure, there's a bit more gear to lug on a fall hike—it's really the only time that I actually take a tent and extra fleece clothing. But to sit out at dusk in front of a warming fire and let all the stress of uncertain times melt away is priceless. And finding a lake to call your very own should be a cinch in the fall. The wilderness is filled with lake options, most of which sustain a population of rainbow and German brown trout.

The last fall trek I took in the wilderness was probably one of the most fulfilling trips I've ever taken. Starting from the Cone Lake trailhead, the dogs and I hit Triangle Lake, 1.8 miles in and one of the largest lakes in the wilderness, in about 15 minutes. I took a short rest to watch the waves ripple across the surface while Scully and Trinity busied themselves log-hopping near the shore.

We continued 1.6 more miles to Turnaround Lake and settled into one of the best lakeside campsites to be found anywhere. The site sits under the cover of lodgepole pine, with a small fire ring positioned right near a granite knob. The lake panorama is punctuated by a large granite point with a lone lodgepole pine, the perfect place to drag a dry fly behind a plastic bubble to entice trout that are cruising the shoreline for a meal.

By nightfall, the steam was rising from the lake, a few snowflakes floated from the sky, and the dogs' breath came out in white bursts. By 9:00 PM I was ready to scrunch into my sleeping bag and zone out for several hours. When I awoke, I was greeted by a 2-inch layer of snow. Everything was crystallized in white. Truly magical.

79. McGowan Lake Trail

Round-trip: 4.4 miles (5.4 miles including Christie Hill)
Hiking time: 3–5 hours (add up to 2 hours for Christie Hill)
Difficulty: Moderate
High point: 6500 feet (6615 feet for Christie Hill)
Elevation gain: 500 feet (950 feet to Christie Hill)
Best hiking time: Winter; hikable year-round

Water: Bring your own

Regulations: Dogs must be leashed in developed areas; elsewhere dogs must be under their owner's control at all times, whether on a leash or under strict voice control

Map: USGS Lassen Peak

Contact: Lassen National Forest, Almanor Ranger District, (530) 258-2141

Getting there: From Red Bluff, take State Route 36 east to the signed Morgan Summit at the junction of SR 36 and the Lassen Park Highway (SR 89), just east of the town of Mineral and northwest of the town of Chester. Turn north onto the highway, go 2 miles, and park at the free clearing where a snow-covered Forest Road 29N22 (your trail) is located.

You've never tried snowshoeing with your dog? Here's your chance to finally get out on snowshoes—it's easy—and have some winter fun with the dogs.

This is a peaceful route that takes you deep into a dark and snow-covered forest, with several clearings for long-distance views to the south. You'll also see huge rock outcroppings and the swift-flowing Nanny Creek, where there's the chance for a snow picnic.

Even in the nearly quiet winter months, this trail allows for great wildlife viewing. Coyotes might be spotted making their way along the creek for a drink, or to ambush the snowshoe hares and mice that venture out from time to time. You might get to see a porcupine or great horned owl in the trunks of the conifers, while the chirps of mountain chickadees and the screech of Steller's jays punctuate the normal silence.

Since you'll be walking on a wide Forest Service road, you'll likely be sharing the trek with cross-country skiers, especially after a big snowstorm blows through. Because of the elevation, the snow falls airy and light—and it tends to get piled on everything in sight.

From the parking area, you'll drop a bit, then begin to climb into a lodgepole pine forest, which then leads to a dense white-fir forest. At just over a mile, swing around a manzanita-covered hillside (you might see snowshoe hare scatter into the cover of dense brush) and you'll catch a great view of Brokeoff Mountain to the north, inside Lassen Volcanic National Park (where, sadly, dogs are not allowed on the trails).

Along the route to Nanny Creek and McGowan Lake (Marc Soares)

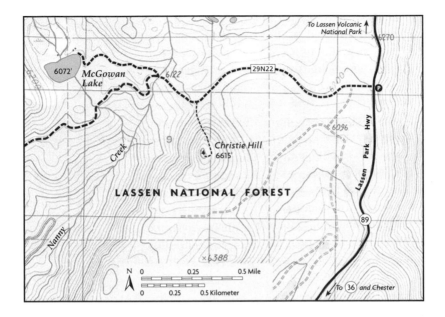

From here, you can climb nearby Christie Hill (6515 feet) to the south. It can be reached from its eastern flanks, then by picking your way safely through the white-fir forest to the crest of the hill. To get the best views of Lassen Peak, you'll need to wend your way through the conifers.

Not into the adventure of climbing a peak in the middle of winter? Stay the course and you'll get to the creek, which is swift and free-flowing from the blockade of several giant volcanic boulders. From here, you descend through incense cedar and Jeffrey pine (the cones won't prick your hands when you run them over the surface, unlike the cones of a ponderosa pine, where the burrs stick sharply out), and the forest opens up. You'll reach Nanny Creek at 1.7 miles, where you can watch the frothy water tumble over snowcapped boulders.

Don't miss going just 0.3 mile farther, where you'll come to an area of multi-trunked cedars in a giant boulder outcropping near McGowan Lake, which is 0.2 mile farther on. From this vantage point, you'll get great views of the Cascade Range to the north and the Sierra Nevada to the south. The outcropping also makes a great place to get out of the elements, enjoy a snack (and maybe some hot chocolate, if so equipped), and rest before returning from whence you came.

80. Lake Almanor Recreation Trail

Round-trip: Up to 19 miles
Hiking time: 3–7 hours or overnight
Difficulty: Easy
High point: 4600 feet
Elevation gain: 300 feet
Best hiking time: Year-round; a great snowshoe route
Water: Bring your own
Regulations: Dogs must be leashed
Map: Lassen National Forest
Contact: Lassen National Forest, Almanor Ranger District, (530) 258-2141

Getting there: From Redding, take Interstate 5 south 35 miles to Red Bluff and take the State Route 36 exit. Turn left onto SR 36 and follow it through town, taking another left at the split junction of SR 36 and SR 99. It's another 78 miles to the intersection of SR 36 and SR 89 near the town of Chester. At the intersection, take SR 89 south 4.6 miles to a plowed (in winter) parking area on the left across from the Humbug Road turnoff.

In summer, the Lake Almanor Recreation Trail is a wide, inviting paved path that meanders along the scenic western shore of this lake, which has 55 miles of shoreline and is 13 miles long and 6 miles wide. The lake was created in 1914 to fuel a hydroelectric plant operated by the Great Western Power Company; its name is a combination of Alice, Martha, and Elinore, the daughters of the company's vice president. Canyon Dam, on the lakeshore, was built in 1927 to harness the North Fork Feather River.

Great Western Power was later bought by Pacific Gas and Electric who, along with the Forest Service, developed this area into the four-season recreation spot it is today. Indeed, you'll find a mix of PG&E and Forest Service campgrounds along the recreation trail, which in the summer is popular with anglers, cyclists, roller-bladers, picnickers (picnic tables and benches dot the entire length of the trail), and dog walkers.

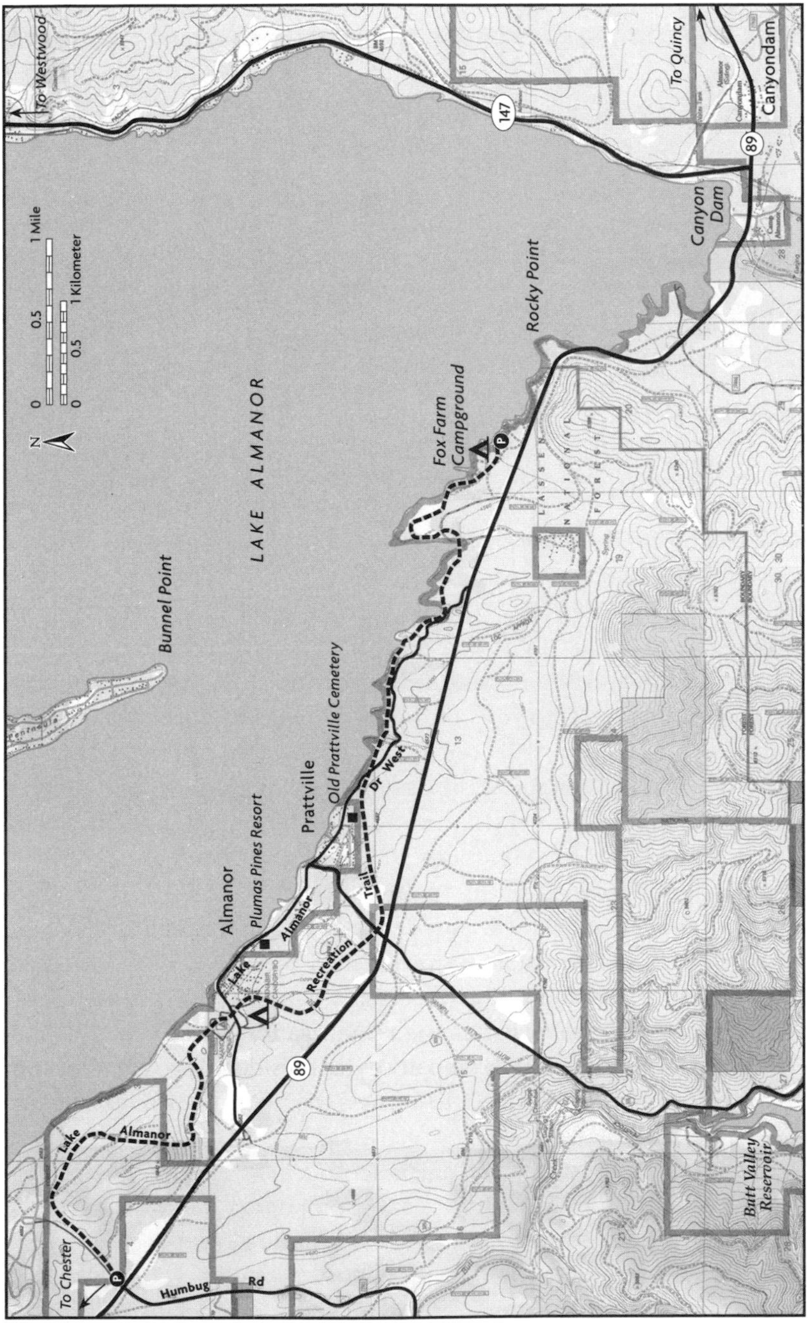

To Westwood

147

To Quincy

Canyondam

Canyon Dam

To Quincy

89

Rocky Point

Canyon Dam

LASSEN NATIONAL FOREST

Fox Farm Campground

N

1 Mile

0.5

0

1 Kilometer

0.5

0

LAKE ALMANOR

Bunnel Point

Dr. West

Old Prattville Cemetery

Prattville

Trail

Almanor

Plumas Pines Resort

Lake Almanor

Recreation

89

Butt Valley Reservoir

Lake Almanor

To Chester

Humbug Rd

Snowshoeing the Lake Almanor Recreation Trail is an experience that shouldn't be missed.

But not in winter. It's at this time that the trail takes on a look of mystery and a sense of adventure. Be sure to bring a fishing rod, since the rainbow and German brown trout fishing is best from November through May, with anglers reportedly catching 4- to 6-pound fish right from the rocky shoreline. Listen for wildlife as well, although much of it departs the winter chill for warmer climes. Still, you'll see and hear plenty of waterfowl as well as shorebirds: the shrill sound of plovers, the chirping of chickadees, the caw of ravens, and the screeches of Steller's jays. Always keep an eye trained for the osprey and bald eagles that hunt for fish in the winter. Or at least, watch the folly as an osprey swoops from on high to take a trout from the chilly water—only to be chased and robbed by a bald eagle. Both species are prevalent on this lake.

But the amount of snowbound adventure and wildlife you take in is up to you: although the trail is 9.5 miles long, you can turn back at any point along the way.

The trail starts 75 yards from the parking area. After a mile of trudging through powdery snow in the shadow of a ponderosa-pine forest and the occasional huge white pine, the trail offers up a glimpse of its magic. Even with 6 feet of snow built up around the lake, you'll recognize that you've entered a series of meadows that dot the path. Looking west, you'll see the Almanor Peninsula and behind that, the white-capped peaks of Little Dyer and Dyer Mountain (which is rumored to be the location of a new, four-season resort that will rival those near Lake Tahoe).

After about a mile, the trail follows the shoreline closely before heading inland again toward the Plumas Pines Resort. It then skirts the Old Prattville Cemetery, crosses Lake Almanor Drive West (watch for traffic), and then again follows the shoreline toward an array of campgrounds (which are closed in winter).

Choose your own turnaround point. You'll find several snow-covered coves that are inviting, with squawking geese—and swooping osprey.

81. Bizz Johnson Trail

Round-trip: 13 miles
Hiking time: 7 hours or overnight
Difficulty: Easy
High point: 4660 feet
Elevation gain: 500 feet
Best hiking time: Year-round
Water: From Boulder Creek
Regulations: Dogs must be leashed in developed areas; elsewhere dogs must be under their owner's control at all times, whether on a leash or under strict voice control
Maps: USGS Susanville, USGS Roop Mountain
Contact: Bureau of Land Management, Eagle Lake Resource Area, (530) 257-0456; Lassen National Forest, Susanville Ranger District, (530) 257-4188

Getting there: From Redding, take State Routes 44/89 about 110 miles to Susanville. To get to the depot, take SR 36 to Susanville and turn south on Weatherlow Street, which soon becomes Richmond Road. After 0.5 mile, park for free across from the depot. Signs will point you to the trail.

This is the way to run a railroad, albeit an abandoned one. The Bizz Johnson Trail links Susanville and the community of Westwood and is a 25-mile multiuse route that follows the rugged Susan River canyon. The

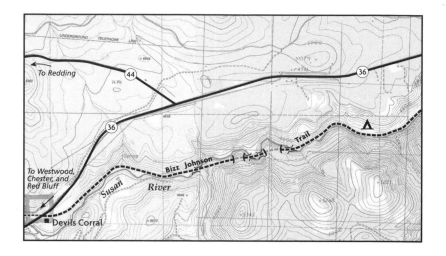

trail is a combined effort between the Lassen Land and Trails Trust, the Bureau of Land Management, the Forest Service, and the Rails-to-Trails Conservancy (a Washington, D.C.–based advocacy group that helps buy old rail right-of-ways).

The historic trail actually is the former right-of-way of the Fernley and Lassen Railroad, built in 1914 to connect a logging mill in Westwood to the railroad's mail line in Fernley, Nevada. The line operated for more than forty years, first run by Fernley and Lassen and later by Central Pacific and Southern Pacific Rail Corporation.

This hike covers the eastern portion of the trail, from the Susanville Railroad Depot to Devils Corral off SR 36, some 6.5 miles away. You certainly could use a car shuttle, or go out and back, or even consider spending the night. Rules include no camping within a mile of a trailhead or near the south side of the road west of Hobo Camp, which is right outside of Susanville. Camping on BLM land is limited to three days; you can stay fourteen days in Lassen National Forest.

In summer, the Susan River is a great place to fish for rainbow trout or to enjoy a quick dip in waters that are quite refreshing. From mid-October through mid-November, the trail comes alive with the golden hues of the cottonwoods and the reds and oranges of the scattered oaks. The Rails-to-Trails Conservancy named the Bizz Johnson one of the eight best trails to catch fall foliage shows in the United States. When winter sets in, there's no need to abandon this trail. Pack the booties, strap on snowshoes, and

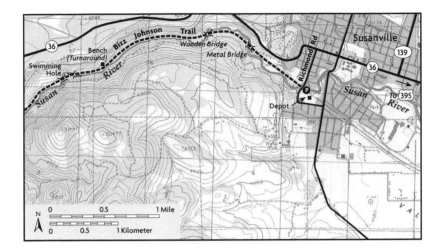

glide along, watching for deer, rabbit, and raccoon tracks in the snow.

The trail is dog- and family-friendly and wide with a gentle slope toward Westwood. The grade rarely exceeds 3 percent along the entire 25.6-mile length.

Start off the first mile with a gentle jaunt through a couple of neighborhoods, before coming to a metal bridge that crosses a great first swimming hole. It's here where you'll see the stark contrast between the dry, sheer rock faces of the Susan River canyon and the lushness of the riparian habitat. You'll cross a small wooden bridge at 1.5 miles that overlooks the gravel bars of the Susan River, where in the summer you'll find the locals swimming, inner-tubing, and fishing for rainbow trout.

At just over 2 miles, the former rail line trail reaches a well-placed bench and several spur trails that lead to the water's edge. Many walkers choose to rest and turn back here, and you'll notice if you press on that you just might have the rest of the trek to yourself. From this point as well, you'll get into the pristine forest views and wild stretches of river.

The dogs and I never (well, never in the summer) miss perhaps the largest and deepest swimming hole along the entire trail at 2.8 miles. It can be found just below a concrete-and-wood bridge. A mile farther, you'll find a nice campsite on the far shore.

After following the Susan River at its level, past the campsite, you'll start to rise well above the rushing water. Cross another bridge at 4.8 miles, then spend some time taking in one of the most interesting features

Bridge over the Susan River (Marc Soares)

of this trek—an old railroad tunnel that stays chilly right through the 100-degree heat of summer. Rail workers used explosives to cut this 150-yard tunnel through the solid cliff face in 1914.

The next 1.5 miles to Devils Corral features more of the same: sheer cliff walls; a wide, inviting path; cool swimming and fishing holes; and slender, long strips of tall grasses along the water's edge. Be sure not to miss this trek in winter, when the scenes are softened by a blanket of snow.

82. North Rim to Middle Trail Loop

Round-trip: 8.1 miles
Hiking time: 4 hours
Difficulty: Strenuous
High point: 1197 feet
Elevation gain: 1452 feet
Best hiking time: Fall through spring
Water: Bring your own, for you and your dog
Regulations: Dogs allowed off leash under strict voice control on trails north of Upper Park Road
Maps: USGS Richardson Springs, USGS Paradise West; park map available online at www.bidwellpark.org
Contact: Chico Creek Nature Center, (530) 891-4671

Getting there: From State Route 99 in Chico, take the SR 32 exit east toward Chester. Go 1.8 miles and turn left on Bruce Road, which continues straight through a series of roundabouts and becomes Manzanita Avenue. Turn right at the third roundabout on Wildwood Avenue, which becomes Upper Park Road. Pass the Chico Municipal Golf Course on the right and the Chico Rod and Gun Club on the left. Enter the Horseshoe Lake parking lot on the left.

With lax leash regulations and awe-inspiring scenery, this loop is the perfect destination for a good, long hike for both you and your four-legged friend. Most of the trails in Upper Bidwell Park have uneven, sometimes loose surfaces as well as hard embedded rocks, so be sure that you and your dog are fit, well prepared, and supplied. There is also little to no shade on this hike, so plan accordingly.

From the north end of the Horseshoe Lake parking lot, follow the sign for the Maidu Trail to Upper North Rim. At the first junction, go right on the Maidu Trail and begin to climb the moderate, switchbacked slopes up the side of the north canyon wall. As you climb, take note of the rock formation near the top of the rim on your right, called Monkey Face.

Near the canyon rim at 0.5 mile, the trail punches a hole through

Paul rests in the shade of an oak tree to escape the temperatures on the plateau.

a dense thicket of brush. Past the thicket, take the signed North Rim Trail to the right. True to its name, the trail works its way along the rim of the deep canyon formed by Big Chico Creek and brings you to many wonderful overlooks, rocky outcroppings, and sheer cliffs along the way.

Look for a lovely spreading oak tree with a flat shady spot underneath on the right side of the trail at just under 1 mile. The tree's canopy is a perfect place to take a break and get out of the direct sunlight for a while. Once you've had a moment to rest, continue your trek east on the North Rim Trail.

While many cliff-top vistas present themselves along the next 1.5 miles, a particularly dramatic one can be found near the 3-mile mark where a narrow notch in the rocks along the rim opens spectacularly and drops away to the canyon floor.

In the spring the wildflowers along this part of the North Rim Trail suddenly burst forth in flurries of color. At just under 3.5 miles, look for the signed junction for the B Trail down the canyon to the right and begin your descent.

The B Trail, built and frequented by mountain bikers, is steep, rocky, and technical in many places, so watch your step. Continue to navigate the trail's rocky switchbacks and at nearly 5 miles, just within sight of Upper Park Road, take the Middle Trail, which splits off to the right.

The Middle Trail paints a perfect swooping ribbon of single-track across the grassy bluffs between Upper Park Road and the sheer cliffs and rocky outcroppings of the North Rim above. Enjoy these last 3 miles of rolling trail, which leads you back to your car at the Horseshoe Lake parking lot.

After this beautiful but long and strenuous hike, you and your dog will surely be ready to cool your feet in the waters of Big Chico Creek, which you can access by driving or walking up the Upper Park service road. Both of you have earned your post-hike rewards with this 8-mile day on the trail.

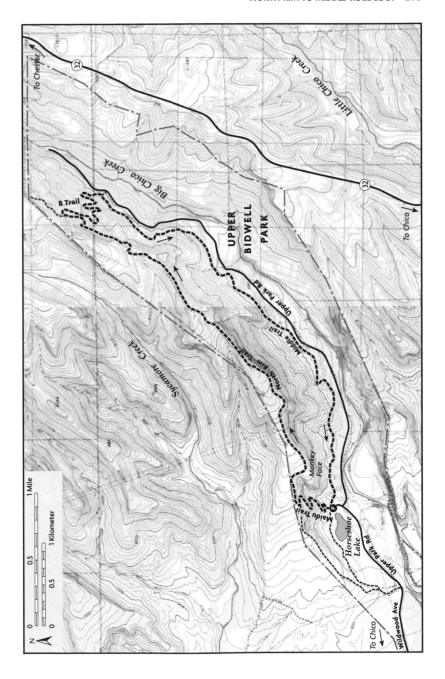

83. Feather Falls

Round-trip: 9 miles (out and back on Upper Loop Trail); 8-mile loop
(returning on Lower Loop Trail)
Hiking time: 4.5 hours or overnight
Difficulty: Moderate
High point: 2427 feet
Elevation gain: 1818 feet
Best hiking time: Year-round
Water: Bring your own, for you and your dog
Regulations: Dogs must be leashed in developed areas; elsewhere
dogs must be under their owner's control at all times, whether
on a leash or under strict voice control
Maps: USGS Forbestown, USGS Brush Creek
Contact: Feather River Ranger District, Plumas National Forest,
(530) 534-6500

Getting there: From State Route 70 in Oroville, take SR 162 east for
just over 8 miles. Turn right on Forbestown Road, drive for 6 miles,
and turn left on Lumpkin Road. Follow Lumpkin Road for 11 miles
and look for the sign for Feather Falls. Turn left at the sign onto Bryant
Ravine Road and continue 1.5 miles to the trailhead, at Feather Falls
Campground.

The road to the falls is narrow, steep, and winding and the hike is long,
but the payoff for this journey is huge. As you and your dog rest at the
falls' dramatic vista point, you'll be awestruck at the images and sounds
of huge sheets of white water cascading off the sheer cliff face.

The trail to the falls is split into Upper and Lower Loop trails. If both
are open, hikers can make them into a big loop or do an out-and-back
along the same trail. As of this writing (late fall 2012) the Lower Loop
is closed for the repair of a damaged bridge. Though shorter, the Lower
Loop involves more climbing and takes about the same amount of time
to navigate. The Upper Loop is mostly smooth and rolling but gets a
moderate rating due to its overall length. An out-and-back on the Upper
Loop Trail will net you about 9 miles of steady hiking.

Begin your hike at the east end of the trailhead parking lot and enjoy

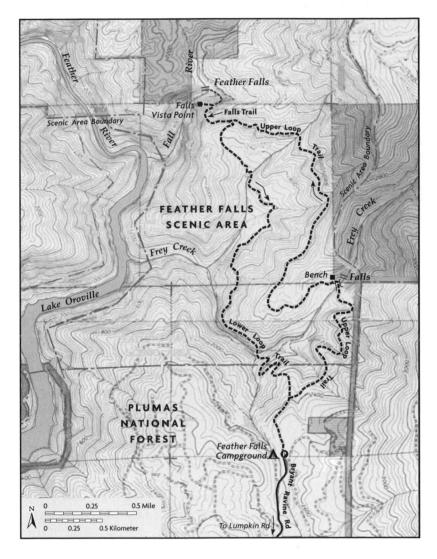

the downhill trek through a shady forest full of California black oaks, ponderosa pines, and incense cedar. Soon after you hit the trail, you'll reach the signed junction for the Upper and Lower Loop trails. If both trails are open, it is decision time. Many people recommend taking the Upper Loop out to the falls and Lower Loop back. The Upper Loop, although longer, is actually easier, with less climbing and a fantastic surface. Either way you go, you are in for a beautiful hike.

The dramatic view of Feather Falls

The Upper Loop Trail winds through the forest, gently descending most of the way with a few slight uphills here and there. Notice several huge madrone trees along the trail with their peeling bark and deep red color.

A handful of stream crossings in the first 2 miles are great places for your dog to take a short rest and drink. After these, water on the trail becomes pretty scarce, so make sure you pack some to keep your pup happy as you hike.

A well-placed wooden bridge and bench at Frey Creek Falls at the 2-mile mark offers a great place to stop, refuel, cool off, and enjoy the sights and sounds of the icy water as it rolls over several tiers of dark, basaltic rock and continues its flow down into the canyon below.

Just past 2.5 miles as you finish a short, gradual uphill section of the trail, take a moment to marvel at Bald Rock Dome miles away across the canyon.

Continue on, and when you reach the junction with the Lower Loop trail at approximately 4 miles, take the signed Falls Trail to the right. Climb the additional half mile to the vista point to see and hear Feather Falls in all its glory. Near the top of the final climb, a trail branches off that leads to the edge of the falls, but, especially with a dog, I would advise against taking it. Be smart and safe—over the last fifty years, a handful of accidental deaths have resulted from people slipping into the water and going over the edge of the falls.

After a nice rest, refuel, and picture-taking session, it is time to retrace your steps back to the trailhead and your car, or exercise your option to return via the Lower Loop if it is open.

APPENDIX: RESOURCES

Books

Mullally, Linda. *Hiking with Dogs: Becoming a Wilderness-Wise Dog Owner.* Helena, MT: Falcon Guides, 1999.

Soares, Marc. *100 Hikes in the San Francisco Bay Area.* Seattle: The Mountaineers Books, 2001.

———. *75 Year-Round Hikes in Northern California.* Seattle: The Mountaineers Books, 2000.

Stienstra, Tom, and Ann Marie Brown. *California Hiking.* Emeryville, CA: Foghorn Press, 2003.

Hiking and Dog-Related Websites

Bay Area Backcountry, www.hknot.com/bab/

Bay Area Hiker, "Where to Take My Dog," www.bahiker.com/doghikes.html

East Bay Regional Park District, www.ebparks.org

First Aid

Acker, Randy, DVM. *Dog First Aid: A Field Guide to Emergency Care for the Outdoor Dog.* Gallatin Gateway, MT: Wilderness Adventure Press, 1999. Dr. Acker also offers a comprehensive dog first-aid kit containing most of the items listed in this book's introduction, all packaged in a convenient fanny pack. For information, contact him at the Sun Valley Animal Center, (800) 699-2663 or online at www.svanimal.com.

Ruffwear Inc. offers prepackaged dog first-aid kits containing the essentials. The packets are available at many outdoor retail shops, or order directly from Ruffwear online at www.ruffwear.com.

Dog Gear

Cascade Designs Inc. (www.cascadedesigns.com) invented the inflatable sleeping pad for hikers thirty years ago and now offers a line of fleece-covered pads just for dogs.

Granite Gear (www.granitegear.com) offers a full line of backpacks for your dog.

Planetdog (www.planetdog.com) makes active gear for your pet, including toys, packable bowls, beds, leashes, leads, and collars. The company donates a portion of its profits to environmental charities.

Ruffwear Inc. (www.ruffwear.com) offers a full line of dog accessories for the active dog. The company makes the popular (and well-worth-the-price) booties for rough environments.

INDEX

THE MOUNTAINEERS, founded in 1906, is a nonprofit outdoor activity and conservation organization, whose mission is "to explore, study, preserve, and enjoy the natural beauty of the outdoors...." The Mountaineers sponsors many classes and year-round outdoor activities in the Pacific Northwest, and supports environmental causes through educational activities, sponsoring legislation and presenting educational programs. The Mountaineers Books supports the organization's mission by publishing travel and natural history guides, instructional texts, and works on conservation and history.

Visit www.mountaineersbooks.org to view our complete list of more than 500 outdoor titles:

 The Mountaineers Books
1001 SW Klickitat Way, Suite 201
Seattle, WA 98134
(800) 553-4453
mbooks@mountaineersbooks.org

 The Mountaineers Books is proud to be a corporate sponsor of The Leave No Trace Center for Outdoor Ethics, whose mission is to promote and inspire responsible outdoor recreation through education, research, and partnerships.
The Leave No Trace program is focused specifically on human-powered (nonmotorized) recreation.
Leave No Trace strives to educate visitors about the nature of their recreational impacts and offers techniques to prevent and minimize such impacts. Leave No Trace is best understood as an educational and ethical program, not as a set of rules and regulations.
For more information, visit www.lnt.org, or call (800) 332-4100.

ABOUT THE AUTHORS

Jason Fator lives in Northern California with his wife and two sons. When he is not hiking with Paul, his Great Dane, he enjoys mountain biking, skiing, and reading. Other interests include playing bass, piano, and guitar. Jason and Thom Gabrukiewicz were co-workers at the *Record Searchlight* newspaper in Redding from 1997 to 2001, and have been friends and hiking buddies ever since.

Thom Gabrukiewicz is a prevention specialist team leader at the Prevention Management Organization of Wyoming in Sheridan. He was formerly the outdoor editor/writer for the *Record Searchlight* in Redding, California, where in twelve years his Outdoors section was judged best in the nation three times by the Outdoor Writers Association of America. He was named California Outdoor Writer of the Year in 2003. Gabrukiewicz now lives at the base of Wyoming's Big Horn Mountain range, with Trinity still faithfully at his side. Scully died of kidney failure in 2009.